Modern England, 1901–1984, Second Edition

CONFERENCE ON BRITISH STUDIES
BIBLIOGRAPHICAL HANDBOOKS

Editor: PETER STANSKY
Consultant Editor: G. R. ELTON

Other books in the series

Anglo-Norman England, 1066–1154 – Michael Altschul
The High Middle Ages in England, 1154–1377 – Bertie Wilkinson
Late-Medieval England, 1377–1485 – Delloyd J. Guth
Tudor England, 1485–1603 – Mortimer Levine
Restoration England, 1660–1689 – William L. Sachse
Late Georgian and Regency England, 1760–1837 – Robert A. Smith
Victorian England, 1837–1901 – Josef L. Altholz

Modern England 1901–1984

Second Edition

ALFRED F. HAVIGHURST

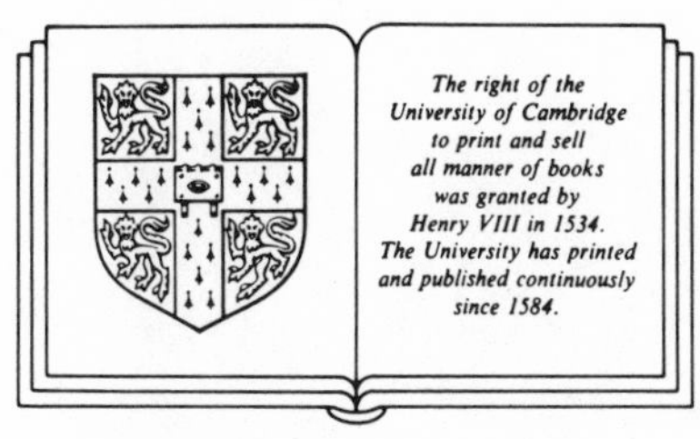
The right of the
University of Cambridge
to print and sell
all manner of books
was granted by
Henry VIII in 1534.
The University has printed
and published continuously
since 1584.

CAMBRIDGE UNIVERSITY PRESS

CAMBRIDGE

NEW YORK NEW ROCHELLE MELBOURNE SYDNEY

For the North American Conference on British Studies

Published by the Press Syndicate of the University of Cambridge
The Pitt Building, Trumpington Street, Cambridge CB2 1RP
32 East 57th Street, New York, NY 10022, USA
10 Stamford Road, Oakleigh, Melbourne 3166, Australia

First published 1987

Printed in the United States of America

Library of Congress Cataloging-in-Publication Data

Havighurst, Alfred F.

Modern England, 1901–1984.

(Conference on British studies bibliographical handbooks)

Rev. ed. of: Modern England, 1901–1970. © 1976.

Includes index.

1. Great Britain – Civilization – 20th century – Bibliography. 2. Great Britain – History – 20th century – Bibliography. I. Havighurst, Alfred F. Modern England, 1901–1970. II. North American Conference on British Studies. III. Title. IV. Series.
Z2020.H38 1988 [DA566.4] 016.941 87–20927

British Library Cataloguing-in-Publication Data

Havighurst, Alfred F.

Modern England, 1901–1984 – 2nd ed.

– (Conference on British Studies bibliographical handbooks).

1. Great Britain – History –
20th century – Bibliography
I. Title II. Series
016.941082 Z2020

ISBN 0 521 30974 3

CONTENTS

PREFACE TO THE SECOND EDITION

This bibliographical handbook is the second edition, revised and extended, of *Modern England, 1901–1970*, published in 1976. Like the other handbooks in this series this book is designed as a ready book of reference and guide for the scholar, for the teacher, for the student, and for the general reader interested in exploring twentieth-century Britain in some depth. It is a bibliography of published material, including primary sources of knowledge (official records, memoirs, autobiographies, diaries, and letters) as well as secondary sources of information (monographs, biographies, and articles). It does not provide direction to unpublished material (in public archives or elsewhere) or on microfilm.

Scholars look forward to publication of the volume in the Oxford series, *Bibliography of Writings on British History, 1914–1985*, now being compiled by Professor K. G. Robbins of the University of Glasgow. He writes me that his bibliography is "in an advanced stage of preparation" but does not now venture to set a date of publication of a book that will render great service, especially to professional historians and to teachers. For less advanced students and general readers, *Modern England, 1901–1984* will continue to be useful as a handbook, at once available on desk or shelf.

The selection of books and articles here presented rests upon a comprehensive search of historical literature published before 1984, though a few important items published in 1984 are included. Of the major aspects of English life only literature per se is excluded. However, biographies of literary figures significant in the social and political life of the period are included.

To cope to a degree with the flood of historical literature that appeared after 1967 when the Public Records Statute opened the archives for the period between the two World Wars and more especially the torrent of publication since 1970, I have somewhat modified principles of selection used in the first edition. I have, to a great extent, avoided overlapping from the previous volume, chronologically, in this series – Josef L. Altholz, *Victorian England, 1837–1901*. Historians had very frequently carried their examination of the nineteenth century down to 1914, especially with relation to foreign relations and economics. For books published before 1968, Altholz should be consulted. More recent publications concerned with the early twentieth century will, of course, be listed in this present volume.

Each book in this series has had its special problems. In the present instance, one is constantly confronted with the difficulty of distinguishing the historical past from the contemporary present. As A. J. P. Taylor put it, history becomes "thicker" as we approach the present. There is more evidence and more comment on that evidence; but is not much of it current events, journalism, or just plain commentary? The closer we approach the present, the thicker or less distinct becomes the material at hand. An illuminating discussion of this problem will be found in C. L. Mowat's *Great Britain Since 1914* (93), Chapter 1, "Since 1914: recent or contemporary?"

There has been one important change in arrangement. A new category, Labour

History, has been introduced in response to the development of its identity and the startling growth of historical literature associated with it. However, an exact definition has yet to be ventured. Its use as a separate category raises a fundamental question and problem. To what extent should the treatment of political, social, and economic aspects of labour be included? For these are all categories of their own. I have chosen to limit the use of Labour History to when it applies to the "working class" as we generally conceive it: a factory worker, a miner, an engineer, a carpenter. I have thought it unwise to separate "labour" from the general area of politics and society. I hope that my use of this new category will be useful, not confusing.

Empire and Commonwealth receive considerable attention since their fortunes have directly affected British life in the twentieth century; but books and articles on the internal history of dominions and colonies have been excluded. Fairly wide coverage is accorded Ireland until formation of the Irish Free State in 1922. For Scotland, items of general interest, associating it with England, will be found. Legal history is under Constitutional and Administrative History. The history of education – an extensive field – is divided: At the elementary and secondary levels it will be found under Social History; higher education and adult education are under Intellectual History. In this last-named category will be found journalism, as well as intellectual discussions of political, economic, and social thought.

Annotations represent my own evaluations, though often influenced by the judgment of others. In particular I have sought to clarify the contents of books where titles are inadequate. Cross references will be found occasionally, in the hope that related material will be easily brought together.

I wish to thank the consultant editors, Professor G. R. Elton and Professor Peter Stansky for their interest, support, and counsel. This new edition as well as the old was largely prepared from the holdings of the following libraries: Amherst College, Smith College, University of Massachusetts, and Harvard University. To the members of their staffs I wish to express my thanks for the countless ways in which they facilitated my task. Finally and especially I wish to express my gratitude and admiration to Rhea Cabin for her extraordinary intelligence and competence in preparing my typescript in its final form.

Amherst, Massachusetts
February, 1987

ALFRED F. HAVIGHURST

ABBREVIATIONS

AHR	*American Historical Review*
BH	*Business History*
BIHR	*Bulletin of the Institute of Historical Research*
BJES	*British Journal of Educational Studies*
BJS	*British Journal of Sociology*
EcHR	*Economic History Review*
EHR	*English Historical Review*
EJ	*Economic Journal*
GJ	*Geographical Journal*
Hist. J.	*Historical Journal*
IHS	*Irish Historical Studies*
IRSH	*International Review of Social History*
JBS	*Journal of British Studies*
JCH	*Journal of Contemporary History*
JEcH	*Journal of Economic History*
JHI	*Journal of the History of Ideas*
JMH	*Journal of Modern History*
JTH	*Journal of Transport History*
PA	*Public Administration*
PP	*Past and Present*
PS	*Political Studies*
SHR	*Scottish Historical Review*
TRHS	*Transactions of the Royal Historical Society*
YBESR	*Yorkshire Bulletin of Economic and Social Research*

EXPLANATORY NOTES

1. In matters of editorial style I have generally followed the practice in the first edition, which previously had generally followed the practice in the preceding volume of this series: Josef L. Altholz, *Victorian England, 1837–1901* (1970).
2. When no place of publication is indicated for a book, the place of publication is London. When a book appeared in two or more places of publication, the location of the copy examined by the compiler is given.
3. If a work appeared under one title in the United Kingdom and under another title in the United States, both titles are normally given.
4. "Printed sources" for each category are generally listed under the names of the authors when they were responsible for original publication; otherwise they are listed under the name of the editor.

I. BIBLIOGRAPHIES

1 Albion, Robert Greenhalgh. *Naval and maritime history: an annotated bibliography*. 4th ed., Mystic, Conn., 1972.

2 American Historical Association. *Recently published articles*. 1976–. Now three times a year; comprehensive by country. Continues the listing begun in the *AHR* in 1936 as 'Other recent publications'; title varies until separate publication in 1976. Incomplete but useful.

3 *Annual bibliography of the history of British art*. 1936–. Begins with 1934 publications. In 1938 the title changes to *Bibliography of British art*.

4 Bain, George Sayers and John Bennett. *Bibliography of British industrial relations, 1971–1979*. N.d.

5 Bayliss, Gwyn M. *Bibliographic guide to the two world wars: an annotated survey of English language reference materials*. 1977.

6 *Bibliographic index: a cumulative bibliography of bibliographies*. Ed. Dorothy Charles et al. Vols. 1–23 relate to 1937–83. Latest is vol. 24, which relates to 1984 (New York, 1985).

7 *A bibliography of the history of Wales*. 2nd ed., Cardiff, 1962.

8 *British national bibliography, 1950–*. 1951–. Weekly list of books published in Great Britain, brought together in annual volumes. Annual cumulative indexes begin in 1976.

9 Bulkley, Mildred E. *Bibliographical survey of contemporary sources for the economic and social history of the war*. Oxford, 1922. On World War I.

10 Carty, James, *Bibliography of Irish history, 1912–1921*. Dublin, 1936. Also his *Bibliography of Irish history, 1870–1911*. Dublin, 1940.

11 Chaloner, William Henry and R. C. Richardson (comps.). *British economic and social history: a bibliographical guide*. Manchester, 1976. 2nd ed. (Manchester, 1984) under title *Bibliography of British economic and social history*.

12 Chrimes, Stanley B. and Ivan A. Roots (eds.). *English constitutional history: a select bibliography* (Helps for Students of History, no. 58). 1958.

13 Cook, Chris and Philip Jones. *Sources in British political history, 1900–1951*. 5 vols. 1975–8.

14 Crombie, Alistair Cameron and Michael A. Hoskin (eds.). *History of science: an annual review of literature, research and teaching*. Cambridge, 1962–. Editorship and subtitle change with vol. XI (1973).

15 *Economic History Review*. 'List of publications on the economic history of Great Britain and Ireland', 1927–. Issued annually; title varies. Thorough coverage of documents, monographs, and articles.

16 Elton, Geoffrey Rudolph (ed.). *The Royal Historical Society's annual bibliography of British and Irish history*. 1976–. Selective. The latest volume is for 1984 (1985).

17 Enser, A. G. S. (ed.). *A subject bibliography of the Second World War: books in English, 1939–1974*. 1977. *A subject bibliography of the Second World War: books in English, 1975–1983*. Aldershot, Hants, 1985.

18 —— *A subject bibliography of the First World War: books in English, 1914–1978*. 1979.

19 Ferguson, Eugene S. (ed.). *Bibliography of the history of technology*. Cambridge, Mass., 1968. 'A reasonably comprehensive introduction to primary and secondary sources'. See also (22).

20 Frewer, Louis B. (ed.). *Bibliography of historical writings published in Britain and the Empire, 1940–1945*. Oxford, 1947. Reprinted, 1974.

21 Frow, Ruth and Edmund and Michael Katanka. *The history of British trade unions: a select bibliography*. 1969. Published by the Historical Association.

22 Goodwin, Jack (ed.). 'Current bibliography in the history of technology', *Technology and Culture*, V– (1964). This first list is for 1962; annual since then; is now the definitive international current bibliography.

23 Gulick, Charles A., Roy A. Ockert, and Raymond J. Wallace (eds.). *History and theories of working-class movements: a select bibliography*. Berkeley, Calif., 1955.

24 Hancock, Philip D. *A bibliography of works relating to Scotland, 1916–1950*. Edinburgh, 1959–60, 2 vols.

25 Hanham, Harold J. (ed.). *A bibliography of British history, 1851–1914*. New York, 1976. Standard.

26 Higham, Robin D. S. (ed.). *A guide to the sources of British military history*. 1972.

27 Historical Association, London. *Annual Bulletin of historical literature*. 1912–. Begins with publications of 1911. Selective. Critical analysis of important books and articles published each year. Some time lag; the latest volume (LXVIII) deals with publications of 1982.

28 'Histories of the First and Second World Wars' (H.M.S.O., Sectional List no. 60). 1967. For commentary see Robin Higham. 'The history of the Second World War, British Official Series', *The Library Quarterly*, XXXIV (July 1964), 240–8.

29 Howard-Hill, Trevor Howard. *Bibliography of British literary bibliographies*. Oxford, 1969. Useful for intellectual and social history.

30 Kellaway, William (ed.). *Bibliography of historical works issued in the United Kingdom, 1957–60*. 1962. *Bibliography of historical works issued in the United Kingdom, 1961–65*. 1967. *Bibliography of historical works issued in the United Kingdom, 1966–70*. 1972.

31 *Labour party bibliography*. 1967. Comprehensive. Material listed is available at Transport House.

32 Lancaster, Joan C., et al. (eds.). *Bibliography of historical works issued in the United Kingdom, 1946–1956*. 1957. *1957–1960*. 1962. *1961–1965*. 1967. *1966–1970*. 1972. *1971–1975*. 1977. Without annotation; includes all countries and all subjects.

33 Maehl, William H., Jr. '"Jerusalem deferred": recent writing in the history of the British labor movement', *JMH*, XLI (Sept. 1969), 335–67. Essential for any serious investigation. Cites earlier review articles on labour movement by Charles Loch Mowat.

34 Martin, Geoffrey H. and Sylvia MacIntyre. *A bibliography of British and Irish municipal history*, I, *general works*. Leicester, 1972.

35 Mathews, William (ed.). *British autobiographies: an annotated bibliography of British autobiographies published or written before 1951*. Berkeley, Calif., 1955.

36 Mowat, Charles Loch. *British history since 1926: a select bibliography* (Helps for Students of History, no. 61). 1960.

37 Mullins, Edward L. C. *Guide to the historical and archaeological publications of societies in England and Wales, 1901–1933*. 1968. Indexes titles and authors.

38 Ottley, George (ed.). *A bibliography of British railway history*. 1983.

39 Perkin, Harold. 'Social history in Britain', *Journal Social History*, X (winter, 1976), 129–43. A bibliographical aid.

40 Rider, Kenneth J. *History of science and technology: a select bibliography for students*. 2nd ed., 1970. Published by the Library Association. Indispensable.

41 Schlatter, Richard (ed.). *Recent views on British history: essays on historical writing since 1966*. New Brunswick, N.J., 1984. Consult Peter Stansky's essay on 1870–1914 and Henry R. Winkler's essay on twentieth century. See also (48).

42 Smith, Harold. *The British labour movement to 1970: a bibliography*. London, 1981.

43 Stephens, W. B. *Sources for English local history*. Manchester, 1973. An 'introduction' to sources; not a detailed guide.

44 Stevenson, Bruce. *Reader's guide to Great Britain: a bibliography*. 1980.

45 Thompson, Theodore R. (ed.). *A catalog of British family histories*. 2nd ed., 1935.

46 Westergaard, John, Anne Weyman, and Paul Wiles (eds.). *Modern British society: a bibliography*. 1977. Includes publications up to 1977.

47 Whitrow, Magda (ed.). *ISIS cumulative bibliography of the history of science formed from ISIS critical bibliographies 1–90, 1913–65*. 1971, 2 vols. Thereafter published annually; indispensable for specialists.

48 Winkler, Henry R. 'Some recent writings on twentieth-century Britain', in Elizabeth C. Furber (ed.), *Changing views on British history: essays on historical writing since 1939*, pp. 289–319. Cambridge, Mass, 1966. See also (41).

49 Winks, Robin W. (ed.). *The historiography of the British Empire–Commonwealth: trends, interpretations and resources.* Durham, N.C., 1966.

50 Woods, Frederick (ed.). *A bibliography of the works of Sir Winston Churchill.* 2nd ed., Toronto, 1969.

51 Wrigley, Chris. *A. J. P. Taylor: a complete annotated bibliography and guide to his historical and other writings.* New York, 1980.

52 *Writings on British history, 1901–.* 1937–. Comprehensive but unannotated. Published thus far: *1901–1933*, ed. Hugh Hale Bellot and Alexander Taylor Milne, 1968–70, 5 vols.; *1934–1945*, ed. Alexander Taylor Milne, 1937–60, 8 vols.; *1946–1948*, ed. Donald James Munro, 1973; *1949–1951*, ed. Donald James Munro, 1975; *1952–1954*, ed. John Merriman Sims, 1975; *1955–1957*, ed. John Merriman Sims and Phyllis May Jacob, 1977; *1958–1959*, ed. Heather J. Creaton, 1977; *1960–1961*, ed. Charles H. E. Philpin and Heather J. Creaton, 1978; *1962–1964*, ed. Heather J. Creaton, 1979; *1965–1966*, ed. Heather J. Creaton, 1981; *1967–1968*, ed. Heather J. Creaton, 1981.

II. CATALOGUES, GUIDES, AND HANDBOOKS

53 *Abstract of labour statistics.* 1894–1937. Periodic reports of the Labour Department of the Board of Trade and later of the Ministry of Labour. Title varies.

54 *The annual register, 1900–.* 1901–. An annual narrative of events (which dates back to 1758) largely from newspaper sources.

55 *Bartholomew's reference atlas of greater London.* 13th ed. Edinburgh, 1968.

56 Bellamy, Joyce M. and John Saville (eds.). *Dictionary of labour biography.* 1970–84, 7 vols. Each volume is self-contained, A to Z.

57 Bickmore, David P. and M. A. Shaw. *The atlas of Great Britain and Northern Ireland.* Oxford, 1963. Superb.

58 Bond, Maurice Francis (comp.). *Guide to the records of Parliament.* 1971. Carries through the session of 1969–70.

59 *Britain 1948/9, an official handbook.* 1948–. Annual; the latest appeared in 1983. Prepared by the Central Office of Information; the best brief reference book.

60 *British labour statistics yearbook 1969–.* H.M.S.O., 1971–. This series follows *British labour statistics: historical abstracts, 1886–1968* (1971) and together form a useful and convenient reference.

61 *British Museum. Subject index of the modern works added . . . in the years 1901–1905.* 1906. Quinquennially, thereafter; title varies.

62 —— *Catalogue of additions to the manuscripts in the British Museum, 1900–.* 1907.

63 —— *The catalogues of the manuscript collections*, ed. T. C. Skeat. Rev. ed., 1962.

64 —— *General catalogue of printed books . . . to 1955.* Photolithographic edition, 1965–6, 263 vols. *Ten year supplement, 1956–1965.* 1968, 50 vols. *Five year supplement, 1966–70.* 1971–2, 26 vols.

65 Butler, David H. E. and Anne Sloman. *British political facts, 1900–1979.* 5th ed., 1980. Includes economic data.

66 *Catalogue of government publications, 1956–.* H.M.S.O., 1957–. Title varies. The latest volume is for publications in 1984 (1985). Continues *Consolidated list of government publications* (1937–). Both assemble *Government publications: monthly list, 1936–.* H.M.S.O., 1937–.

67 *Census reports of Great Britain, 1901–1931* (Guides to Official Sources, no. 2). H.M.S.O., 1951. For subsequent censuses, consult *Census of England and Wales, preliminary report.* H.M.S.O. See also (66).

68 Cheney, Christopher Robert (comp.). *Handbook of dates for students of English history* (Royal Historical Society Guides and Handbooks, no. 4). 1945. Reprinted, 1985.

69 C[okayne], G[eorge] E. *The complete peerage of England, Scotland, Ireland, Great*

Britain and the United Kingdom, extant, extinct, or dormant, rev. by Vicary Gibbs. New ed., 1910–59, 13 vols. in 14. Title and editors vary. Vol. 13, ed. H. A. Doubleday and Lord Howard de Walden, is *Peers created 1901–1938*. 1940. Best guide to peerage.

70 Craig, Frederick W. S. (ed.). *British electoral facts 1885–1975*. 1976. Very useful for General Elections. See also Craig's *Boundaries of parliamentary constituencies, 1885–1972* (1972).

71 *Crockford's clerical directory for 1860–*. 1860–. Annual or semiannual; 'a statistical book of reference for facts relating to the clergy and the church'.

72 *The dictionary of national biography. Second supplement*. 1912, 3 vols. Short biographies of 'noteworthy persons' who died 1910–11. *Supplement, 1912–1921*. 1927. *Supplement, 1922–1930*. 1937. *Supplement, 1931–1940*. 1949. *Supplement, 1941–1950*. 1959. *Supplement, 1951–1960*. 1971. *Supplement, 1961–1970*. 1981. An epitome is in *The concise dictionary:* pt. II, *1901–1960*. 1971.

73 Di Roma, Edward and Joseph A. Rosenthal. *A numerical finding list of British command papers, published 1833–1961/62*. New York, 1967.

74 [Dod, Charles Roger Phipps]. *Dod's parliamentary companion, 1901–*. 1901–. Inaugurated in 1832, the latest volume (the 161st ed.) was published in 1974. And now see *Who's Who of British members of Parliament, 1919–1945*, ed. Michael Stenton and Stephen Lees, which is a revision of Dod. Three volumes have appeared. Atlantic Highlands, N.J., 1978–9.

75 Ford, Percy and Grace Ford. *A breviate of parliamentary papers, 1900–1916*. Oxford, 1957. *1917–39*. Oxford, 1951. *1940–54*. Oxford, 1961.

76 —— *A guide to parliamentary papers: what they are; how to find them; how to use them*. 3rd ed., Shannon, Ireland, 1972.

77 —— and Diana Marshallsay. *Select list of parliamentary papers, 1955–1964*. Shannon, Ireland, 1970.

78 *General Index to the bills, reports and papers printed by order of the House of Commons and to the reports and papers presented by command 1900 to 1948–9*. H.M.S.O., 1960.

79 *Guide to the contents of the Public Record Office*. 1963–8, 3 vols. Replaces M. S. Giuseppi, *A guide to the manuscripts preserved in the Public Record Office*. 1923–4, 2 vols.

80 *Guide to the historical publications of the societies of England and Wales (BIHR*, suppls. I–XIII). 1929–46.

81 Harrison, Royden John, et al. (eds.). *The Warwick guide to British Labour Periodicals, 1790–1970*. 1977.

82 Hazlehurst, Cameron and Christine Woodland. *A guide to the papers of British Cabinet ministers, 1900–1951* (Royal Historical society: Guides and Handbooks, suppl. series, no. 1). 1974. Locates and describes.

83 Herwig, Holger H. and Neil M. Heyman. *Biographical dictionary of World War I*. 1982.

84 *Historical abstracts, 1775–1945: bibliography of the world's periodical literature*. Santa Barbara, Calif., 1955–. A quarterly, assembled in annual volumes, providing a useful abstracting service; author and subject indexes.

85 Historical Manuscripts Commission. *Record repositories in Great Britain*. 5th ed., 1973. Informs the researcher 'where the record material available... may be found, and what organisations will help him to approach and use it'.

86 *Jane's Fighting Ships, 1984–5*. 1984. The most recent volume in a long series; title and editorship vary. Indispensable.

87 Kendall, Maurice George (ed.). *The sources and nature of the statistics of the United Kingdom*. 1952–7, 2 vols. A reprint of articles in the *Journal of the Royal Statistical Society* beginning in 1949.

88 London and Cambridge Economic Service. *Key statistics of the British economy, 1900–1966*. N.d. Excellent for quick reference.

89 MacLeod, Roy M., James R. Friday, and Carol Gregor. *The corresponding societies of the British Association for the Advancement of Science, 1883–1922*. 1974. Archival study.

90 Mitchell, Brian R. and Phyllis Deane. *Abstract of British historical statistics.* Cambridge, 1962. Statistical material to 1938. Supplemented by Brian R. Mitchell and H. G. Jones, *Second abstract of British historical statistics.* Cambridge, 1971.

91 Mitchell, Jean B. (ed.). *Great Britain: geographical essays.* Cambridge, 1962. Authoritative; fascinating.

92 Morgan, Paul. *Oxford libraries outside the Bodleian; a guide.* Oxford, 1973.

93 Mowat, C. L. *Great Britain since 1914.* 1977. Classified guide to historical materials available for twentieth-century Britain.

94 Munby, Alan Noel L. *Cambridge College libraries: aids for research students.* 2nd ed., Cambridge, 1962.

95 Munby, Denys Lawrence. *Inland transport statistics, Great Britain, 1900–1970.* Oxford, 1978.

96 National Film Library. *Catalog:* I, *Silent News Films, 1895–1933.* 2nd ed., 1965.

97 Palmer, Samuel, et al. (eds.). *Palmer's index to 'The Times' newspaper (London), 1790–1941.* Corsham, 1868–1943. Quarterly vols. Kraus reprint, Vaduz, 1965–6, 83 vols.

98 Pemberton, John F. *British official publications.* New York, 1971. 'A practical guide'.

99 PEP (Political and Economic Planning). This 'independent, non-party organisation', inaugurated in 1931, has published some 50 books and 500 broadsheets. For a listing, see *Annual report, 1969–1970.* N.d. 'A bridge between research and policy making'. Baltimore, Md., 1973.

100 Pine, Leslie Gilbert. *The new extinct peerage, 1884–1971, containing extinct, abeyant, dormant & suspended peerages with genealogies and arms.* Baltimore, Md., 1973.

101 Powicke, F. Maurice and E. B. Fryde (eds.). *Handbook of British chronology.* 2nd ed., 1961.

102 Public Record Office Handbooks. H.M.S.O. Includes: No. 4, *List of Cabinet Papers, 1880–1914.* 1964. No. 6, *List of papers of the Committee of Imperial Defence, to 1914.* 1964. No. 9, *List of Cabinet Papers, 1915 and 1916.* 1966. No. 10, *Classes of departmental papers for 1906–1939.* 1966. No. 11, *The records of the Cabinet Office to 1922.* 1966. No. 13, *The records of the Foreign Office, 1782–1939.* 1969. No. 14, *Records of interest to social scientists, 1919–1939, introduction.* 1971. No. 15, *The Second World War, a guide to documents in the Public Record Office.* 1972.

103 Rodgers, Frank. *A guide to British Government publications.* New York, 1980.

104 Scholes, Percy A. *The concise Oxford dictionary of music.* Ed. John Owen Ward. 2nd ed., 1964. 3rd. ed., Michael Kennedy, 1980.

105 Stamp, L. Dudley and Stanley H. Beaver. *The British Isles: a geographic and economic survey.* 5th ed., 1963.

106 *The statesman's year book: statistical and historical annual of the states of the world.* 1864–. 122nd ed. (1985–6) was published in 1985. Invaluable for quick reference.

107 *Statistical abstract of the United Kingdom.* 1856–. Succeeded by *Annual abstract of statistics.* 1948–. Latest volume is for 1979. Issued by Central Statistical Office.

108 Steinberg, Sigfrid H. and I. H. Evans (eds.). *Steinberg's dictionary of British history.* 2nd ed., 1971.

109 Stewart, James D., et al. (eds.). *British union catalogue of periodicals: a record of the periodicals of the world from the seventeenth century to the present day in British libraries.* 1955–8, 4 vols. Suppl. vols. (title slightly changed) with titles of new periodicals. 1962–.

110 *The subject index to periodicals.* 1915–61. Quarterly since 1954. From 1962 known as *British humanities index.* 1962–. The most recent volume is for 1979 (1980). The best guide to articles on British history.

111 *The Times.* London. *Annual index to The Times, 1906–.* 1907–. In 1914 the title changes to *The official index.* More complete than (97), available on microfilm.

112 —— *Obituaries from The Times, 1951–1960, 1961–1970, 1971–1975.* Comp. Frank C. Roberts. Reading, 1975–9.

113 *The Times guide to the House of Commons*. 1980. The latest volume in a series that has appeared after each General Election since 1900. Title varies slightly; includes biographies of M.P.'s as well as results of the polls.
114 *Urban history yearbook, 1978*, ed. Harold James Dyos. Leicester, 1978. The first volume was for 1974. Leicester, 1974. Includes reports on conferences, reviews, bibliographies, register of research in progress.
115 Vogel, Robert. *A breviate of British diplomatic blue books, 1919–1939*. 1963. Continues Temperley, Harold W. V. and Lillian M. Penson, *A century of diplomatic blue books, 1814–1914*. Cambridge, 1938.
116 Whitaker, Joseph. *An almanack for the year of our Lord . . . 1901*. 1901–. Annual; the most recent edition appeared in 1986. A useful book of reference for Britain and the Commonwealth.
117 Whitmore, John B. *A genealogical guide: an index to British pedigrees in continuation of Marshall's Genealogist's Guide* (1903). 1947–53, 4 pts.
118 *Who's who, 1985–1986: annual biographical dictionary*. 1985. Indispensable for contemporary biography. See also *Who was who*. 1919–80, 7 vols. Embraces 1897–1980.
119 Williams, Trevor Illtyd (ed.). *A biographical dictionary of scientists*. 2nd ed., 1974.
120 *Willing's press guide, 1977*. 1977. Annual since 1899.

III. GENERAL SURVEYS

121 Bartlett, Christopher John. *A history of postwar Britain, 1945–74*. New York, 1977.
122 Beloff, Max. *Wars and welfare: Britain, 1914–1945*. 1984.
123 Harvie, Christopher. *No gods & precious few heroes: Scotland, 1914–1980*. 1981.
124 Havighurst, Alfred F. *Britain in transition: the twentieth century*. 4th ed. Chicago, 1985. Originally, *Twentieth-century Britain*. 1962, 1966.
125 Kellas, J. G. *Modern Scotland: the nation since 1870*. 1968.
126 Lloyd, Trevor O. *Empire to welfare state: English history, 1906–1967*. 2nd ed. 1979.
127 Lyons, F. S. L. *Ireland since the famine*. New York, 1971.
128 Marriott, John A. R. *Modern England: 1885–1945: a history of my own times*. 4th ed. 1960.
129 Marwick, Arthur. *Britain in our century: images and controversies*. 1984.
130 Medlicott, William M. *Contemporary England, 1914–1964: with epilog, 1964–1974*. 1976.
131 Morgan, Kenneth O. *Rebirth of a nation: Wales, 1880–1980*. Oxford, 1981.
132 Mowat, Charles Loch. *Britain between the wars, 1918–1940*. 1955. The best general treatment of the interwar years.
133 Pelling, Henry. *Modern Britain, 1885–1955*. 1960.
134 Robbins, Keith. *The eclipse of a great power: modern Britain, 1870–1975*. New York, 1983.
135 Sampson, Anthony. *The changing anatomy of Britain*. 1981.
136 Spender, John A. *Great Britain: empire and commonwealth, 1886–1935*. 1936. In its day one of the best treatments.
137 Taylor, Alan J. P. *English history, 1914–1945* (Oxford History of England, XV). 1965. Brilliant; not always reliable.

IV. CONSTITUTIONAL AND ADMINISTRATIVE HISTORY

1. Printed sources

138 Amery, Leopold S. *Thoughts on the constitution*. 2nd ed., 1953. By an articulate and independent Conservative.

139 Beaverbrook, William Maxwell Aitken, 1st Baron. *Abdication of King Edward VIII*. Ed. Alan J. P. Taylor. 1966.
140 Cumpston, Ina M. (ed.). *The growth of the British Commonwealth, 1880–1932*. 1973. Documents with commentary.
141 Dawson, Robert MacGregor (ed.). *The development of dominion status, 1900–1936*. 1937. Documents with commentary.
142 Halsbury, Hardinge Stanley Giffard, 1st Earl of. *Halsbury's laws of England*. Various eds. from 1900 to 1973.
143 Hardinge, Helen Mary. *Loyal to three kings*. 1967. A memoir of Alec Hardinge, principal private secretary to Edward VIII; useful for abdication crisis.
144 Headlam, Cecil (ed.). *The Milner papers*, vol. II. *South Africa, 1899–1905*. 1933.
145 Jones, Philip (ed.). *Britain and Palestine, 1914–1948: archival sources for the history of the British mandates*. 1979.
146 Keir, David Lindsay and Frederick H. Lawson (eds.). *Cases in constitutional law*. 6th ed. Oxford, 1979. Standard collection.
147 *The law reports . . . ; ten years digest, 1901–1910; all the cases reported in the Law Reports and in the Weekly Notes*. 1911. Continues for ten- and twenty-year periods. Set of 12 vols., reprinted in 1981.
148 Le May, Godfrey H. L. *British government, 1914–1953: select documents*. 1955. A very useful collection; no commentary.
149 Lowther, James William, 1st Viscount Ullswater. *A Speaker's commentaries*. 1925, 2 vols. Lowther was speaker of the House of Commons, 1905–21.
150 Mansergh, Nicholas (ed.). *Documents and speeches on Commonwealth affairs, 1931–1952*. 1953, 2 vols. *1952–1962*. 1963.
151 —— and E. W. R. Lumby (eds.). *Constitutional relations between Britain and India: the transfer of power, 1942–7*. I–III and VI. 1970–6. Documents.
152 Minogue, Martin (ed.). Documents on Contemporary British Government, I, *British government and constitutional change*. II, *Local government in Britain*. 1977.
153 Morrison, Herbert. *Government and parliament: a survey from the inside*. 2nd ed., 1959. By a prominent Labour leader.
154 *The Parliamentary debates, 1900–1908*. 1900–8. Lords and Commons are together.
155 *The Parliamentary debates: House of Lords*. 1909–.
156 *The Parliamentary debates: House of Commons*. 1909–.
157 Perham, Margery F. *Colonial sequence, 1930–1949: a chronological commentary upon British colonial policy especially in Africa*. 1967. 'Occasional writings' from various sources. Continued by *Colonial sequence, 1949–1969*. 1970.
158 Ponsonby, Frederick, 1st Lord Sysonby. *Recollections of three reigns*. Ed. Colin Welch. 1952. Court life under Victoria, Edward VII, and George V.
159 Smuts, Jan Christian, 1870–1950. *Selections from the Smuts papers*. Ed. W. K. Hancock and Jean Van der Poel. 7 vols. 1966–73.
160 Windsor, Duke of. *A king's story: memoirs of the Duke of Windsor*. New York, 1957. Concerning his abdication.
161 Wiseman, Herbert Victor. *Parliament and the executive: an analysis with readings*. 1966.

2. Surveys

162 Bradley, Kenneth B. *The living Commonwealth*. 1961. Popular; worth reading.
163 Chester, Daniel N. (ed.). *The organisation of British central government, 1914–1956*. 1957. A survey by a study group at the Royal Institute of Public Administration.
164 Cross, Colin. *The fall of the British Empire, 1918–1968*. 1968.
165 Gordon, Donald C. *The moment of power: Britain's imperial epoch*. Englewood Cliffs, N.J., 1970. A survey, well-informed, interpretative; emphasis on India.
166 Gordon Walker, Patrick. *The Commonwealth*. 1962. Informed and perceptive.
167 Hall, Hessel Duncan. *Commonwealth: A history of British Commonwealth of Nations*. 1971. Massive; very useful.

168 Judd, Denis and Peter Slinn. *The evolution of the modern Commonwealth, 1902–1980*. 1982. Brief; excellent; for general reader.
169 Keith, Arthur Berriedale. *The constitution of England from Victoria to George VI*. 1940, 2 vols.
170 Knaplund, Paul. *Commonwealth and empire, 1901–1955*. 1956.
171 McIntyre, W. David. *The Commonwealth of Nations: origins and impacts, 1869–1971*. Minneapolis, Minn., 1978. Excellent bibliography.
172 Mansergh, Nicholas. *The Commonwealth experience*, I, *The Durham Report to the Anglo-Irish treaty;* II, *From British to multiracial Commonwealth*. 1982.
173 Porter, Bernard. *The lion's share: a short history of British imperialism, 1850–1970*. 1975. Popular; well done.
174 Robson, William A. *The development of local government*. 3rd ed., 1954.
175 Smellie, Kingsley B. *A hundred years of English government*. 2nd ed., 1950. Takes the story to 1949.
176 —— *A history of local government*. 4th ed., 1968. Largely on twentieth century; see also Bryan Keith-Lucas and Peter G. Richards, *A history of local government in the twentieth century*. 1979.

3. Monographs

177 Abramovitz, Moses and Vera F. Eliasberg. *The growth of public employment in Great Britain*. Princeton, N.J., 1957.
178 Beloff, Max. *Imperial sunset*, I., *Britain's liberal empire 1897-1921*. 1969. A second volume is forthcoming.
179 Benewick, Robert. *The Fascist movement in Britain*. Rev. ed., 1972. First published in 1969 as *Political violence and public disorder*. See also Colin Cross. *The Fascists in Britain*. 1961.
180 Berkeley, Humphry. *The power of the prime minister*. 1968. Develops the thesis that prime ministerial government replaced cabinet government under Lloyd George. See also (308).
181 Blake, Robert. *A history of Rhodesia*. 1978. See also (270).
182 Blom-Cooper, Louis and Gavin Drewey. *Final appeal: a study of the House of Lords in its judicial capacity*. 1972.
183 Brand, Jack. *Local government reform in England, 1888–1974*. 1974.
184 Broad, C. Lewis. *The abdication: twenty-five years after; a reappraisal*. 1961.
185 Bromhead, Peter A. *Private members' bills in the British parliament*. 1956.
186 —— *The House of Lords and contemporary politics, 1911–1957*. 1958.
187 Browne, Douglas G. *The rise of Scotland Yard: a history of the Metropolitan Police*. 1956.
188 Buckland, Patrick. *The factory of grievances: devolved government in Northern Ireland, 1921–39*. New York, 1979.
189 Bulmer-Thomas, Ivor. *The growth of the British party system*. 2nd ed., 2 vols. New York, 1967.
190 Burk, Kathleen (ed.). *War and the state: the transformation of British government, 1914–1919*. 1982. Essays.
191 Callahan, Raymond A. *Churchill: retreat from empire*. Wilmington, Del., 1984.
192 Canning, Paul. *British policy toward Ireland, 1921–1941*. 1985.
193 Chadwick, John. *The unofficial Commonwealth: the story of Commonwealth foundation, 1965–1980*. 1982.
194 Chester, Daniel N. and Nona Bowring. *Questions in parliament*. Oxford, 1962.
195 Christoph, James B. *Capital punishment and British politics: the British movement to abolish the death penalty, 1945–57*. 1962.
196 Daalder, Hans. *Cabinet reform in Britain, 1914–1963*. Stanford, Calif., 1963.
197 Darwin, John. *Britain, Egypt and the Middle East; imperial policy in the aftermath of war, 1918–1922*. New York, 1981.
198 Drummond, Ian. *Imperial economic policy, 1917–1939*. 1974.
199 Eaves, John. *Emergency powers and the parliamentary watchdog: Parliament and the executive in Great Britain, 1939–1951*. 1957.
200 Edwards, Owen Dudley, et al. *Celtic nationalism*. 1968.
201 Ehrman, John. *Cabinet government and war, 1890–1940*. Cambridge, 1958. See also (302).

202 Fox, Lionel W. *The English prisons and Borstal systems.* 1952. Since the Criminal Justice Act (1948), with historical background.

203 Fraser, Robert (ed.). *The new Whitehall series.* 1955–70, 14 vols. 'To provide authoritative descriptions of the present work of the major departments of the Central Government'.

204 Fry, Geoffrey Kingdon. *Statesmen in disguise: the changing role of the administrative class of the British home civil service, 1853–1966.* 1969.

205 Gallagher, John. *Decline, revival and fall of the British Empire.* 1982.

206 Gann, Lewis H. and Peter Duignan, et al. (eds.). *Colonialism in Africa, 1870–1960.* 1969–73, 5 vols. Excellent chapters on Britain's role.

207 Garner, Joe. *The Commonwealth office, 1925–1968.* 1978. Garner had been the permanent undersecretary.

208 Gifford, Prosser and William Roger Louis (eds.). *Britain and Germany in Africa: imperial rivalry and colonial rule.* New Haven, Conn. 1967.

209 —— *France and Britain in Africa: imperial rivalry and colonial rule.* New Haven, Conn., 1971.

210 Ginsberg, Morris (ed.). *Law and opinion in England in the 20th century.* 1959. Essays.

211 Goldsworthy, David. *Colonial issues in British politics, 1945–1961.* Oxford, 1971.

212 Halperin, Vladimir. *Lord Milner and the empire: the evolution of British imperialism.* [1952].

213 Hamilton, William B., et al. (eds.). *A decade of the Commonwealth 1955–1964.* 1966. Twenty-four articles by various authors.

214 Hancock, William Keith. *Survey of Commonwealth affairs:* I, *Problems of nationality, 1918–1936*; II, *Problems of economic policy, 1918–1939.* 1937, 1942.

215 Hanham, Harold J. *Scottish nationalism.* 1969. Detailed historical context.

216 Hansard Society. *Parliamentary reform, 1933–60: a survey of suggested reforms.* 1961.

217 Hanson, Albert H. *Parliament and public ownership.* 1961.

218 Hardie, Frank. *The political influence of the British monarchy, 1868–1952.* New York, 1970.

219 Hicks, Ursula K. *British public finances: their structure and development, 1880–1952.* 1954.

220 Hodson, Henry V. *The great divide: Britain, India, Pakistan.* 1970. Informed; well written.

221 Holland, R. F. *Britain and the Commonwalth alliance, 1918–1939.* Atlantic Highlands, N.J., 1981.

222 Howe, Roland. *The story of Scotland Yard: a history of the C.I.D. from the earliest times to the present day.* 1965. Popular.

223 Inglis, Brian. *Abdication.* New York, 1966. Concerning Edward VIII.

224 Jeffrey, Keith and Peter Hennessy. *States of emergency: British Governments and strike breaking since 1919.* Boston, 1983.

225 Jenkins, Roy H. *Mr. Balfour's poodle: an account of the struggle between the House of Lords and the government of Asquith.* 1954.

226 Jennings, W. Ivor. *Cabinet government.* 3rd ed., Cambridge, 1959. See also his *Parliament.* 2nd ed., Cambridge, 1957.

227 Judd, Denis, *Balfour and the British Empire: a study in imperial evolution, 1874–1932.* 1968.

228 Keith-Lucas, Bryan and Peter G. Richards. *A history of Local Government in the twentieth century.* 1979.

229 Kendle, John Edward. *The Round Table movement and imperial unions.* Toronto, 1975.

230 Le May, Godfrey H. L. *British supremacy in South Africa, 1899–1907.* Oxford, 1965.

231 Louis, William Roger. *Imperialism at Bay: The United States and Great Britain and the decolonization of the British empire, 1941–1945.* Oxford, 1978.

232 —— *The British empire in the Middle East, 1945–1951: Arab Nationalism, the United States and postwar imperialism.* Oxford, 1984.

233 Mackenzie, John M. *Propaganda and empire: the manipulation of British public opinion, 1880–1960.* Manchester, 1984.

234 Mansergh, Nicholas. *Survey of British Commonwealth affairs: problems of external policy, 1931–1939*. 1952.

235 —— *Survey of British Commonwealth affairs: problems of wartime co-operation and post-war change, 1939–1952*. 1958.

236 Martin, John P. and Gail Wilson. *The police: a study in manpower: the evolution of the service in England and Wales. 1829–1965*. 1969. Reliable.

237 Miller, John Donald Bruce. *Survey of Commonwealth affairs: problems of expansion and attrition, 1953–1969*. 1974. Detailed.

238 Moore, R. J. *The Crisis of Indian unity, 1917–1940*. Oxford, 1974. See also his *Churchill, Cripps and India, 1939–1945*. Oxford, 1979. Also his *Escape from empire: the Attlee Government and the Indian problem*. Oxford, 1983.

239 Morgan, Janet P. *The House of Lords and the Labour Government, 1964–1970*. Oxford, 1975.

240 Mossek, M. *Palestine immigration policy under Sir Herbert Samuel: British, Zionist and Arab attitudes*. 1979.

241 Naylor, John F. *Sir Maurice Hankey, the Cabinet secretariat and the custody of Cabinet secrecy*. Cambridge, 1984.

242 Nimocks, Walter. *Milner's young men: the 'kindergarten' in Edwardian imperial affairs*. Durham, N.C., 1968.

243 Norton, Philip. *The Commons in perspective*. 1981.

244 Pandey, Bishwa N. *The break-up of British India*. 1969. General study, 1900–47.

245 Paton, Herbert J. *The claim of Scotland*. 1968. Her claim 'to govern herself' is treated in the context of recent history.

246 Peacock, Alan T. and Jack Wiseman. *The growth of public expenditure in the United Kingdom*. Princeton, N.J., 1961. Developments since 1890.

247 Perham, Margery F. *The colonial reckoning: end of imperial rule in Africa in the light of British experience*. 1976.

248 Pugh, Martin. *Electoral reform in war and peace, 1906–1918*. 1978.

249 Pyrah, Geoffrey B. *Imperial policy and South Africa, 1902–1910*. Oxford, 1955.

250 Redcliffe-Maud, Lord and Bruce Wood. *English local government reformed*. 1974.

251 Reese, Trevor R. *The history of the Royal Commonwealth Society, 1868–1968*. Oxford, 1968.

252 Richards, Peter Godfrey. *The reformed local government system*. 1975.

253 Rizvi, S. A. G. *Linlithgow and India: a study of British policy and the political impasse in India, 1936–1943*. 1978.

254 Robson, William A. (ed.). *Civil service in Britain and France*. 1956. Essays.

255 Ross, James Frederick Stanley. *Elections and electors*. 1955. Critical study of parliamentary representation during 1918–35 with proposals for reform.

256 Rumbold, Sir Algernon. *Watershed in India, 1914–1922*. 1979.

257 Sencourt, Robert. *The reign of Edward VIII*. 1962. See also (223).

258 Sparks, Richard F. *Local prisons: the crisis in the English penal system*. 1971. Based on studies in 1960s.

259 Stacey, Frank. *British government, 1966–1975: years of reform*. Oxford, 1975. Invaluable.

260 Stevens, Robert. *Law and politics: the House of Lords as a judicial body, 1800–1976*. Chapel Hill, N.C., 1968.

261 Thompson, L. M. *The unification of South Africa, 1902–1910*. Oxford, 1960.

262 Thornton, A. P. *The imperial idea and its enemies*. 1959.

263 Turner, John A. *Lloyd George's secretariat*. 1980.

264 Walkland, S. A. (ed.). *The House of Commons in the twentieth century: essays by members of the Study of Parliament Group*. Oxford, 1979.

265 Wasserstein, Bernard. *The British in Palestine: the mandatory government and the Arab–Jewish conflict, 1917–1929*. 1978.

266 Wheare, Kenneth C. *The Statute of Westminster and Dominion status*. 5th ed., 1953. Concerns the statute of 1931.

267 —— *The constitutional structure of the Commonwealth*. Oxford, 1960.

268 Wigley, Philip G. *Canada and the transition to the Commonwealth, 1917–1926*. 1977.

269 Williams, David. *Keeping the peace: the police and public order*. 1967.

270 Windrich, Elaine. *Britain and the politics of Rhodesian independence.* New York, 1978.
271 Wolpert, Stanley A. *Morley and India, 1906–1910.* Berkeley, Calif., 1967.
272 Woolf, Cecil and Jean Moorcraft Wilson (eds.). *Authors take sides on the Falklands.* 1982.

4. Biographies

273 Battiscombe, Georgina. *Queen Alexandra.* 1969.
274 Birkenhead, Frederick W. F. Smith, 2nd Earl of. *Walter Monckton: The life of Viscount Monckton of Brenchley.* 1969. Useful for Edward VIII.
275 Donaldson, Frances, *Edward VIII.* 1974. See (160) and (274).
276 Duff, David. *Elizabeth of Glamis.* 1973. Biography of the present queen mother.
277 Fox, A. Wilson. *The Earl of Halsbury, lord high chancellor (1823–1921).*1929.
278 Gopal, Sarvepalli. *Jawaharial Nehru.* 3 vols. Cambridge, 1979–84.
279 Hancock, W. K. *Smuts: the sanguine years, 1870–1919.* 1962. *Smuts: the fields of force, 1919–1950.* 1968.
280 Hough, Richard. *Mountbatten.* 1981. But now see also Philip Ziegler. *Mountbatten.* New York, 1985.
281 Hyde, H. Montgomery. *Norman Birkett: the life of Lord Birkett of Ulverston.* 1964.
282 Jackson, Robert. *The chief: the biography of Gordon Hewart, lord chief justice of England, 1922–40.* 1959.
283 Judd, Denis. *King George VI: 1895–1952.* 1982. See (291).
284 Lacey, Robert. *Majesty: Elizabeth II and the House of Windsor.* 1977.
285 Lee, Sidney. *King Edward VII.* II, *The Reign.* New York, 1927. But see also Philip Magnus. *King Edward the Seventh.* 1964. The best biography.
286 Magnus, Philip. *Kitchener: portrait of an imperialist.* 1958.
287 Marlowe, John. *Milner: apostle of empire.* 1976. Use with A. M. Gollin, *Proconsul in politics: a study of Lord Milner in opposition and power.* 1964.
288 Nicolson, Harold. *King George the fifth: his life and reign.* 1952. One of the best biographies of royalty. A more recent biography is Kenneth Rose. *Kind George V.* 1983.
289 Perham, Margery F. *Luggard: the years of authority, 1898–1945: the second part of the life of Frederick Dealtry Lugard.* 1960. Lugard was an outstanding colonial administrator.
290 Pope-Hennessy, James. *Queen Mary, 1867–1953.* 1959.
291 Wheeler-Bennett, John W. *King George VI: his life and reign.* 1958. See (283).

5. Articles

292 Berry, C. L. 'The coronation oath and the Church of England', *Journal of Ecclesiastical History,* XI (April 1960), 98–105.
293 Bogdanor, Vernon. 'The English constitution and devolution', *Political Quarterly,* L (Jan.–Mar. 1979), 36–49.
294 Bromhead, Peter A. 'Mr. Wedgwood Benn, the peerage and the constitution', *Parliamentary Affairs,* XIV (autumn 1961), 493–506.
295 Brookshire, Jerry H. 'Clement Attlee and Cabinet reform, 1930–1945', *Hist. J.,* XXIV (no. 1, 1980), 175–88.
296 Caldwell, J. A. M. 'The genesis of the Ministry of Labour', *PA,* XXXVII (winter 1959), 367–91.
297 Close, David H. 'The collapse of resistance to democracy: Conservatives, adult suffrage and Second Chamber reform, 1911–1928', *Hist. J.,* XX (no. 4, 1977), 893–918.
298 Crewe, Ivor, et al. 'Partisan dealignment in Britain, 1964–1974', *British Journal of Political Science,* VII (1977), 129–90.
299 Crozier, Andrew J. 'The establishment of the Mandates system, 1919–25', *JCH,* XIV (July 1979), 483–513.
300 Darwin, John. 'Imperialism in decline? Tendencies in British imperial policy between the Wars', *Hist. J.,* XXIII (no. 3, 1980), 657–79.

301 Ehrman, John. 'Lloyd George and Churchill as war ministers', *TRHS*, 5th ser., XI (1961), 101–15. Valuable comparative treatment.
302 Finer, Herman. 'The British Cabinet, the House of Commons and the war', *Political Science Quarterly*, LVI (Sept. 1941), 321–60.
303 Gibbon, I. G. 'Recent changes in the local government of England and Wales', *American Political Science Review*, XXIII (Aug. 1929), 633–56.
304 Gwyn, William B. 'The ombudsman in Britain: a qualified success in Government reform', *PA*, LX (summer 1982), 177–95.
305 Lowe, R. 'The Ministry of Labour, 1916–1924: a graveyard of social reform', *PA*, LII (winter 1974), 415–38.
306 Meadows, Martin. 'Constitutional crisis in the United Kingdom: Scotland and the devolution controversy', *Review of Politics*, XXXIX (January 1977), 41–59.
307 Meredith, David. 'The British government and colonial economic Policy, 1919–1939', *EcHR*, 2nd ser., XXVIII (August 1975), 484–99.
308 Morgan, Kenneth O. 'Lloyd George's premiership: a study in prime ministerial government,' *Hist. J.*, XIII (no. 1, 1970), 130–57.
309 Nottage, Raymond and Freida Stack. 'The Royal Institute of Public Administration, 1939–1972', *PA*, L (winter 1972), 419–46.
310 Robertson, James C. 'British policy in East Africa, March 1891 to May 1935', *EHR*, XCIII (Oct. 1978), 835–44.
311 Ross, James Frederick Stanley. 'Women and parliamentary elections', *BJS*, IV (1953), 14–24.
312 Schwarz, John E. 'Exploring a new role in policy making: the British House of Commons in the 1970s', *American Political Science Review*, LXXIV (March 1980), 23–37.
313 Weston, Corinne Comstock. 'The Liberal leadership and the Lords' veto, 1907–1910', *Hist. J.*, XI (no. 3, 1968), 508–37.
314 Willcox, Temple. 'Towards a Ministry of Information', *History*, LXIX (Oct. 1984), 398–414.
315 Willson, F. M. G. 'The routes of entry of new members of the British Cabinet, 1868–1958', *PS*, VII (no. 3, 1959), 222–32.
316 —— 'The organisation of British central government, 1955–1961', *PA*, XL (summer 1962), 159–206.
317 Wiseman, Herbert Victor. 'Regional government in the United Kingdom', *Parliamentary Affairs*, XIX (winter 1965–6), 56–82. A historical treatment, largely after 1940.
318 Wylie, Diana. 'Confrontation over Kenya: the Colonial Office and its critics, 1918–1940', *Journal of African History*, XVII (no. 3, 1977), 427–47.

V. POLITICAL HISTORY

1. Printed sources

319 Addison, Christopher. *Four and a half years: a personal diary from June 1914 to January 1919*. 1934, 2 vols. By a prominent officer of state.
320 Amery, Leopold S. *My political life*. 1953–5, 3 vols. By a statesman prominent in the twenties.
321 Asquith, Herbert Henry, 1st Earl of Oxford and Asquith. *Fifty years of parliament*. 1926, 2 vols. A personal history.
322 —— *Memories and reflections, 1852–1927*. Boston, 1928, 2 vols.
323 —— *Letters of the Earl of Oxford and Asquith to a friend*. [Ed. Desmond MacCarthy]. 1933–4, 2 vols.
324 —— *Letters to Venetia Stanley*. Ed. Michael and Eleanor Brock. 1982.
325 Attlee, Clement, Earl Attlee. *As it happened*. 1954. A disappointing autobiography, especially on domestic affairs. Attlee is more perceptive in his *The Labour Party in perspective*. 1937.
326 Barker, Bernard (ed.). *Ramsay MacDonald's political writings*. 1972.
327 Barnes, George N. *From workshop to War Cabinet*. 1924.
328 Bealey, Frank. 'Negotiations between the Liberal Party and the Labour Rep-

resentation Committee before the General Election of 1906'. *BIHR*, XXIX (1956), 261–74. Documents.

329 —— (ed.). *The social and political thought of the British Labour Party*. 1970. Extracts from one hundred speeches and writings, 1900–67.

330 Beattie, Alan (ed.). *English party politics*, II, *The twentieth century*. 1970. Documents with commentary.

331 Bevan, Aneurin. *In place of fear*. New ed., 1961. First published in 1952; a statement of Bevan's political and social philosophy.

332 Birrell, Augustine. *Things past redress*. 1937. Autobiography.

333 Boothby, Robert J. G., Baron Boothby. *I fight to live*. 1947. Autobiography (1919–41) by a Conservative supporter of Churchill in the 1930s.

334 Braithwaite, William J. *Lloyd George's ambulance wagon: being the memoirs of William J. Braithwaite, 1911–1912*. Ed. Henry N. Bunbury. 1957. 'The inside story of the preparation and passage through Parliament of the National Insurance Act of 1911', by a civil servant in the Inland Revenue Dept.

335 Briggs, Asa (ed.). *They saw it happen*. IV, an anthology of eyewitnesses' accounts of events in British history, 1897–1940. Oxford, 1960.

336 Brockway, Fenner. *Inside the left: thirty years of platform, press, prison and parliament*. 1942. Autobiographical, to 1939.

337 Brown, George, Baron George-Brown. *In my way*. 1970. Political memoirs of a Labour leader in the sixties.

338 Butler, Richard Austen, Baron. *The art of the possible: the memoirs of Lord Butler, K.G., C.H.* (1971). A fascinating and significant autobiography. See also his *Art of Memory: friends in perspective*. 1982.

339 Castle, Barbara. *The Castle diaries, 1964–70*. 1984. *The Castle diaries, 1974–76*. 1980. By a Labour politician.

340 Chamberlain, Austen. *Down the years*. (1934). 'Random recollections' of men and events. See also his *Politics from the inside: an epistolary chronicle, 1906–1914*. 1936.

341 Channon, Henry. *'Chips', the diaries of Sir Henry Channon*. Ed., Robert Rhodes James. 1967. Selections from fascinating diaries of a leading social figure and an M.P., 1935–58.

342 Churchill, Randoph S. and Martin Gilbert. *Winston S. Churchill*, companion vols., I–VI. Boston, Mass., 1967–83. Accompany (663).

343 Churchill, Winston Spencer. *The world crisis, 1914–1918*. New York, 1923–7, 4 vols. *The aftermath (the world crisis, 1918–1928)*. New York, 1929. Copious documents. See also Robin Prior, *Churchill's World Crisis as History*. 1983.

344 —— *Secret Session Speeches*. Comp. Charles Eade. 1946. Five speeches during World War II not recorded at the time.

345 —— *The war speeches of the Rt. Hon. Winston S. Churchill*. Ed. Charles Eade. 1951–2, 3 vols.

346 —— *His complete speeches, 1897–1963*. Ed. Robert Rhodes James. New York, 1974, 8 vols. The definitive collection; for some speeches outside Parliament only extracts are given; consult (344).

347 Clynes, John R. *Memoirs*. 1937, 2 vols. Useful account by a Labour leader.

348 Cooper, Duff, 1st Viscount Norwich. *Old men forget*. 1963. Autobiographical.

349 Craig, Frederick W. S. (ed.). *British General Election manifestoes*, 1918–66. Chichester, 1970.

350 Cross, Colin (ed.). *Life with Lloyd George: the diary of A. K. Sylvester, 1931–45*. 1975. Sylvester was Lloyd George's secretary.

351 Crossman, Richard Howard Stafford. *The diaries of a Cabinet minister*. 1975–7, 3 vols. On 1964–70. Useful biographical notes. For a shortened version, consult Anthony Howard, ed., *Richard Crossman: The Crossman diaries: selections from the diaries of a Cabinet minister, 1964–1970*. 1979.

352 Crozier, William P. *Off the record: political interviews, 1933–1943*. Ed. Alan J. P. Taylor. 1973. The editor of the *Manchester Guardian* interviews leading political figures.

353 Cummings, Michael. *The uproarious years: a pictorial post-war history, with an introduction by Hugh Massingham*. 1954. Cartoons from the *Daily Express*.

354 Dalton, Hugh. *Call back yesterday: memoirs, 1887–1931*. 1953. *The fateful years:*

memoirs, 1931–45. 1957. *High tide and after; memoirs, 1945–1960*. 1962. Based on diaries.

355 Eccles, David McAdam, 1st Baron. *Life and politics: a moral diagnosis*. 1967.

356 [Eden, Anthony]. *The memoirs of Anthony Eden: full circle*. 1960. *Facing the dictators*. 1962. *The reckoning*. 1965. *Full circle* is essential for the Suez crisis, 1956.

357 Esher, Reginald Brett, 1st Viscount. *Journals and letters of Reginald Viscount Esher*. Ed. Maurice V. Brett and Oliver Sylvain Baliol Brett, 3rd Viscount Esher. 1934–8, 4 vols. See also (681).

358 Fitzroy, Almeric. *Memoirs*. 6th ed. [1925], 2 vols. Spans 1898–1923. He was clerk of the Prioy Council.

359 Gilbert, Martin. *Plough my own furrow: the story of Lord Allen of Hurtwood as told through his writings and correspondence*. 1965.

360 Gooch, George P. *Under six reigns*. 1958. Reminiscence.

361 Grigg, P. J. *Prejudice and judgment*. 1948. By a civil servant (from 1913) and Cabinet member.

362 Grimond, Jo. *Memoirs*. 1979. By the leader of the Liberal Party, 1965–7.

363 Haldane, Richard Burdon, Viscount Haldane. *An autobiography*. New York, 1919. See also his *Before the war*. 1920.

364 Hamilton, Mary Agnes. *Remembering my good friends*. 1944. Valuable for Labour politics.

365 [Hobhouse, Sir Charles]. *Inside Asquith's Cabinet, from the diaries of Sir Charles Hobhouse*. Ed. E. I. David. 1977.

366 Hurd, Douglas. *End to promises: sketch of a government, 1970–4*. 1979. By a Cabinet member under Heath.

367 James, Robert Rhodes (ed.). *Memoirs of a Conservative: J. C. C. Davidson's memoirs and papers, 1910–1937*. 1969. Useful on Baldwin.

368 Johnston, Thomas. *Memories*. 1952. Excellent on Labour and Scotland.

369 Jones, Thomas. *A diary with letters, 1931–1950*. 1954. Useful on Cliveden set.

370 —— *Whitehall Diary*. Ed. Keith Middlemas. 1969–71, 3 vols. Embraces 1916–30.

371 Kilmuir, D. P. Maxwell Fyfe, Earl of. *Political adventure: the memoirs of the Earl of Kilmuir*. 1964. By a Conservative politician and law officer of the crown.

372 [King, Cecil]. *The Cecil King diary, 1965–1970*. 1972. By a prominent newspaper proprietor. Continued by his *Cecil King diaries, 1970–4*. 1975.

373 Labour Party. *Report of the . . . annual conference*. 1901–. Title varies.

374 Lansbury, George. *My life*. 1928. Autobiography of a Labour Party leader.

375 Lee, Jennie. *Tomorrow is a new day*. 1942. Autobiographical; in the USA published as *This great journey* (1942).

376 Lloyd George, David. *War memoirs of David Lloyd George*. Boston, Mass., 1933–7, 6 vols. Very significant though unreliable.

377 Long, Walter, 1st Viscount Long of Wraxall. *Memories*. New York, n.d. By a Conservative politician; a member of the Cabinet, 1895–1905, 1915–21.

378 Low, David. *Years of wrath: a cartoon history, 1932–1945*. 1949. Largely reprinted from the London *Evening Standard*.

379 Lucy, Henry. *The diary of a journalist*. 1920–3, 3 vols. On Parliament, 1885–1916. Very useful.

380 Lyttleton, Oliver, Viscount Chandos. *The memoirs of Lord Chandos*. 1962. By an industrialist and a Conservative politician.

381 MacArdle, Dorothy. *The Irish Republic: a documented chronicle of the Anglo–Irish conflict and the partitioning of Ireland with a detailed account of the period, 1916–1923*. 1937.

382 MacDonald, J. Ramsay. *The socialist movement*. 1911. Cf. companion vols. in Home University Library series: Lord Hugh Cecil. *Conservatism*. [1912]. Leonard T. Hobhouse. *Liberalism*. 1911.

383 Macmillan, Harold. *Winds of change, 1914–1939*. 1966. *The blast of war, 1939–1945*. 1967. *Tides of fortune, 1945–1955*. 1969. *Riding the storm, 1956–1959*. 1971. *Pointing the way, 1959–1961*. 1972. *At the end of the day, 1961–1963*. 1973. These volumes of autobiography are revealing as to Macmillan himself; otherwise disappointing.

384 —— *War Diaries; politics and war in the Mediterranean, January 1943–May 1945*. 1984.

385 Maurice, Nancy (ed.). *The Maurice case: from the papers of Major-General Sir Frederick Maurice*. [Hamden, Conn.], 1972. Concerns the controversy in May 1918 over Maurice's letter to the press concerning British troop strength.

386 Miliband, Ralph and John Saville (eds.). *The socialist register, 1964–*. 1964–. Annual. Analysis of contemporary events, with a long chapter on Britain. Latest volume is for 1981.

387 Minney, Rubeigh J. *The private papers of Hore-Belisha*. 1960.

388 Morgan, Kenneth O. *Lloyd George: family letters, 1885–1936*. 1973.

389 Morley, John. *Recollections*. New York, 1917, 2 vols. Disorganized, but valuable.

390 —— Viscount Morley of Blackburn. *Memorandum on resignation, August 1914*. New York, 1928. A classic document.

391 Morrison, Herbert, Baron Morrison of Lambeth. *Herbert Morrison: an autobiography*. 1960. Weak on Labour Government of 1945–51.

392 Mosley, Oswald. *My life*. 1968. Tiresome and turgid, but revealing.

393 Murray, Arthur C. *Master and brother: Murrays of Elibank*. 1945. Memoir.

394 Newton, Thomas Wodehouse Legh, 2nd Baron. *Retrospection*. 1941. Lord Newton was a diplomat, politician, and author.

395 O'Connor, Thomas P. *Memoirs of an old parliamentarian*. New York, 1929, 2 vols. O'Connor was a Member of Parliament, 1885–1929. See also (2609).

396 Pakenham, Francis Aungier, 7th Earl of Longford. *Born to believe: an autobiography*. 1953. See also his *Five lives*. 1964. And his *The grain of wheat*. 1974.

397 Pankhurst, Emmeline. *My own story*. 1914. By a militant suffragette.

398 Parmoor, Charles Alfred Cripps, 1st Baron. *A retrospect: looking back over a life of more than eighty years*. 1936. By a Conservative politican who switched to Labour.

399 *Political party year books, 1885–1948*. 128 vols. Includes *The constitutional year book, 1885–1939* of the Conservative Party; *The Labour year book, 1895–1948; The Liberal yearbook, 1887–1939*. Reprint, Harvester Press, Hassocks, Sussex. Publication concluded, 1974.

400 Pollitt, Harry. *Serving my time: an apprenticeship to politics*. 1940. By a secretary general and chairman of the British Communist Party. See also John Mahon, *Harry Pollitt*. 1976.

401 Ponsonby, Arthur, Baron. *Falsehood in war-time*. 1928. Documents.

402 Pritt, Denis N. *The autobiography of D. N. Pritt*. 1965–6, 3 vols. Carries Pritt from Toryism to Marxism.

403 Ramsden, John (ed.). *Real old Tory politics: the political diaries of Sir Robert Sanders, Lord Bayford, 1910–35*. 1984.

404 *Report of the Royal Commission on the poor laws and the relief of distress*. 1909. Authorized by Parliament in 1905.

405 Riddell, George Allardice, Baron. *Lord Riddell's war diary, 1914–1918*. [1923]. Also *More pages from my diary, 1908–1914*. 1934.

406 Sacks, Benjamin. *J. Ramsay MacDonald in thought and action*. Albuquerque, N. Mex., 1952. Digest of MacDonald's writings and speeches.

407 Salter, James Arthur, 1st Baron. *Memoirs of a public servant*. 1961. See also Salter's *Slave of the lamp: a public servant's notebook*. 1967.

408 Samuel, Herbert Louis, 1st Viscount. *Memoirs*. 1945. Published in the USA as *Grooves of change: a book of memoirs*. New York, 1946. See also (652).

409 Shinwell, Emmanuel. *Conflict without malice*. 1955. Autobiographical. See also his *The Labour story*. 1963.

410 Snowden, Philip. *An autobiography*. 1934, 2 vols.

411 Stansky, Peter (ed.). *The Left and war: British Labour Party and World War I*. New York, 1969. Documents.

412 Stevenson, Frances. *The years that are past*. 1967. By Lloyd George's secretary and mistress. See also her *Lloyd George: a diary*. Ed. Alan J. P. Taylor. 1971. And *My darling pussy: the letters of Lloyd George and Frances Stevenson, 1913–1941*. Ed. A. J. P. Taylor. 1975.

413 Swanwick, Helena M. L. *Builders of peace: being ten years' history of the Union of Democratic control.* 1973. First published in 1924.
414 Swinton, Philip Cunliffe-Lister, 1st Earl. *Sixty years of power: some memories of the men who wielded it.* 1966. From Balfour to Alec Douglas-Home.
415 Templewood, Samuel Hoare, Viscount. *Nine troubled years.* 1954. Indispensable for 'appeasement' and other matters of state, 1931–40.
416 Tiltman, H. Hessell. *James Ramsay MacDonald: Labor's man of destiny.* 1929. Useful for quotations, from writings and speeches, to 1924.
417 Wedgwood, Rt. Hon. Josiah C. *Memoirs of a fighting life.* 1941. Liberal who turned Labourite.
418 Wigg, George, Baron. *George Wigg.* 1972. Autobiography of a Liberal politician.
419 Williams, Philip M. (ed.). *The diary of Hugh Gaitskell, 1945–1956.* 1983.
420 Williams, Shirley. *Politics is for people.* 1981.
421 Wilson, Harold. *The Labour government, 1964–1970: a personal record.* 1971. *The final term: the Labour government, 1974–76.* 1979.
422 Wilson, Trevor (ed.). *The political diaries of C. P. Scott, 1911–1928.* 1970.
423 Winterton, Edward Turnour, Earl. *Fifty tumultous years.* 1955. Reminiscences of the years 1904–54 by a politician and journalist.
424 Woolton, Frederick James Marquis, Earl of. *Memoirs.* 1959. Woolton was chairman of the Conservative Party in a crucial period, 1945–51.

2. Surveys

425 Barnett, Correlli. *The collapse of British power.* 1972.
426 Beloff, Max. *Wars and welfare: Britain, 1914–1945.* 1984.
427 Blake, Robert. *The Conservative Party from Peel to Thatcher.* 1985. Rev. from 1st ed., 1970.
428 ——*The decline of power, 1915–1964.* 1985.
429 Boyd, Francis. *British politics in transition, 1945–63.* 1964.
430 Brand, Carl F. *British Labour's rise to power: eight studies.* 1941.
431 —— *The British Labour Party: a short history.* 1974.
432 Calvocoressi, Peter. *The British experience, 1945–75.* New York, 1978.
433 Childs, David. *Britain since 1945: a political history.* New York, 1980.
434 Cole, G. D. H. *History of the Labour party from 1914.* 1948.
435 Cook, Chris. *A short history of the Liberal Party, 1900–1976.* 1976.
436 James, Robert Rhodes. *The British revolution: British politics, 1880–1939.* 1976–7, 2 vols.
437 Leys, Colin. *Politics in Britain: an introduction.* 1983.
438 Lindsay, T. F. and Michael Harrington. *The Conservative Party, 1918–1970.* 1974. Excellent short treatment.
439 Lyons, Francis S. L. *Ireland since the famine.* New York, 1971. Includes excellent treatment of the twentieth century. See also his Ford Lectures in 1970: *Culture and Anarchy in Ireland, 1890–1939.* Oxford, 1979.
440 McElwee, William. *Britain's locust years, 1918–1940.* 1962.
441 McFarlane, Leslie J. *British politics, 1918–1964.* 1965.
442 Macintosh, John Pitcairn. *British prime ministers in the twentieth century.* 1977–8, 2 vols.
443 Moore, Roger F. *The emergence of the Labour Party, 1880–1924.* 1978.
444 Pugh, Martin. *Making of modern British politics, 1867–1939.* New York, 1982.
445 Ramsden, John. *The age of Balfour and Baldwin, 1902–1940.* 1978.
446 Sked, Alan and Chris Cook. *Post-war Britain: a political history.* 1979. General treatment of years 1945–79.
447 Thomas, Neville Penry. *A history of British politics from the year 1900.* 1956.

3. Monographs

448 Adams, R. J. Q. *Arms and the wizard: Lloyd George and the Ministry of Munitions, 1915–1916.* College Station, Tex., 1978.

449 Anderson, Gerald D. *Fascists, communists and the National Government: civil liberties in Great Britain, 1931–1937*. Columbia, Mo., 1983.
450 Barker, Elizabeth. *Churchill and Eden at war*. New York, 1978.
451 Barker, Rodney. *Education and politics, 1900–1951: a study of the Labour Party*. Oxford, 1972.
452 —— *Political ideas in modern Britain*. 1978.
453 Barry, E. Eldon. *Nationalization in British politics: the historical background*. 1965.
454 Bassett, Reginald. *Nineteen thirty-one: political crisis*. 1958. Holds that MacDonald was not disloyal to the Labour Party.
455 Bealey, Frank and Henry Pelling. *Labour and politics, 1900–1906: a history of the Labour Representation Committee*. 1958.
456 Beaverbrook, William Maxwell Aitken, 1st Baron. *Politicians and the war, 1914–1916*. New York, 1928. But see Peter Fraser, 'Lord Beaverbrook's fabrications in *Politicians and the war, 1914–1916*', *Hist. J.*, XXV (1982), 147–66.
457 —— *Men and power, 1917–1918*. 1956.
458 —— *The decline and fall of Lloyd George*. 1963. On the events of 1921–2.
459 Beer, Samuel H. *British politics in the collectivist age*. New York, 1969.
460 —— *Britain against itself: the political contradictions of collectivism*. 1982.
461 Beloff, Max and Gillian Peele. *The government of the United Kingdom: political authority in a changing society*. New York, 1980.
462 Bentley, Michael. *The Liberal mind, 1914–1929*. 1977.
463 Berrington, Hugh B. *Backbench opinion in the House of Commons, 1945–55*. Oxford, 1973. See also (516).
464 Birch, Alan Harold. *Political integration and disintegration in the British Isles*. 1977.
465 Blewett, Neal. *The peers, the parties and the people: the General Elections of 1910*. 1972. Detailed.
466 Bogdanor, Vernon. *The people and the party system: the referendum and electoral reform in British politics*. 1981.
467 —— *Liberal party politics*. 1983. A collection of essays of great value.
468 Booker, Christopher. *The seventies: portrait of a decade*. 1980.
469 Boyce, D. G. *Englishmen and Irish troubles: British public opinion and the making of Irish policy, 1918–1922*. Cambridge, Mass., 1972.
470 Buckland, Patrick. *Irish unionism*, I, *The Anglo-Irish and the new Ireland, 1885–1922*; II, *Ulster Unionism and the origins of Northern Ireland, 1886–1922*. Dublin, 1972–3.
471 Bunyan, Tony. *The history and practice of the political police in Britain*. 1976.
472 Burk, Kathleen (ed.). *War and the state: the transformation of the British government, 1914–1919*. 1982. Essays.
473 Butler, David E. *The British General Election of 1951*. 1952. *The British General Election of 1955*. 1955.
474 —— *The electoral system in Britain since 1918*. 2nd ed., Oxford, 1963.
475 —— *The British General Election of 1979*. 1980.
476 —— *The General Election of 1983*. 1984.
477 —— and Dennis Kavanagh. *The British General Election of February 1974*. 1974. *The British General Election of October 1974*. 1975.
478 —— and Anthony King. *The British General Election of 1964*. 1965. *The British General Election of 1966*. 1966.
479 —— and Uwe Kitzinger. *The 1975 referendum*. New York, 1976.
480 —— and Michael Pinto-Duschinsky. *The British General Election of 1970*. 1971.
481 —— and Richard Rose. *The General Election of 1959*. 1960.
482 —— and Anne Stoneau. *British political facts, 1900–1979*. 5th ed., 1980. Scrupulously exact.
483 Campbell, John. *Lloyd George: the goat in the wilderness, 1922–1931*. 1977.
484 Carberry, Thomas F. *Consumers in politics: a history and general review of the Co-operative Party*. Manchester, 1969.
485 Challinor, Raymond. *The origins of British Bolshevism*. 1977.
486 Chester, Lewis, et al. *The Zinoviev letter*. Philadelphia, 1968.

POLITICAL HISTORY

487 Clarke, Peter F. *Lancashire and the new Liberalism*. Cambridge, 1971. Significant regional study.

488 —— *Liberals and Social Democrats*. Cambridge, 1979. Extraordinary bibliography.

489 Cline, Catherine Ann. *Recruits to Labour: the British Labour Party, 1914–31*. Syracuse, N.Y., 1963.

490 Coates, David. *Labour in power: a study of the Labour Government, 1974–1979*. 1980.

491 Coffey, Thomas M. *Agony at Easter: the 1916 Irish uprising*. New York, 1969.

492 Cole, George D. H. *History of the Labour Party from 1914*. 1948. Important.

493 Colvin, Ian. *The Chamberlain Cabinet*. 1971. Based on Cabinet papers.

494 Cook, Chris. *The age of alignment: electoral politics in Britain, 1922–1929*. Toronto, 1975.

495 —— and John Ramsden (eds.). *By-elections in British politics*. 1973. Twelve essays.

496 —— and Ian Taylor (eds.) *The Labour Party: an introduction to its history, structure and politics*. 1980. Essays.

497 Cowling, Maurice. *The impact of Labour, 1920–24: the beginning of modern British politics*. Cambridge, 1970. Important study, in detail of these years.

498 Craton, Michael and Herbert W. McCready. *The great Liberal revival, 1903–6*. 1966. Useful for the polls.

499 Cregier, Don. M. *Bounder from Wales: Lloyd George's career before the First World War*. 1976.

500 Crosby, Gerda Richards. *Disarmament and peace in British politics, 1914–1919*. 1957.

501 Curran, Joseph M. *The birth of the Irish Free State, 1921–1923*. University, Ala., 1980.

502 Dangerfield, George. *The strange death of Liberal England*. New York, 1935. Brilliant and stimulating but not altogether reliable.

503 —— *The damnable question: a study in Anglo-Irish relations*. Boston, 1969. Not always reliable.

504 Das, Manmath N. *India under Morley and Minto: politics behind revolution, repression and reform*. 1964. Based on Morley and Minto papers.

505 Davies, Hywel. *The Welsh Nationalist Party, 1925–1945: a call to nationhood*. 1983.

506 Davies, W. Watkin. *Lloyd George, 1863–1914*. 1939. Well done.

507 Donaldson, Frances. *The Marconi scandal*. 1962. The most reliable account.

508 Dowse, Robert E. *Left in the centre: the Independent Labour Party, 1893–1940*. 1966. Sympathetic treatment of its decline.

509 Eatwell, Roger. *The 1945–51 Labour Governments*. 1979. Cf. (600).

510 Eckstein, Harry. *Pressure group politics: the case of the British Medical Association*. Stanford, Calif., 1960.

511 Einzig, Paul. *Decline and fall? Britain's crisis in the sixties*. 1969. A general assessment; no documentation.

512 Emy, H. V. *Liberals, radicals and social politics, 1892–1914*. Cambridge, 1973. Additional detail based on original sources.

513 Fair, John D. *British interparty conferences: a study of the process of conciliation in British politics, 1867–1921*. Oxford, 1980.

514 Fergusson, James. *The Curragh incident*. 1964. The best treatment.

515 Fine, Samuel Edward. *Changing British party system, 1945–1979*. Washington, D.C., 1980.

516 Finer, Samuel E., Hugh B. Berrington, and David J. Bartholomew. *Backbench opinion in the House of Commons, 1955–59*. Oxford, 1961. On matters of defence. See also (463).

517 Freeden, Michael. *The new Liberalism: an ideology of social reform*. 1978.

518 Gainer, Bernard. *The alien invasion: the origins of the Aliens Act of 1905*. Ithaca, N.Y., 1972.

519 Goldie, Grace Wyndham. *Facing the nation: television and politics, 1936–1976*. 1977.

520 Gollin, Alfred M. *Balfour's burden: Arthur Balfour and imperial preference*. 1965.

521 Guinn, Paul. *British strategy and politics, 1914 to 1918*. Oxford, 1965. Relations between generals and politicians.
522 Gwynn, Denis. *The history of partition (1912–1925)*. Dublin, 1950. As good a general account as we have.
523 Halévy, Elie. *A history of the English people in the nineteenth century*, V, *Imperialism and the rise of labour*; VI, *The rule of democracy, 1905–1914*. Trans. Edward Ingram Watkin. 2nd ed., 1951–3. This celebrated work still stands up well.
524 Hankey, Maurice P. A., 1st Baron. *The supreme command, 1914–1918*. 1961, 2 vols. By the secretary of the War Cabinet.
525 Harrison, Brian. *Separate spheres: the opposition to women's suffrage in Britain*. 1978.
526 Haseler, Stephen. *The Gaitskellites: revisionism in the British Labour Party, 1951–64*. 1969. Thorough.
527 Hazlehurst, Cameron. *Politicians at war, July 1914 to May 1915*. 1971.
528 Hodder-Williams, Richard. *Public opinion polls and British politics* 1970. Analysis since 1945.
529 Hoffman, John D. *Conservative Party in opposition, 1945–51*. 1964.
530 Hohmen, Helen Fisher. *The development of social insurance and minimum wage legislation in Great Britain*. Boston, Mass., 1933.
531 Hope, James F. *A history of the 1900 parliament*. 1907. On 1900–1.
532 Hume, Leslie Parker. *The National Union of Women's Suffrage Societies, 1897–1914*. New York, 1982.
533 Hyam, Ronald P. *Elgin and Churchill at the Colonial Office*. 1905–8. New York, 1968. Gives Elgin his due.
534 [Illingworth, Percy H.]. *The government record, 1906–1913: seven years of Liberal legislation and administration*. 1913. Detailed account by Liberal Party Publication Department.
535 Irving, Clive, et al. *Scandal '63: a study of the Profumo affair*. 1963.
536 Jackson, Robert J. *Rebels and whips: an analysis of dissension, discipline and cohension in British political parties*. 1968. Analysis of period 1945–64.
537 Jalland, Patricia. *The Liberals and Ireland: the Ulster question in British politics to 1914*. 1980.
538 James, Robert Rhodes. *Ambitions and realities: British politics, 1964–1970*. 1972.
539 Janosik, Edward G. *Constituency Labour Parties in Britain*. 1968. Based on 1964 General Election.
540 Jenkins, Peter. *The battle of Downing Street*. 1970. The 'political crisis' of June 1969. Instant history, stimulating.
541 [Johnson, Francis]. *The I.L.P. in war and peace: a short account of the party from its foundation to the present day*. 1942.
542 Johnson, Paul Barton. *Land for heroes: the planning of British reconstruction*. Chicago, Ill., 1968. Important.
543 Jupp, James. *The radical Left in Britain, nineteen thirty-one to nineteen forty-one*. 1982.
544 Kellas, James G. *The Scottish political system*. Cambridge, 1973. Includes recent political history.
545 Kendall, Walter. *The revolutionary movement in Britain in 1900–1921: the origins of British communism*. 1969.
546 Kinnear, Michael. *The British voter: an atlas and survey since 1885*. Ithaca, N.Y., 1968. 'A study of the economic and social background of politics'. Goes through the General Election of 1966.
547 —— *The fall of Lloyd George: the political crisis of 1922*. 1973. His view is challenged by McKibbin. See (568).
548 Klugman, James. *History of the Communist Party of Great Britain*. 1969, 2 vols. Strongly partisan. Cf. (593).
549 Kogan, David and Maurice Kogan. *The battle of the Labour Party*. 1982. Largely on 1979–82.
550 Koss, Stephen E. *John Morley at the India Office, 1905–1910*. 1969.
551 —— *Lord Haldane, scapegoat for Liberalism*. New York, 1969. A controversial contribution to the political crisis of May 1915.
552 —— *Non-conformity in modern British politics*. 1975.

553 Lapping, Brian. *The Labour Government, 1964–70*. 1970. Instant history.
554 Lawlor, Sheila. *Britain and Ireland, 1914–1923*. Totowa, N.J., 1983.
555 Lebzelter, Gisela C. *Political anti-Semitism in England, 1918–1939*. 1978.
556 Lee, John Michael. *The Churchill coalition, 1940–1945*. Hamden, Conn., 1980.
557 Levin, Bernard. *The pendulum years: Britain and the sixties*. 1970. A wide examination–political, economic, social.
558 Lewis, Ben W. *British planning and nationalization*. New York, 1952. Developments during 1945–51.
559 Longford, 7th Earl of (Francis Aungier Pakenham) and Anne McHardy. *Ulster*. 1981.
560 —— *Eleven at No. 10: a personal view of prime ministers, 1931–1984*. 1984.
561 Lunn, Kenneth and Richard C. Thurlow (eds.). *British Fascism: essays on the radical right in inter-war Britain*. 1980.
562 Lyman, Richard. *The first Labour government, 1924*. [1957]
563 McBriar, A. M. *Fabian socialism and English politics, 1884–1918*. Cambridge, 1962.
564 McCallum, Ronald B. and Alison Readman. *The British General Election of 1945*. 1945. See also Henry Pelling. 'The 1945 General Election reconsidered', *HJ*, XXIII (no. 2, 1980), 399–414.
565 McCarran, M. Margaret Patricia. *Fabianism in the political life of Britain, 1919–1931*. 2nd ed., Chicago, 1954. Complete, but sometimes misleading.
566 Maccoby, Simon. *English radicalism: the end?* 1961. Concerns 1906–31.
567 McHenry, Dean E. *His Majesty's Opposition: structure and problems of the British Labor Party, 1913–1938*. Berkeley, Calif., 1940.
568 McKibbin, Ross. *Evolution of the Labour Party, 1910–1924*. 1974. The best account.
569 McKie, David and Chris Cook (eds.). *The decade of disillusion: British politics in the sixties*. 1972. Essays by various writers.
570 Marcus, Geoffrey. *Before the lamps went out: Britain's golden age, Christmas 1913–August 1914*. Boston, 1965. A very sensitive account.
571 Matthew, Henry C. G. *The Liberal Imperialists: the ideas and politics of a post-Gladstonian elite*. 1973. Largely restricted to leadership.
572 Middlemas, Robert Keith. *the Clydesiders: a left wing struggle for parliamentary power*. 1965. The role of Glasgow Independent Labour Party members of Parliament, 1922–3.
573 Miliband, Ralph. *Parliamentary socialism: a study in the politics of Labour*. 2nd ed., 1972. A general view since 1906.
574 Minkin, Lewis. *The Labour Party Conference*. Manchester, 1980.
575 Miller, William Lockley. *Electoral dynamics in Britain since 1918*. New York, 1977.
576 —— *The end of British politics? Scots and English political behaviour in the seventies*. Oxford, 1981.
577 Morgan, David. *Suffragists and Liberals: the politics of women's suffrage in England*. 1975. See also Andrew Rosen. *Rise up women: the militant campaign of the Women's Social and Political Union, 1903–1914*. 1974.
578 Morgan Kenneth O. *David Lloyd George: Welsh radical as world statesman*. Cardiff, 1964.
579 —— *Wales in British politics*. 1970.
580 —— *The age of Lloyd George: the Liberal Party and British politics, 1880–1929*. 2nd ed., 1978. Best brief treatment.
581 —— *Consensus and disunity: the Lloyd George coalition Government, 1918–1922*. Oxford, 1979.
582 —— *Labour in power, 1945–51*. 1984. Fine bibliography.
583 Morris, A. J. Anthony. *Radicalism against war, 1906–1914*. Totowa, N.J., 1972. See also his *Edwardian radicalism, 1900–1914*. 1974.
584 —— *The scaremongers: the advocacy of war and rearmament, 1896–1914*. 1984.
585 Murray, Bruce K. *The people's budget, 1909–10: Lloyd George and Liberal politics*. 1980.
586 Nicholas, Herbert G. *The British General Election of 1950*. 1951.
587 Northedge, F. S. and Audrey Wells. *Britain and soviet communism: the impact of a revolution*. Atlantic Highlands, N.J., 1982.

588 Norton, Philip. *Dissension in the House of Commons, 1974–1979*. 1980. See also his *Conservative dissidents: dissent within the parliamentary Conservative Party, 1970–74*. 1978.

589 Pakenham, Francis, 7th Earl of Longford. *Peace by ordeal: an account from first-hand sources of the negotiation and signature of the Anglo–Irish Treaty*. 2nd ed., Cork, 1951.

590 Parkinson, Roger. *Blood, toil, tears and sweat: the war history from Dunkirk to Alamein, based on the War Cabinet papers of 1940 to 1942*. 1973. Continued by his *A day's march nearer home: the war history from Alamein to VE Day based on the War Cabinet papers of 1942–1945*. New York. 1974.

591 Peele, Gillian and Chris Cook (eds.). *The politics of reappraisal, 1918–1939*. 1975. Essays by various writers.

592 Pelling, Henry. *A short history of the Labour Party*. 1961. Interesting judgments.

593 —— *The British Communist Party: a historical profile*. 1975. Reliable. Cf. (548).

594 —— *The Labour governments, 1945–51*. 1984. With excellent bibliography.

595 Penniman, Howard R. (ed.). *Britain at the polls: the parliamentary elections of 1974*. 1975.

596 Phillips, Gregory D. *The diehards: aristocratic society and politics in Edwardian England*. Cambridge, Mass., 1979. Concerns the Parliament Act of 1911.

597 Pierson, Stanley. *British socialists: the journey from fantasy to politics*. Cambridge, Mass., 1979.

598 Plowden, William. *The motor car and politics, 1896–1970*. 1971. Well researched and well argued.

599 Poirier, Philip P. *The advent of the British Labour Party*. 1958. Excellent.

600 Pritt, Denis N. *The Labour Government, 1945–51*. 1963. Hostile account. Cf. (509) and (582).

601 Pulzer, Peter G. J. *Political representation and elections: parties and voting in Great Britain*. 1967. On the period 1945–66.

602 Punnett, Robert M. *Front-bench opposition: the role of the leader of the Opposition, the shadow Cabinet and shadow Government in British politics*. 1973. Principally in 1951–70 period.

603 Ramsden, John. *The making of the Conservative Party policy: the Conservative research department since 1929*. 1980.

604 Rasmussen, Jorgen Scott. *The Liberal Party: a study of retrenchment and revival*. [1965]. Published in the USA as *Retrenchment and revival: a study of the contemporary British Liberal Party*. Tucson, Ariz. [1964]. On developments since 1945.

605 Raymond, John (ed.). *The Baldwin Age*. 1960. Interesting, useful essays on political, economic, and cultural themes by various authors.

606 Rees, Goronwy. *A chapter of accidents*. 1972. Mainly concerning Guy Burgess and Donald Maclean.

607 Remple, Richard A. *Unionists divided: Arthur Balfour, Joseph Chamberlain and the Unionist free traders*. 1972.

608 Richards, Peter G. *Honourable members: a study of the British backbencher*. 1959.

609 —— *Parliament and conscience*. 1970. Discussion of issues in private Member Bills dealing with capital punishment, homosexuality, divorce, abortion, Sunday entertainment, and censorship in the theatre.

610 Riddell, Peter. *The Thatcher government*. Oxford, 1983. Thoughtful.

611 Rodgers, W. T. (ed.). *Hugh Gaitskill, 1906–1963*. 1964. Not biographical.

612 Rowland, Peter. *The last Liberal governments: the promised land, 1905–1910*. 1968. See also his *The last Liberal governments: unfinished business, 1911–1914*. 1971. Comprehensive.

613 Russell, A. K. *Liberal landslide: the General Election of 1906*. 1973.

614 Scally, Robert James. *The origins of the Lloyd George coalition: the politics of social imperialism, 1900–1918*. 1975.

615 Scanlon, John. *Decline and fall of the Labour Party*. [1932]. A contemporary view; polemical.

616 Searle, Geoffrey R. *The quest for national efficiency: a study in British politics and political thought, 1899–1914*. Berkeley, Calif., 1971.

617 Seldon, Anthony. *Churchill's Indian summer: the Conservative Government, 1951–55*. 1981.

618 Shrimsley, Anthony. *The first hundred days of Harold Wilson*. New York, 1965. Interesting instant history.
619 Simpson, Bill. *Labour, the unions and the party: a study of the trade unions and the British Labour movement*. 1973.
620 Skidelsky, Robert. *Politicians and the slump: the Labour Government of 1929–1931*. 1967.
621 Snyder, William P. *The politics of British defense policy, 1945–1962*. Columbus, Ohio, 1964.
622 Stacey, Frank. *The British ombudsman*. Oxford, 1971.
623 Stevenson, John and Chris Cook. *The slump: society and politics during the depression*. 1977.
624 Stewart, Anthony Terrence Quincey. *The Ulster crisis*. 1967. Excellent on the crisis of 1911–14.
625 Swartz, Marvin. *The Union of Democratic Control in British politics during the First World War*. Oxford, 1971. Largely from manuscript sources.
626 Taylor, Alan J. P., et al. *Churchill revised: a critical assessment*. New York, 1969. Churchill considered as statesman, politician, historian, military strategist, and 'the man'.
627 —— (ed.). *Lloyd George: Twelve essays*. New York, 1971.
628 Thompson, Laurence Victor. *1940*. New York, 1966.
629 Thomson, George Malcolm. *The twelve days: 24 July to 4 August 1914* 1964. Follows British policy and opinion.
630 Townshend, Charles. *British campaign in Ireland, 1919–1921: the development of political and military policies*. 1975. See also his 'The Irish Republican army and the development of guerrilla warfare, 1916–1921', *EHR*, XCIV (Apr. 1979), 318–45.
631 Wald, Kenneth D. *Crosses on the ballot: patterns of British voter alignment since 1885*. Princeton, N.J. 1983.
632 Walker, M. *The National Front*. 1977.
633 Warde, Alan. *Consensus and beyond: development of Labour Party strategy since the Second World War*. Manchester, 1982.
634 Watkins, K. W. *Britain divided: the effect of the Spanish Civil War on British public opinion*. 1963.
635 Williams, Desmond (ed.). *The Irish struggle, 1916–1926*. 1966. Fifteen scholarly essays by various authors.
636 Willis, Irene Cooper. *England's holy war: a study of English liberal idealism during the great war*. New York, 1928. In England published in three volumes: *How we went to war*. 1919. *How we got on with the war*. 1920. *How we came out of the war*. 1921.
637 Wilson, Arnold. *Old age pensions: a historical and critical study* 1941.
638 Wilson, Trevor. *The downfall of the Liberal Party, 1914–1935*. Ithaca, N.Y., 1966. Concludes that developments during World War I were mainly responsible.
639 Winter, J. M. *Socialism and the challenge of war: ideas and politics in Britain, 1912–1918*. 1974.
640 Younger, Calton. *Ireland's civil war*. 1968. Especially 1920–3; uses Cabinet papers.

4. Biographies

641 Adam, Colin Forbes. *Life of Lord Lloyd*. 1948.
642 Adams, William S. *Edwardian portraits*. 1957. Concerning Edward VII, W. S. Blunt, Sir Robert Baden-Powell, Lord Leverhulme, and E. D. Morel.
643 Allen, Bernard M. *Sir Robert Morant: a great public servant*. 1934.
644 Amery, Julian. *The life of Joseph Chamberlain*, IV–VI. 1951–69. Completes J. L. Garvin. *The life of Joseph Chamberlain*, I–III. 1932–4. For later and more sophisticated biographies, see (697).
645 Arnold, Bruce. *Margaret Thatcher: a study in power*. 1984. The best study so far. Cf. Angela Levin. *Margaret Thatcher*. 1981.
646 Aster, Sidney. *Anthony Eden*. New York, 1976.
647 Bartram, Peter. *David Steel, his life and politics*. 1981.

648 Birkenhead, Frederick W. F. Smith, 2nd Earl of. *F. E.: the life of F. E. Smith, First Earl of Birkenhead.* 1959.
649 —— *Halifax: the life of Lord Halifax.* 1965. The best biography.
650 Blake, Robert E. *The unknown prime minister: the life and times of Andrew Bonar Law, 1858–1923.* One of the best political biographies.
651 Bonham Carter, Violet. *Winston Churchill as I knew him.* 1965. Published in the USA as *Winston Churchill–an intimate portrait.* N.Y., 1965.
652 Bowle, John. *Viscount Samuel: a biography.* 1984. See also (408).
653 Brendon, Piers. *Winston Churchill: a biography.* 1984. Brief; worthwhile.
654 Brittain, Vera. *Pethick-Lawrence–a portrait.* 1963.
655 Brodrick, Alan Houghton. *Near to greatness: a life of the 6th Earl of Winterton.* 1965.
656 Brown, Kenneth D. *John Burns.* 1977. The best, so far.
657 Bullock, Alan Louis Charles. *The life and times of Ernest Bevin.* 3 vols.–1960, 1967, 1983.
658 Butler, James R. M. *Lord Lothian (Philip Kerr), 1882–1940.* 1960. Information concerning the Round Table Group.
659 Calton, David. *Anthony Eden.* 1981.
660 Campbell, John. *F. E. Smith, First Earl of Birkenhead.* 1983.
661 —— *Roy Jenkins: a biography.* New York, 1983.
662 Churchill, Randolph S. *Lord Derby, 'King of Lancashire': the official life of Edward, 17th Earl of Derby, 1865–1948.* 1959.
663 —— and Martin Gilbert. *Winston S. Churchill.* New York, 1966–83, 6 vols. Presently to 1941: in progress; the official life. See also (342).
664 Churchill, Winston S. *Great contemporaries.* Essays written 1929–37; Includes George V, Rosebery, Shaw, Joseph Chamberlain, John Morley, Asquith, and Curzon.
665 Cline, Catherine Ann. *E. D. Morel, 1873–1924: the strategies of protest.* 1980.
666 Cole, Margaret. *Makers of the labour movement.* 1948. Biographical sketches including those of Blatchford, Hardie, S. Webb, Arthur Henderson, George Lansbury, and H. G. Wells.
667 Cooke, Colin. *The life of Richard Stafford Cripps.* 1957. 'Official'.
668 Cosgrove, Patrick. *R. A. Butler: an English life.* 1981.
669 Craig, Mary. *Longford: a biographical portrait.* 1978.
670 Cross, Colin, *Philip Snowden.* 1966. Inadequate, but the best there is.
671 Cross, J. A. *Sir Samuel Hoare: a political biography.* 1977.
672 —— *Lord Swinton.* Oxford, 1982.
673 Dickie, John. *The uncommon commoner: a study of Sir Alec Douglas-Home.* 1964.
674 Dilks, David. *Neville Chamberlain.* Vol. I: *Pioneering and reform, 1869–1929.* 1984. Cf. Keith Feiling. *The life of Neville Chamberlain.* 1946. And Iain MacLeod. *Neville Chamberlain.* 1961.
675 Donoughe, Bernard and G. W. Jones. *Herbert Morrison: portrait of a politician.* 1973. 'Official', sympathetic, thorough.
676 Dugdale, Blanche E. C. *Arthur James Balfour, First Earl of Balfour.* 1936, 2 vols. For many years the standard. But now cf. Kenneth Young. *Arthur James Balfour: the happy life of the politician, prime minister, statesman and philosopher, 1848–1930.* 1963. See also Max Egremont. *Balfour.* 1980. It is more personal than the following, which is also excellent: Sydney H. Zebel. *Balfour, a political biography.* Cambridge, 1973.
677 Fisher, Herbert A. L. *James Bryce (Viscount Bryce of Dechmont, O.M.).* New York, 1927, 2 vols.
678 Fisher, Nigel. *Iain Macleod.* 1973.
679 —— *Harold Macmillan, a biography.* 1982.
680 Foot, Michael. *Aneurin Bevan: a biography.* 1962–73, 2 vols. But see also Mark Jenkins. *Bevanism: Labour's high tide.* Nottingham, 1980.
681 Fraser, Peter. *Lord Esher: a political biography.* 1973. See also (357).
682 Gooch, George P. *Life of Lord Courtney.* 1920.
683 Grigg, John. *The Young Lloyd George.* 1973. *The people's champion, 1902–1911.* 1978. *Lloyd George: from peace to war, 1912–1916.* 1985.
684 Gwynn, Denis. *The Life of John Redmond.* 1932.
685 Hamer, David A. *John Morley: Liberal intellectual in politics.* Oxford, 1968.

686 Hamilton, Mary Agnes. *Arthur Henderson: a biography.* 1938.
687 Harris, Kenneth. *Attlee.* 1982.
688 Hoggart, Simon and David Leigh. *Michael Foot: a portrait.* 1981.
689 Hutchinson, George. *Edward Heath.* 1970. Journalistic; informative. See also Margaret Laing, *Edward Heath, prime minister.* 1972.
690 Hyde, H. Montgomery. *Carson, the Life of Sir Edward Carson, Lord Carson of Duncairn.* 1953. Cf. (706).
691 —— *Lord Reading: the life of Rufus, First Marquess of Reading.* 1967.
692 —— *Baldwin: the unexpected prime minister.* 1973. Cf. (741).
693 Isaacs, Gerald Rufus, 2nd Marquess of Reading. *Rufus Isaacs, First Marquess of Reading, 1860–1914.* 1942–5, 2 vols.
694 James, Robert Rhodes. *Rosebery: a biography of Archibald Philip, fifth Earl of Rosebery.* 1963. Now the standard.
695 —— *Churchill: a study in failure, 1900–1939.* 1970.
696 —— *Victor Cazalet.* 1976.
697 Jay, Richard. *Joseph Chamberlain: a political study.* 1981. See also Denis Judd. *Radical Joe: a life of Joseph Chamberlain.* 1977. Cf. (644).
698 Jenkins, Roy. *Asquith: portrait of a man and of an era.* 1964. Cf. (701).
699 Johnson, Alan Campbell. *Sir Anthony Eden: a biography.* Rev. ed., 1955.
700 Jones, Thomas. *Lloyd George.* Cambridge, Mass., 1951. Still useful.
701 Koss, Stephen E. *Sir John Brunner: a radical plutocrat, 1842–1919.* Cambridge, 1970.
702 —— *Asquith.* 1976. Now the best biography.
703 Lewis, Roy. *Enoch Powell: principle in politics.* 1979. Useful. Better than Andrew Roth, *Enoch Powell: Tory tribune.* 1970.
704 Lysaght, Charles Edward. *Brendan Bracken.* 1979.
705 McNair, John. *James Maxton, the beloved rebel.* 1955.
706 Marjoribanks, Edward and Ian Colvin. *The life of Lord Carson.* 1932–6, 3 vols. Cf. (691).
707 Marquand, David. *Ramsay MacDonald.* 1977. Now standard.
708 Masterman, Lucy. *C. F. G. Masterman: a biography.* 1939. Includes diary entries and much correspondence.
709 Maurice, Sir Frederick. *Haldane, 1858–1928: the life of Viscount Haldane of Cloan.* 1929, 2 vols. See also (726).
710 Middlemas, Keith and John Barnes. *Baldwin: a biography.* 1969. Cf. (741).
711 Mitchell, David. *Queen Christabel: a biography of Christabel Pankhurst.* 1979.
712 Morgan, Kenneth. *Portrait of a progressive: political career of Christopher, Viscount Addison.* Oxford, 1980.
713 Morgan, Ted. *Churchill: young man in a hurry, 1874–1915.* 1982.
714 Morris, A. J. A. *C. P. Trevelyan, 1870–1958: portrait of a radical.* 1979.
715 Mosley, Nicholas. *Rules of the game: Sir Oswald and Lady Cynthia Mosley, 1896–1933.* 1982.
716 Pakenham, Francis Aungier, 7th Earl of Longford and Thomas P. O'Neill. *Eamon de Valera.* 1970.
717 Pelling, Henry. *Churchill.* 1974. More analytical than (663).
718 Petrie, Charles. *The life and letters of Sir Austen Chamberlain.* 1939–40, 2 vols.
719 Pope-Hennessy, James. *Lord Crewe, 1858–1945: the likeness of a Liberal.* 1955.
720 Postgate, Raymond W. *The life of George Lansbury.* 1951. See (374).
721 Reid, B. L. *The lives of Roger Casement.* New Haven, 1976. Cf. Roger Sawyer. *Casement, the flawed hero.* 1984. And Brian Inglis. *Roger Casement.* New York, 1973.
722 Roskill, Stephen W. *Hankey: man of secrets.* 1970–4, 3 vols. Authorized biography based on Hankey's diary and other papers.
723 Rowland, Peter. *David Lloyd George: a biography.* 1976. Best single-volume biography.
724 Skidelsky, Robert. *Oswald Mosley.* 1975.
725 Smith, Janet Adam. *John Buchan: a biography.* 1965.
726 Sommer, Dudley. *Haldane of Cloan, his life and times, 1856–1928.* 1960. Weak on Haldane at the War Office, but generally more adequate than (709).
727 Spender, John A. *The life of the Right Hon. Sir Henry Campbell-Bannerman,*

G.C.B. Boston, Mass., 1924, 2 vols. For many years the standard work; now in many ways superseded by (739).

728 —— and Cyril Asquith. *Life of Herbert Henry Asquith, Lord Oxford and Asquith.* 1932, 2 vols. But see (698) and (702).

729 Spiers, Edward M. *Haldane: an army reformer*. Edinburgh, 1980.

730 Sykes, Christopher. *Nancy: the life of Lady Astor*. New York, 1972.

731 Taylor, Alan J. P. *Beaverbrook*. 1972. Fascinating and provocative.

732 Taylor, Robert. *Lord Salisbury*. 1975. Excellent brief life.

733 Trevelyan, George Macaulay. *Grey of Falloden: the life and letters of Sir Edward Grey, afterwards Viscount Grey of Falloden*. Boston, 1937. Still of great interest though superseded in scholarship by (1066).

734 Vernon, Betty D. *Ellen Wilkinson, 1891–1947*. 1982. Biography of a feminist and politician.

735 Wedgwood, C. Veronica. *The last of the Radicals: Josiah Wedgwood, M.P.* 1951.

736 Wheeler-Bennett, John W. *John Anderson, Viscount Waverly*. 1962.

737 Williams, Philip M. *Hugh Gaitskell: a political biography*. 1979. Informative but uncritical. See also Geoffrey McDermott. *Leader lost: a biography of Hugh Gaitskell.* 1972.

738 Wilson, Duncan. *Leonard Woolf: a political biography*. 1978.

739 Wilson, John. *CB: a life of Sir Henry Campbell-Bannerman*. 1973. More scholarly detail than (727).

740 Young, Kenneth. *Churchill and Beaverbrook: a study in friendship and politics.* 1966. Narrative, 1910–65, based largely on Beaverbrook papers.

741 —— *Stanley Baldwin*. 1976. An improvement over G. M. Young. *Stanley Baldwin*. 1972.

5. Articles

742 Addison, Paul. 'The political beliefs of Winston Churchill', *TRHS*, 5th ser., 30 (1980), 23–47.

743 Bassett, Reginald. 'Telling the truth to the people: the myth of the Baldwin "Confession"', *Cambridge Journal*, II (Nov. 1948), 84–95. On Baldwin's speech in parliament, Nov. 12, 1936.

744 Beer, Samuel H. 'The representation of interests in the British government: historical background', *American Political Science Review*, LI (Sept. 1957), 613–50.

745 Benewick, R. J., et al. 'The floating voter and the Liberal view of representation', *PS*, XVII (1969), 177–95. Examination of voting behaviour and political opinion, 1950–62.

746 Bentley, Michael. 'Liberal politics and the Grey conspiracy of 1921', *Hist. J.*, XX (no. 2, 1977), 461–78.

747 Bernstein, George L. 'Liberalism and the progressive alliance in the constituencies, 1900–1914: three case studies', *Hist. J.*, XXVI (no. 3, 1983), 617–40.

748 Bisceglia, Louis R. 'Norman Angell and the "pacifist" muddle', *BIHR*, XLV (May 1972), 104–21.

749 Blewett, Neal. 'Free fooders, Balfourites, whole hoggers: factionism within the Unionist Party, 1906–1910', *Hist. J.*, XI (no. 1, 1968), 95–124.

750 Brown, Kenneth D. 'The Labour Party and the unemployment question, 1906–1910', *Hist. J.*, XIV (no. 3, 1971), 599–616.

751 Chamberlain, Chris. 'The growth of support for the Labour party in Britain', *BJS*, XXIV (Dec. 1973), 474–89. Sociological study of Labour Party's growth in the 1920s.

752 Clarke, Peter F. 'The end of laissez-faire and the politics of cotton', *Hist. J.*, XV (no. 3, 1972), 493–512.

753 Close, David H. 'Conservatives and coalition after the First world War', *JMH*, XLV (June 1973), 240–60.

754 —— 'The collapse of resistance to democracy: Conservatives, adult suffrage and second chamber reform', *Hist. J.*, XX (no. 4, 1977), 893–918.

755 —— 'The realignment of the British electorate in 1931', *History,* LVII (Oct. 1982), 393–404.
756 Crewe, Ivor, et al. 'Partisan realignment in Britain, 1964–1974', *British Journal of Political Science*, VII (April 1977), 129–90. Carefully done.
757 Crowe, Edward. 'Cross-voting in the British House of Commons: 1945–76', *Journal of Politics*, XLII (May 1980), 487–510.
758 Douglas, Roy. 'The background to the "Coupon" election arrangements', *EHR*, LXXXVI (April 1971), 318–36.
759 —— 'The National Democratic Party and the British Workers' League', *Hist. J.*, XV (no. 3, 1972), 533–52. Minority attitudes towards the First World War in Labour Party and socialist groups.
760 Dunbabin, J. P. D. 'British elections in the 19th and 20th centuries: a regional approach', *EHR*, XLV (April 1980), 241–67.
761 Dutton, D. J., 'The Unionist Party and social policy', *Hist. J.*, XXIV (no. 4, 1981), 871–84.
762 Edgar, David. 'Racism, Fascism and the politics of the National Front', *Race and Class*, XIX (Autumn 1977), 111–31.
763 Emy, H. V. 'The impact of financial policy on English party politics before 1914', *Hist. J.*, XV (no. 1, 1972), 103–31.
764 Epstein, Leon D. 'New M.P.s and the politics of the PLP', *PS*, X (1962), 121–9. Study of the Parliamentary Labour Party after 1952.
765 —— 'The nuclear deterrent and the British election of 1964', *JBS*, V (no. 2, 1966), 139–63.
766 Fair, John D. 'The Conservative basis for the formation of the National Government of 1931', *JBS*, XIX (spring 1980), 142–64.
767 —— 'The second Labour Government and the politics of electoral reform, 1929–1931', *Albion*, XIII (fall 1981), 276–301.
768 Franklin, Mark N. and Anthony Mughan. 'The decline of class voting in Britain: problems of analysis and interpretation', *American Political Science Review*, LXXII (June 1978), 523–34.
769 Fraser, Peter. 'Unionism and tariff reform: the crisis of 1906', *Hist. J.*, V (no. 2, 1962), 149–66.
770 —— 'British war policy and the crisis of Liberalism in May 1915', *JMH*, LIV (March 1982), 1–26.
771 Gilbert, Bentley B. 'Health and politics: the physical deterioration report of 1904', *Bulletin of the History of Medicine*, XXXIX (1965), 143–53.
772 —— 'David Lloyd George: the reform of British landholding and the budget of 1914', *Hist. J.*, XXI (no. 1, 1978), 117–41.
773 Golant, W. 'The emergence of C. R. Attlee as leader of the Parliamentary Labour Party in 1935', *Hist. J.*, XIII (no. 2, 1970), 318–32.
774 —— 'C. R. Attlee in the first and second Labour governments', *Parliamentary Affairs*, XXVI (summer 1973), 318–35.
775 Gollin, Alfred. 'Freedom or control in the First World War (the great crisis of May 1915)', *Historical Reflections*, II (winter 1975), 135–55.
776 Gooch, John. 'The Maurice debate 1918', *JCH*, III (Oct. 1968), 211–28.
777 Harrop, Martin. 'The changing British electorate', *Political Quarterly*, LIII (Oct.–Dec. 1982), 385–402. Study of the period 1951–82.
778 Hart, Michael. 'The Liberals, the war and the franchise', *EHR*, XCVII (Oct. 1982), 820–32.
779 Hazlehurst, Cameron. 'Asquith as a prime minister, 1908–1916', *EHR*, LXXXV (July 1970), 502–31.
780 Heller, Richard. 'East Fulham revisited', *JCH*, VI (no. 3, 1971), 172–96. Cf. (821).
781 Hobsbawm, Eric J. 'The British Communist Party', *Political Quarterly*, XXV (no. 1, 1954), 30–43. General information.
782 —— 'Some reflections on "the break up of Britain"', *New Left Review*, CV (Sept.–Oct. 1977), 3–23. An answer to Marxist militants.
783 Jacobson, Peter D. 'Rosebery and Liberal Imperialism, 1899—1903', *JBS*, XIII (Nov. 1973), 83–107.
784 Jalland, Patricia and John Stubbs. 'The Irish question after the outbreak of

war in 1914: some unfinished party business', *EHR*, XCVI (Oct. 1981), 778–807.

785 Kendle, J. E. 'The Round Table Movement and Home Rule all round', *Hist. J.*, XI (no. 2, 1968), 332–53.

786 Layton, Henry. 'The young Conservatives, 1945–70', *JCH*, VIII (Apr. 1973), 143–56.

787 Lemieux, Peter H. 'Political issues and Liberal support in the February 1974, British General Election', *PS*, XXV (Sept. 1977), 323–42.

788 Lyman, Richard W. 'James Ramsay MacDonald and the leadership of the Labour Party, 1918–1922', *JBS*, II (Nov. 1962), 132–60.

789 —— 'The British Labour Party: the conflict between socialist ideals and practical politics between the wars', *JBS*, V (Nov. 1965), 140–52.

790 McEwen, J. M. 'The coupon election of 1918 and Unionist members of Parliament', *JMH*, XXXIV (Sept. 1962), 294–306.

791 —— 'The struggle for mastery in Britain: Lloyd George versus Asquith, December 1916', *JBS*, XVIII (fall 1978), 131–56.

792 —— 'Northcliffe and Lloyd George at war, 1914–1918', *Hist. J.*, XXIV (Sept. 1981), 651–72.

793 McGill, Barry. 'Asquith's predicament, 1914–1918', *JMH*, XXXIX (Sept. 1967), 283–303. Uses Cabinet papers.

794 McKibbin, Ross. 'The economic policy of the second Labour Government, 1927–1931', *PP*, LXVIII (1975), 95–123.

795 Marder, Arthur J. 'Winston is back: Churchill at the Admiralty, 1939–1940', *EHR*, suppl., V (1972). Cf. Stephen W. Roskill. 'Marder, Churchill and the Admiralty, 1939–42', *Journal of the Royal United Service Institute for Defense Studies*, CXVII (Dec. 1972), 49–53. Also Roskill's comment in *Times Literary Supplement* (13 Dec. 1974), 1415–16.

796 Marwick, Arthur J. B. 'The Independent Labour Party in the nineteen-twenties', *BIHR*, XXXV (1962), 62–74. Uses unpublished material.

797 —— 'Middle opinion in the thirties: planning, progress and political "agreement"', *EHR*, LXXIX (Apr. 1964), 285–98.

798 —— 'The Labour Party and the welfare state in Britain, 1900–1948', *AHR*, LXXIII (Dec. 1967), 380–403.

799 Mason, A. 'The government and the general strike, 1926', *IRSH*, XIV (pt. 1, 1969), 1–21.

800 Matthew, H. C. G., R. I. McKibbin, and J. A. Kay. 'The franchise factor in the rise of the Labour party', *EHR*, LXXXXI (Oct. 1976), 721–52.

801 Morgan, Kenneth O. 'The New Liberalism and the challenge of Labour: the Welsh experience, 1885–1929', *Welsh History Review*, 6 (June 1973), 288–312.

802 Morris, Andrew J. Anthony. 'The English Radicals' campaign for disarmament and the Hague Conference of 1907', *JMH*, XLIII (Sept. 1971), 367–93.

803 —— 'Haldane's army reforms, 1906–8: the deception of the Radicals', *History*, new ser., LVI (1971), 17–34.

804 Mowat, Charles Loch. 'Baldwin restored', *JMH*, XXVII (June 1955), 169–74. A review article. For subsequent treatment see (710, 780).

805 Murray, Bruce K. 'The politics of the "People's Budget"', *Hist. J.*, XVI (Sept. 1973), 555–70.

806 Pelling, Henry, 'The 1945 General Election reconsidered', *Hist. J.*, XXIII (no. 2, 1980), 339–414.

807 —— 'Politics of the Osborne Judgment', *Hist. J.*, XXV (no. 4, 1982), 889–909.

808 Petter, Martin. 'The Progressive Alliance', *History*, LVIII (Feb. 1973), 45–59. Lib–Lab relations, 1906–14.

809 Pimlott, Ben. 'The Socialist League: intellectuals and the Labour left in the 1930s', *JCH* VI (no. 3, 1971), 12–38.

810 Prynn, D. L. 'Common Wealth–a British "third party" of the 1940s', *JCH*, VII (nos. 1–2, 1972), 169–79.

811 Pugh, Martin D. 'Politicians and the women's vote, 1914–1918', *History*, LIX (1974), 358–74.

812 Pugh, Michael. 'Pacifism and politics in Britain, 1931–1935', *Hist. J.*, XXIII (no. 3, 1980), 641–56.
813 Rasmussen, Jorgen Scott. 'Government and intra-party opposition: dissent within the Conservative Parliamentary party in the 1930s', *PS*, XIX (1971), 172–83.
814 —— 'The role of women in British parliamentary elections', *Journal of Politics*, XXXIX (Nov. 1977), 1044–54.
815 Richards, Noel J. 'The Education Bill of 1906 and the decline of political nonconformity', *Journal of Ecclesiastical History*, XXIII (Jan. 1972), 49–63.
816 Rose, Norman. 'The resignation of Anthony Eden', *Hist. J.*, XXV (no. 4, 1982), 911–31.
817 [*Round Table]*. 'Empire to Commonwealth, 1910–1970', *Round Table*, Diamond Jubilee Number, no. 240 (Nov. 1970), 375–617. Articles by specialists.
818 Searle, G. R. 'The Edwardian Liberal Party and Business', *EHR*, XCVIII (Jan. 1983), 28–60. A question about the significance of "New Liberalism".
819 Shapiro, Stanley. 'The Great War and reform: Liberals and Labor, 1917–1919', *Labor History*, XII (summer 1971), 323–44.
820 Sires, Ronald V. 'The beginnings of British legislation for old-age pensions', *JEcH*, XIV (no. 3, 1954), 229–53.
821 Stannage, C. T. 'The East Fulham by-election, 25 October 1933', *Hist. J.*, XIV (no. 1, 1971), 165–200. Cf. (780).
822 Taylor, H. A. 'The proportional decline hypothesis in English elections', *Journal of the Royal Statistical Society*, ser. A, CXXXV (1972), 365–9. Tested from General Elections, 1950–70.
823 Tsuzuki, Chushichi. 'The "Impossible Revolt" in Britain', *IRSH*, I (pt. 3, 1956), 377–97. origins of the Socialist Labour Party and of the Socialist Party of Great Britain, 1900–4.
824 Wald, Kenneth D. 'Class and the vote before the Great World War', *British Journal of Political Science*, VIII (no. 4, 1978), 441–57.
825 Weiner, Sanford L. 'The competition for certainty: the polls and the press in Britain', *Political Science Quarterly*, XCI (Winter 1976–77), 673–96.
826 Williamson, Philip. 'Safety first: Baldwin, the Conservative Party, and the 1929 General Election', *Hist. J.*, XXV (no. 2, 1982), 385–409.
827 Winter, J. M. 'Arthur Henderson, the Russian Revolution and the reconstruction of the Labour Party', *Hist. J.*, XV (no. 4, 1972), 753–73.

VI. FOREIGN RELATIONS

1. Printed sources

828 Adamthwaite, Anthony P. *The making of the Second World War*. 1979. Documents with commentary.
829 Angell, Norman. *The great illusion: a study of the relation of military power in nations to their economic and social advantages*. 1910. Classic.
830 Buchanan, George. *My mission to Russia and other diplomatic memories*. 1923. 2 vols. Buchanan was ambassador to Tsarist Russia and to Italy.
831 Cecil, Robert, 1st Viscount Cecil of Chelwood. *A great experiment: an autobiography*. New York, 1941. Significant in studying Britain and the League of Nations.
832 Craigie, Sir Robert. *Behind the Japanese mask*. [1946]. By the ambassador to Japan for 1937–42.
833 David, Edward (ed.). *Inside Asquith's Cabinet: from the diaries of Charles Hobhouse*. 1977. For 1904–16.
834 Dickinson, G. Lowes. *The international anarchy, 1904–1914*. 1926. By a humanist, historian, and philosophical writer.
835 Dilks, David (ed.). *The Diaries of Sir Alexander Cadogan O.M., 1938–1945*. 1971. Cadogan was permanent undersecretary in Foreign Office.
836 Eayrs, James (ed.). *The Commonwealth and Suez: a documentary survey*. 1964.
837 Evans, Trefor E. (ed.). *The Killearn Diaries, 1934–1946*. 1972. Lord Killearn

(Sir Miles Lampson) was British ambassador to Egypt during World War II.

838 Gladwyn, Hubert Miles Gladwyn. Jebb, Baron. *Memoirs of Lord Gladwyn* 1972.

839 Glubb, John Bagot. *Britain and the Arabs: a study of fifty years, 1908–1958.* 1959. By the officer commanding the Arab Legion in Jordan.

840 Gooch, George P. and Harold W. V. Temperley (eds.). *British documents on the origins of the war, 1898–1914.* 1926–38, 11 vols. Standard.

841 [Goschen, Edward]. *The diary of Edward Goschen, 1900–1914.* Ed. Christopher H. D. Howard. 1980. Goschen was ambassador to Austria, 1905–8, and to Germany, 1908–14.

842 Grenville, J. A. S. (ed.). *The major international treaties, 1914–1973; A history and guide with texts.* 1974. Invaluable.

843 Grey, Edward, Viscount Grey of Falloden. *Twenty-five years, 1892–1916.* New York, 1925, 2 vols. By the foreign secretary, 1905–16.

844 Gwynn, Stephen (ed.). *The letters and friendships of Sir Cecil Spring Rice.* 1930, 2 vols. Spring Rice was ambassador to the USA, 1913–18.

845 Hankey, Maurice P. A., 1st Baron. *The supreme control at the Paris Peace Conference, 1919: a commentary.* 1963.

846 Hardinge, Charles, Baron. *Old diplomacy: the reminiscences of Lord Hardinge of Penshurst.* 1947.

847 Harvey, John (ed.). *Diplomatic diaries of Oliver Harvey, 1937–1940.* 1970. Harvey was private secretary to Eden and Halifax.

848 Henderson, Neville. *Failure of a mission: Berlin, 1937–1939.* New York, 1940. See also (1069).

849 Hoare, Samuel J. G., Viscount Templewood. *Ambassador on special mission.* 1946. Mission to Spain, 1940–4.

850 Howard, Esme, Lord Howard of Penrith. *Theatre of life.* Boston, Mass., 1935–6, 2 vols. Howard was in the Foreign Service during 1885–1930; was ambassador to the USA, 1924–30.

851 Jones, Philip (ed.). *Britain and Palestine, 1914–1948: archival sources for the history of the British mandate.* 1979.

852 Kimball, Warren (eds). Churchill and Roosevelt: the complete correspondence. Princeton, N.J., 1984, 3 vols.

853 Kirkpatrick, Ivone. *The inner circle.* 1959. Memoirs: Kirkpatrick was high commissioner to Germany, 1950–3, and permanent undersecretary of foreign affairs, 1953–7.

854 Knatchbull-Hugessen, Sir Hughe. *Diplomat in peace and war.* 1949. Ambassador to China, Turkey, and Belgium.

855 Koss, Stephen E. (ed.). *The anatomy of an antiwar movement: the pro-Boers.* Chicago, 1973. Readings with commentary.

856 Lawrence, Thomas E. *Seven pillars of wisdom: a triumph.* 1925. An abbreviated version of *Revolt in the desert.* 1927.

857 Lockhart, Bruce. *British agent.* New York, 1933. On his activities in Malaya, Russia, Poland, Czecho-Slovakia. Published in England as *Memoirs of a British agent.* 1932.

858 Morel, E. D. *Truth and the war.* 1916. Reprint with introduction by Catherine Ann Cline. New York, 1972.

859 Nicolson, Harold. *Peacemaking 1919: being reminiscences of the Paris Peace Conference.* Boston, Mass., 1933. Nicolson served with the British delegation.

860 Ponsonby, Arthur, Baron. *Democracy and diplomacy–a plea for popular control of foreign policy.* 1915. Ponsonby, a lifelong pacifist, was a Radical Liberal (later, a Laborite) in politics.

861 Riddell, George Allardice, Baron. *Intimate diary of the Peace Conference and after.* 1933. Riddell was a newspaper proprietor and confidante of Lloyd George.

862 Ross, Graham (ed.). *The foreign office and the Kremlin: British documents on Anglo–Soviet relations, 1941–45.* 1984.

863 *Stalin's correspondence with Churchill, Attlee, Roosevelt and Truman, 1941–45.* 1958.

864 Strang, William, 1st Baron. *Home and abroad.* 1956. An account of a significant role in the Foreign Office, 1919–53.

865 Temperley, Arthur C. *The whispering gallery of Europe*. 1938. Autobiography (to 1936) of a noted diplomat; he was permanent undersecretary in the Foreign Office, 1930–8.
866 Watt, Donald Cameron. *Documents on the Suez crisis*. 1957. Selected documents with commentary.
867 Wheeler-Bennett, John Wheeler, et al. (eds.). *Documents on international affairs*. 1929–73. An annual series for the years 1928–63 by various editors, sponsored by the Royal Institute of International Affairs.
868 Woodward, Ernest Llewellyn. *British foreign policy in the Second World War*. 5 vols. 1970–6.
869 —— and William N. Medlicott, et al. *Documents on British foreign policy, 1919–1939*. Three series. 1947–. Latest volume published in 1982. Documents from Foreign Office archives.
870 Young, Kenneth. *Diaries of Sir Robert Bruce Lockhart*. Vol. 1 (1915–38). New York, 1975.

2. Surveys

871 Barker, Elizabeth. *Britain in a divided Europe, 1945–1970*. 1971.
872 Foot, Michael R. D. *British foreign policy since 1898*. 1956.
873 Frankel, Joseph. *British foreign policy, 1945–1973*. 1975.
874 Gooch, George P. 'British foreign policy' in his *Studies in diplomacy and statecraft*. 1942, pp. 86–107. Brilliant.
875 Haigh, Anthony. *Congress of Vienna to Common Market: an outline of British foreign policy, 1815–1972*. 1973. Largely on twentieth century.
876 Hayes, Paul. *The twentieth century, 1880–1939: modern British foreign policy*. 1978.
877 Medlicott, William N. *British foreign policy since Versailles, 1919–1963*. 2nd ed., 1968. A standard work.
878 Northedge, Frederick S. *The troubled giant: Britain among the powers, 1916–1939*. 1966.
879 —— *Descent from power: British foreign policy, 1945–73*. 1974.
880 Reynolds, Philip A. *British foreign policy in the inter-war years*. 1954.
881 Toynbee, Arnold J., et al. *Survey of international affairs*. 1925–. Begins with 1920; the latest volume (for 1962) is by D. C. Watt. 1970. Consolidated index volume, 1920–38. 1967.
882 Ward, Adolphus W. and George P. Gooch (eds.). *Cambridge history of British foreign policy, 1783–1919*. Vol. III, 1866–1919. Cambridge, 1923.
883 Woodhouse, Christopher M. *British foreign policy since the Second World War*. 1961.

3. Monographs

884 Abadi, Jacob. *Britain's withdrawal from the Middle East, 1947–1971: the economic and strategic imperative*. Princeton, N.J., 1983.
885 Addison, Paul. *The road to 1945: British politics and the Second World War*. 1975. Brilliant.
886 Alexander, George Martin. *Prelude to the Truman doctrine: British policy in Greece, 1944–1947*. New York, 1982.
887 Arnot, R. Page. *The impact of the Russian Revolution in Britain*. 1967.
888 Aster, Sidney. *1939: the making of the Second World War*. 1973. Detailed.
889 Auty, Phyllis and Richard Clogg. *British policy toward war-time resistance in Yugo-Slavia and Greece*. New York, 1976.
890 Barker, Elizabeth. *British policy in South-east Europe in the Second World War*. 1976.
891 —— *Churchill and Eden at war*. New York, 1978.
892 —— *The British between the super powers, 1945–50*. 1983.
893 Barker, Rachel. *Conscience, government and war: conscientious objection in Great Britain, 1939–45*. Boston, 1982.
894 Bartlett, Christopher J. *The Long retreat: a short history of British defence policy, 1945–70*. 1972.

895 Bassett, Reginald. *Democracy and foreign policy: a case history. The Sino–Japanese dispute, 1931–33.* 1952.

896 Beloff, Max. *Lucien Wolf and the Anglo–Russian Entente.* 1951. Lecture.

897 —— *New dimensions in foreign policy: a study in administrative experience, 1947–1959.* 1961.

898 Bennett, Jeremy. *British broadcasting and the Danish resistance movement, 1940–1945.* 1966.

899 Boardman, Robert and A. J. R. Groom (eds.). *The management of Britain's external relations.* 1973. Chapters by various writers. Investigates questions growing out of Britain's changing international situation since 1945.

900 Boyle, Andrew. *The climate of treason: five who spied for Russia.* 1979. Informing: directed at a general reading public.

901 Braddon, Russell. *Suez: splitting of a nation.* 1973. What Suez meant to the British.

902 Bridge, F. R. *Great Britain and Austria–Hungary, 1906–1914: a diplomatic history.* 1972. See also (1076)

903 Buckley, Roger. *Occupation diplomacy: Britain, the United States and Japan, 1945–1952.* 1982.

904 Busch, Briton Cooper. *Britain and the Persian Gulf, 1894–1914.* Berkeley, Calif, 1967.

905 —— *Britain, India and the Arabs, 1914–1921.* Berkeley, Calif., 1971.

906 —— *Mudros to Lausanne: Britain's frontier in West Asia, 1918–1923.* Albany, N.Y., 1976.

907 Calder, Kenneth J. *Britain and the origins of the New Europe, 1914–1918.* 1976.

908 Carlton, David. *MacDonald versus Henderson: the foreign policy of the second Labour Government.* New York, 1970.

909 Carr, Edward H. *Britain: a study of foreign policy from the Versailles Treaty to the outbreak of war.* 1939. Brief essay; interesting observations representing a prewar view of a noted historian.

910 Carter, Gwendolen M. *The British Commonwealth and international security: the role of the Dominions, 1919–1939.* Toronto, 1947.

911 Ceadel, Martin. *Pacifism in Britain, 1914–1945: the defining of a faith.* 1980.

912 Chapman, Maybelle Kennedy. *Great Britain and the Baghdad Railway, 1888–1914* (Smith College Studies in History, 31). Northampton, Mass., 1948.

913 Clifford, Nicholas, R. *Retreat from China: British policy in the Far East, 1937–1941.* Seattle, Wash., 1967.

914 Coates, William P. and Zelda K. Coates. *A history of Anglo–Soviet relations.* 2 vols.–1945, 1958.

915 Cohen, Michael J. *British policy in Mesopotamia, 1903–1914.* Oxford, 1976.

916 —— *Palestine, a retreat from the mandate: the making of British policy, 1936–45.* New York, 1978.

917 Collier, Basil. *The lion and the eagle: British and Anglo–American strategy, 1900–1950.* 1972.

918 Collins, Robert O. *King Leopold, England and the Upper Nile, 1899–1909.* 1968.

919 —— *Shadows in the grass; Britain in the southern Sudan, 1918–1956.* 1983.

920 Colvin, Ian G. *Vansittart in office: an historical survey of the origins of the Second World War based on the papers of Sir Robert Vansittart.* 1965. Published in the USA as *None so blind: a British diplomatic view of the origins of World War II.* New York, 1965.

921 Conwell-Evans, Thomas P. *Foreign policy from a back bench, 1904–1918: a study based on the papers of Lord Noel Buxton.* 1932. See also Mosa Anderson. *Noel Buxton, a life.* 1952.

922 Cowling, Maurice. *The impact of Hitler: British politics and British policy, 1933–1940.* 1975. Contentious.

923 Craig, Gordon A. and Felix Gilbert (eds.). *The diplomats, 1919–1939.* Princeton, N.J., 1953. Essays.

924 Darby, Philip. *British defence policy east of Suez, 1947–1968.* 1973.

925 Darwin, John. *Britain, Egypt and the Middle East: imperial policy in the aftermath of war, 1918–1922.* New York, 1981.

926 Dilks, David (ed.). *Retreat from power: studies in Britain's foreign policy of the twentieth century.* 1981, 2 vols. Essays.

927 Dockrill, Michael L. and J. Douglas Gould. *Peace without promise: Britain and the Peace Conferences, 1919–1923*. Hamden, Conn., 1981.

928 Douglas, Roy A. *The advent of war, 1939–40*. New York, 1979. *New alliances, 1940–41*. New York, 1982. *From war to cold war, 1942–48*. New York, 1981.

929 Edwards, Jill. *The British government and the Spanish civil war, 1936–1939*. New York, 1979. Replaces earlier treatment.

930 Egerton, George W. *Great Britain and the creation of the League of Nations: strategy, politics and international organization, 1914–1919*. Chapel Hill, N.C., 1978.

931 Endicott, Stephen Lyon. *Diplomacy and enterprize: British China policy, 1930–1937*. 1976.

932 Epstein, Leon D. *British politics in the Suez crisis*. 1964.

933 Fabunmi, L. A. *The Sudan in Anglo-Egyptian relations: a case study in power politics, 1880–1956*. 1960.

934 Fest, Wilfried. *Peace or partition: the Hapsburg monarchy and British policy, 1914–1918*. 1978.

935 Fitzsimons, Matthew A. *The foreign policy of the British Labour Government, 1945–1951*. Notre Dame, Ind., 1953.

936 Fowler, W. B. *British–American relations, 1917–18: the role of sir William Wiseman*. Princeton, N.J., 1969. Wiseman was the Foreign Office liaison officer in the USA.

937 Friedman, Irving S. *British relations with China: 1931–1939*. New York, 1940. Deserves attention.

938 Friedman, Isaiah. *The question of Palestine, 1914–1918: British Jewish–Arab relations*. 1973.

939 Fry, Michael G. *Lloyd George and foreign policy*. Vol. I. 1890–1916. Montreal, 1977.

940 Gates, Eleanor. *End of the affair: the collapse of the Anglo-French alliance, 1939–1940*. 1981.

941 George, Margaret. *The warped vision: British foreign policy, 1933–1939*. Pittsburgh, Pa., 1965. Based on printed sources.

942 Gilbert, Martin. *The roots of appeasement*. 1966. Study of period, 1914–39.

943 Gooch, George P. *Before the war: studies in diplomacy*. 1936–8, 2 vols.

944 Goodhart, Philip. *Fifty ships that saved the world: the foundations of the Anglo-American alliance*. 1965. Concerning the agreement of 1940 on bases and destroyers.

945 Gordon, Michael R. *Conflict and consensus in Labour's foreign policy, 1914–1965*. Stanford, Calif., 1969. Emphasis on post–1945.

946 Gorodetsky, Gabriel. *Stanford Cripps' Mission to Moscow, 1940–42*. 1984.

947 Gottlieb, Wolfram W. *Studies in secret diplomacy during the First World War*. 1957.

948 *Great Britain and Egypt, 1914–1951*. Information Papers, no. 19, Royal Institute of International Affairs. 1936. New and rev. ed., 1952.

949 *Great Britain and Palestine, 1915–1945*. Information Papers, no. 20, Royal Institute of International Affairs. 1946.

950 Griffiths, Richard. *Fellow travellers of the right: British enthusiasts for Nazi Germany, 1933–9*. 1983.

951 Haggie, Paul. *Britannia at bay: the defence of the British Empire against Japan, 1931–1941*. Oxford, 1981.

952 Hale, Oron James. *Publicity and diplomacy, with special reference to England and Germany, 1890–1914*. 1940. Significant study.

953 Halpern, Paul G. *The Mediterranean naval situation, 1908–1914*. Cambridge, Mass., 1971. Archival study of the policy of Britain and others.

954 Hanak, Harry. *Great Britain and Austria–Hungary during the First World War: a study in the formation of public opinion*. 1962.

955 Hathaway, Robert M. *Ambiguous partnership: Britain and America, 1944–47*. New York, 1981.

956 Hauser, Oswald. *England und das Dritte Reich*. Ersterband, 1933–6. Stuttgart, 1972.

957 Heller, Joseph. *British policy toward the Ottoman Empire, 1908–1914*. 1983.

958 Hinsley, Francis Harry (ed.). *British foreign policy under Sir Edward Grey*. 1977. Twenty-one scholarly essays.
959 Howard, Michael. *The continental commitment*. 1972. Ford Lecture, 1971.
960 Jordan, William M. *Great Britain, France and the German problem, 1918–1939*. 1943. Thorough and scholarly.
961 Kaarsted, Tage. *Great Britain and Denmark, 1914–1920*. 1979. Trans. of Danish ed. (1974).
962 Kedourie, Elie. *England and the Middle East: the destruction of the Ottoman Empire, 1914–1921*. 1956.
963 Kennedy, John F. *Why England slept*. 1940. A study of the 1930s that attracted wide attention.
964 Kennedy, Malcolm D. *The estrangement of Great Britain and Japan, 1917–35*. Manchester, 1969.
965 Kennedy, Thomas C. *The hound of conscience: a history of the No-Conscription Fellowship, 1914–1919*. Fayetteville, Ark., 1981.
966 Kersandy, François. *Churchill and de Gaulle*. 1981.
967 Klieman, Aaron S. *Foundations of British policy in the Arab world: the Cairo Conference of 1921*. Baltimore, Md., 1970.
968 Lammers, Donald Ned. *British foreign policy, 1929–1934: the problem of Soviet Russia*. Stanford, Calif., 1960.
969 —— *Explaining Munich: the search for motive in British policy* (Hoover Institution Studies, 16). Stanford, Calif. 1966.
970 Lee, Bradford A. *Britain and the Sino–Japanese war, 1937–1939: a study in the dilemmas of British decline*. Stanford, Calif., 1973. Fine scholarship with an invaluable bibliographical note.
971 Lloyd, Selwyn. *Suez 1956: a personal account*. 1978.
972 Louis, William Roger. *Great Britain and Germany's last colonies, 1914–1919*. Oxford, 1967.
973 —— *British strategy in the Far East, 1919–1939*. Oxford, 1971. Thorough, lucid.
974 Lowe, Cedric J. and M. L. Dockrill. *The mirage of power: British foreign policy, 1902–22*. 1972, 3 vols. Documents in Vol. III.
975 Lowe, Peter. *Great Britain and Japan, 1911–1915: a study of British foreign policy*. 1969.
976 —— *Great Britain and the origins of the Pacific War: a study of British policy in East Asia, 1937–1941*. Oxford, 1977.
977 MacDonald, C. A. *The United States, Britain and appeasement, 1936–1939*. 1981.
978 McLean, David. *Britain and her buffer state: the collapse of the Persian Empire, 1890–1914*. 1979.
979 Maclean, Donald. *British foreign policy: the years since Suez, 1956–1968*. 1970.
980 McNeill, William Hardy. *America, Britain and Russia, their cooperation and conflict, 1941–1946*. 1953.
981 Maddox, William P. *Foreign relations in British Labour politics . . ., 1900–1924*. Cambridge, Mass., 1934.
982 Mander, John. *Great Britain or Little England*. 1963.
983 Manderson-Jones, Ronald B. *The special relationship: Anglo–American relations and western unity, 1947–56*. New York, 1972.
984 Mansfield, Peter. *The British in Egypt*. New York, 1972. A popular account of developments, 1882–1956.
985 Martin, David A. *Pacifism: an historical and sociological study*. New York, 1965. With particular reference to Britain, 1914–45; excellent bibliography.
986 Martin, Laurence W. *Peace without victory: Woodrow Wilson and the British Liberals*. New Haven, Conn., 1958.
987 Masterman, John C. *The double-cross system in the war of 1939 to 1945*. 1972. An account of British intelligence.
988 Mathews, Joseph James. *Egypt and the formation of the Anglo–French Entente of 1904*. Philadelphia, Pa., 1939.
989 Medlicott, William N. *Britain and Germany: the search for agreement 1930–1937*. 1969. Creighton lecture, 1968.
990 Meehan, Eugene J. *The British left wing and foreign policy: a study of the influence*

of ideology. New Brunswick, N.J., 1960. During World War II and on to 1951.

991 Middlemas, Keith. *Diplomacy of illusion: the British government and Germany, 1937–39*. 1972.

992 Miller, Kenneth E. *Socialism and foreign policy: theory and practice in Britain to 1931*. The Hague, 1967. For discussion of the issues, see Barbara Malament. Book review in *JMH*, 42 (June 1970), 280–4.

993 Monger, George. *The end of isolation: British foreign policy, 1900–1907*. 1963.

994 Monroe, Elizabeth. *Britain's moment in the Middle East, 1914–1971*. 1981.

995 Montgelas, Maximilian Garnerin, Count. *British foreign policy under Sir Edward Grey*. Trans. William C. Dreher, ed. Harry Elmer Barnes. New York, 1928. An influential book during the years of revisionism.

996 Naylor, John F. *Labour's international policy: The Labour Party in the 1930s*. Boston, 1969. Detail rather than analysis.

997 Nelson, Harold I. *Land and power: British and allied policy on Germany's frontiers, 1916–19*. 1963.

998 Nevakivi, Jukka. *Britain, France and the Arab Middle East, 1914–1920*. 1969.

999 Newman, Simon. *March 1939: the British guarantee to Poland: a study in the continuity of British foreign policy*. Oxford, 1976.

1000 Nicholas, Herbert George. *Britain and the U.S.A.* Baltimore, Md., 1963. On period 1938–1960.

1001 Nicolson, Harold. *Curzon: the last phase, 1919–1925: a case study in post-war diplomacy*. 1934.

1002 Nish, Ian H. *The Anglo–Japanese alliance: the diplomacy of two island empires, 1894–1907*. 1966. Nish's work is learned and skillful.

1003 —— *Alliance in decline: a study in Anglo–Japanese relations, 1908–23*. 1972.

1004 —— (ed.). *The Anglo–Japanese alienation, 1919–52: papers of the Anglo-Japanese conference on the history of the Second World War*. 1982.

1005 Nutting, Anthony. *No end of a lesson: the story of Suez*. 1967. One of best accounts.

1006 Orde, Anne. *Great Britain and International security, 1920–1926*. 1978.

1007 Ovendale, Ritchie (ed.). *The foreign policy of the British Labour Governments, 1945–51*. 1984.

1008 Parkinson, Roger. *Peace for our time: Munich to Dunkirk: the inside story*. 1971.

1009 Perkins, Bradford. *The great rapprochement: England and the United States, 1895–1914*. 1969. An admirable synthesis.

1010 Plass, Jens B. *England zwischen Russland und Deutschland: der persische Golf in der britischen Vorkriegspolitik, 1899–1907*. Hamburg, 1966.

1011 Porter, Brian. *Britain and the rise of Communist China: a study of British attitudes, 1945–1954*. 1967.

1012 Pribram, Alfred Francis. *Austria–Hungary and Great Britain, 1908–1914*. Trans. Ian F. D. Morrow. 1921. See also Pribram's *England and the international policy of the European Great Powers, 1871–1914* (Ford Lectures, 1929). 1931.

1013 Rappaport, Armin. *The British press and Wilsonian neutrality*. Stanford, Calif., 1951.

1014 Reynolds, David. *The creation of the Anglo–American alliance, 1937–1941*. 1981.

1015 Robbins, Keith. *Munich, 1938*. Thorough analysis of British policy. 1968.

1016 —— *The abolition of war: the "peace movement" in Britain, 1914–1919*. Cardiff, 1976.

1017 Rock, William R. *Appeasement on trial: British foreign policy and its critics, 1938–1939*. Hamden, Conn., 1966. See also his *British appeasement in the 1930s*. 1977.

1018 Rolo, P. J. V. *Entente Cordiale: the origins and negotiation of the Anglo–French agreements of 8 April, 1904*. 1969.

1019 Rose, N. A. *The gentile Zionists: a study in Anglo–Zionist diplomacy, 1929–1939*. 1973.

1020 Rose, Saul. *Britain and South-east Asia*. Baltimore, Md., 1962.

1021 Rothwell, Victor H. *British war aims and peace diplomacy, 1914–1918*. Oxford, 1971.

1022 —— *Britain and the Cold War, 1941–7*. 1982.

1023 Rowse, A. Leslie. *All Souls and appeasement*. 1961. 'Evidence', not 'history', Rowse calls it. Published in the USA as *Appeasement: a study in political decline, 1933–1939*. New York, 1963.

1024 Sherman, Ari Joshua. *Island Refuge: Jewish refugees from the Third Reich*. Berkeley, Calif., 1975.

1025 Sluglett, Peter. *Britain in Iraq, 1914–32*. Oxford, 1976.

1026 Stein, Leonard. *The Balfour Declaration*. 1961.

1027 Steiner, Zara S. *The Foreign Office and foreign policy, 1898–1914*. 1969.

1028 —— *Britain and the origins of the First World War*. 1977.

1029 Strong, Kenneth. *Men of intelligence: a study of the roles and decisions of the chiefs of intelligence from World War I to the present day*. 1970.

1030 Sykes, Christopher. *Crossroads to Israel*. New York, 1965. On Great Britain and Zionism.

1031 Taylor, Alan J. P. *The Origins of the Second World War*. 1961. 2nd ed., 'with a reply to critics', n.d. See also William Roger Louis (ed.). *Origins of the Second World War: A. J. P. Taylor and his critics*. 1972. See also (1089).

1032 Temperley, Harold W. V. (ed.). *History of the Peace Conference of Paris*. 1920–4, 6 vols. Compressive and impressive.

1033 Thomas, Hugh. *The Spanish Civil War*. 1961. Full account of British policy.

1034 —— *The Suez affair*. 1967. Published in the USA as *Suez*. New York, 1967. The crisis of 1956.

1035 Thomas, R. T. *Britain and Vichy: the dilemma of Anglo–French relations, 1940–42*. 1979.

1036 Thorne, Christopher G. *The approach of war, 1938–1939*. 1967. A good synthesis.

1037 —— *The limits of foreign policy: the West, the League and the Far Eastern crisis, 1931–1933*. 1972. Follows Britain's role carefully.

1038 Tillman, Seth P. *Anglo–American relations at the Paris Peace Conference of 1919*. Princeton, N.J., 1961.

1039 Trotter, Ann. *Britain and East Asia, 1933–47*. 1975.

1040 Tucker, William Rayburn. *The attitude of the British Labour Party towards European and collective security problems, 1920–1939*. Genève, 1950.

1041 Ullman, Richard H. *Anglo–Soviet relations, 1917–1921*. 1961–72, 3 vols. In the main a study of British politics; as such it is thorough and absorbing.

1042 Walder, David. *The Chanak affair*. 1969. The best treatment of the Anglo–Turkish crisis of 1922.

1043 Wasserstein, Bernard. *The British in Palestine: the mandatory government and the Arab–Jewish conflict, 1917–1929*. 1978.

1044 Watt, Donald Cameron. *Britain looks to Germany: British opinion and policy towards Germany since 1945*. 1965.

1045 —— *Personalities and policies. Studies in the formulation of British foreign policy in the twentieth century*. Notre Dame, Ind., 1975. Reprint of 1965 ed. Aims to 'bridge gap' between history and political science.

1046 Weber, Frank G. *The evasive neutral: Germany, Britain and the quest for a Turkish alliance in the Second World War*. Columbia, Mo., 1979.

1047 Wheeler-Bennett, Sir John. *Munich: prologue to tragedy*. 1948.

1048 White, Stephen. *Britain and the Bolshevik revolution: a study in the politics of diplomacy, 1920–1924*. 1979. An excellent sequel to Ullman (1041).

1049 Willert, Arthur. *The road to safety: a study in Anglo–American relations*. 1952. Concerns Sir William Wiseman and British diplomacy in Washington, D. C. during World War I.

1050 Williams, Ann. *Britain and France in the Middle East and North Africa, 1914–1967*. 1968. Good general account with excellent bibliography.

1051 Williamson, Samuel R., Jr. *The politics of grand strategy: Britain and France prepare for war, 1904–1914*. Cambridge, Mass., 1969. Probably the best as well as the most complete treatment. Useful description of manuscript collections.

1052 Windrich, Elaine. *British Labour's foreign policy*. Stanford, Calif., 1952. Cf. Barbara Malament. Book review in *JMH*, 42 (June 1970), 280–4.

1053 Winkler, Henry R. *The League of Nations movement in Great Britain*. New Brunswick, N.J., 1952. An important book.

1054 Wolfers, Arnold. *Britain and France between two wars: conflicting strategies of peace since Versailles*. New York, 1940. Reflects the atmosphere of the 1930s.

1055 Woodward, Ernest Llewellyn. *British foreign policy in the second world war*. 1970–6, 5 vols. Part of the 'official history' of the war; clear, comprehensive with complete documentation.

4. Biographies

1056 Aldington, Richard. *Lawrence of Arabia: a biographical enquiry*. 1955. A critical examination.

1057 Busch, Briton Cooper. *Hardinge of Penshurst: a study in the old diplomacy*. Hamden, Conn., 1981.

1058 Douglas-Home, Charles. *Evelyn Baring: the last proconsul*. 1978.

1059 Gilbert, Martin. *Sir Horace Rumbold: portrait of a diplomat, 1869–1941*. 1973.

1060 Hendrick, Burton J. *The life and letters of Walter H. Page*. New York, 1922–5, 3 vols. Page was the American ambassador to Great Britain, 1913–18.

1061 Leslie, Shane. *Mark Sykes: his life and letters*. 1923.

1062 Liddell Hart, Basil Henry. *'T. E. Lawrence': in Arabia and after*. 1934. Eulogistic. Cf. (1056).

1063 Mosley, Leonard. *Curzon: the end of an epoch*. 1960. Brief, readable.

1064 Newton, Thomas Wodehouse Legh, 2nd Baron. *Lord Lansdowne: a biography*. 1929. Hardly adequate.

1065 Nicolson, Harold. *Sir Arthur Nicolson, Bart., First Lord Carnock: a study in the old diplomacy*. 1930. Nicolson was ambassador to Russia, 1906–10, and undersecretary for foreign affairs, 1910–16.

1066 Robbins, Keith. *Sir Edward Grey: a biography of Lord Grey of Falloden*. 1971. On Grey's official role, replaces (733).

1067 Ronaldshay, Lawrence John Lumley Dundas, Earl of. *The life of Lord Curzon*. 1928, 3 vols. the 'official' biography and still the only complete life. Inadequate.

1068 Rose, Norman. *Vansittart: study of a diplomat*. 1978. See also Vansittart's autobiography (to 1936): *The mist procession*. 1958.

1069 Strauch, Rudi. *Sir Neville Henderson: Britischer Botschafter in Berlin von 1937 bis 1939*. Bonn, 1959. See also (848).

1070 Waterfield, Gordon. *Professional diplomat: Sir Percy Loraine of Kirkharle Bt., 1880–1961*. 1973. A career diplomat.

1071 Wrench, Thomas Wodehouse Legh, 2nd Baron. *Lord Lansdowne: a biography*. 1929. Needs to be redone.

5. Articles

1072 Aulach, Harindar. 'Britain and the Sudeten issue, 1938: the evolution of a policy', *JCH*, XVIII (Apr. 1983), 233–59.

1073 Beloff, Max. 'The special relationship: an Anglo–American myth'. In Martin Gilbert (ed.). *A Century of Conflict, 1850–1950*. 1966, pp. 151–71.

1074 Bosworth, Richard. 'Britain and Italy's acquisition of the Dodecanese, 1912–1915', *Hist. J.*, XIII (no. 4, 1970), 683–705.

1075 —— 'The British press, the Conservatives and Mussolini, 1920–34', *JCH*, V (no. 2, 1970), 163–82.

1076 Bridge, F. R. 'The British declaration of war on Austria–Hungary in 1914', *Slavonic and East European Review*, XLVII (July 1969), 401–22. See also (902).

1077 Butterfield, Herbert. 'Sir Edward Grey in July 1914', *Historical Studies* (papers read before the sixth Conference of Irish Historians), V (1965), 1–25.

1078 Carlton, David. 'The Anglo–French compromise on arms limitation, 1928', *JBS*, VIII (May 1969), 141–62.

1079 Cassels, Alan. 'Repairing the *Entente Cordiale* and the New Diplomacy', *Hist. J.*, XXIII (1980), 133–53. After World War I.

1080 Ceadel, Martin. 'The first British referendum: the Peace Ballot, 1934–35', *EHR*, XCV (1980), 810–39. See also his 'The King and Country debate,

1933: student politics, pacifism and the dictators', *Hist. J.*, XXII (no. 2, 1979), 397–422.

1081 Cohen, Michael J. 'British strategy and the Palestine question, 1936–39', *JCH*, VII (nos. 3–4, 1972), 157–83. Based on Colonial Office and Cabinet Office papers.

1082 Conway, John S. 'The Vatican, Great Britain and relations with Germany, 1938–1940,' *Hist. J.*, XVI (Mar. 1973), 147–67.

1083 Cooper, M. B. 'British policy in the Balkans, 1908–9', *Hist. J.*, VII (no. 2, 1964), 258–79.

1084 Craig, Gordon A. 'High tide of appeasement: the road to Munich, 1937–1938', *Political Science Quarterly*, 65 (Mar. 1950), 20–37.

1085 Crowe, Sibyl Eyre. 'Sir Eyre Crowe and the Locarno Pact', *EHR*, LXXXVII (Jan. 1972), 49–74.

1086 Darwin, J. G. 'The Chanak crisis and the British Cabinet', *History*, LXV (Feb. 1980), 32–48.

1087 Dilks, David. 'The twilight war and the fall of France: Chamberlain and Churchill in 1940', *TRHS*, 5th ser., XXVIII (1979), 61–86.

1088 Dowse, Robert E. 'The Independent Labour Party and foreign politics: 1918–23' *IRSH*, VII (1962), 33–46.

1089 Dray, W. H. 'Concepts of causation in A. J. P. Taylor's account of the origins of the Second World War', *History and Theory*, XVII (no. 2, 1978), 149–74. See also (1031).

1090 Dubin, Martin David. 'Toward the concept of collective security: the Bryce Group's "Proposals for the Avoidance of War", 1914–1917', *International Organization*, 24 (1970), 288–318.

1091 Edwards, E. W. 'Great Britain and the Manchurian Railways Question, 1909–1910', *EHR*, LXXXI (Oct. 1966), 740–69.

1092 Edwards, Peter. 'The Austen Chamberlain–Mussolini meetings', *Hist. J.*, XIV (no. 1, 1971), 153–64. Account of five meetings, 1924–9, based on the Chamberlain papers, Cabinet papers, British and Italian Foreign Office documents.

1093 Egerton, George W. 'The Lloyd George Government and the creation of the League of Nations', *AHR*, LXXIX (Apr. 1974), 419–44. Detailed examination on basis of Cabinet and Lloyd George papers. See (930).

1094 —— 'Britain and the "Great Betrayal": Anglo–American relations and the struggle for United States ratification of the Treaty of Versailles, 1919–1920', *Hist. J.*, XXI (no. 4, 1978), 885–911.

1095 Elcock, H. J. 'Britain and the Russo–Polish frontier, 1919–1921', *Hist. J.*, XII (no. 1, 1969), 137–54.

1096 Fest, W. B. 'British war aims and German peace feelers during the First World War (Dec. 1916–Nov. 1918)', *Hist J.*, XV (no. 2, 1972), 285–308. Based on Lloyd George and Cabinet papers.

1097 Fieldhouse, H. N. 'Noel Buxton and A. J. P. Taylor's "The trouble-makers"'. In Martin Gilbert (ed.). *A century of conflict, 1850–1950*. 1966, p. 175–98.

1098 Fox, John P. 'Britain and the Inter-allied Military Commission of Control', *JCH*, IV (Apr. 1969), 143–64. Based on Foreign Office and Cabinet documents.

1099 Goold, J. Douglas. 'Lord Hardinge and the Mesopotamia expedition and inquiry, 1914–1917', *Hist. J.*, XIX (Dec. 1976), 919–45.

1100 Gowen, Robert Joseph. 'Great Britain and the twenty-one demands of 1915: cooperation versus effacement', *JMH*, XLIII (Mar. 1971), 76–106. The 'demands' were made by Japan on China.

1101 Hall, H. Duncan. 'The genesis of the Balfour Declaration of 1926', *Journal of Commonwealth Political Studies*, I (1961–3), 169–93.

1102 Halpern, Paul G. 'The Anglo–French–Italian naval convention of 1915', *Hist. J.*, XIII (no. 1, 1970), 106–29.

1103 Hanak, H. 'Sir Stafford Cripps as British ambassador in Moscow May 1940 to June 1941', *EHR*, XCIV (Jan. 1979), 48–70.

1104 —— 'Sir Stafford Cripps as British ambassador in Moscow June 1941–Jan. 1942', *EHR*, XCVII (Apr. 1982), 232–44.

1105 Hill, Leonidas. 'Three crises, 1938–39', *JCH*, III (Jan. 1968), 113–44. Use with (1031).

1106 Jankowski, James. 'The government of Egypt and the Palestine Question, 1936–1939', *Middle East Studies*, XVII (Oct. 1981), 427–53.

1107 Johnson, Douglas. 'Austen Chamberlain and the Locarno agreements', *University of Birmingham Historical Journal*, VIII (1961), 62–81.

1108 Kernek, Sterling. 'Distractions of peace during the war: the Lloyd George's government's reactions to Woodrow Wilson, December 1916–November 1918', *Transactions of American Philosophical Society*, n.s., LXV (1975), 5–114.

1109 Kettenacker, Lother. 'The Anglo–Soviet alliance and the problem of Germany, 1914–1945', *JCH*, XVII (July 1982), 435–58.

1110 Klein, Ira. 'Britain, Siam and the Malay Peninsula, 1906–1909', *Hist.J.*, XII (no. 1, 1969), 119–36. Uses Foreign Office papers.

1111 —— 'Anglo–Russian Convention and the problem of central Asia, 1907–1914', *JBS*, II (Nov. 1971), 126–47.

1112 Koch, H. W. 'The Anglo–German alliance negotiations: missed opportunity or myth?', *History*, n.s., LIV (no. 3, 1969), 378–92. On 1898–1901.

1113 Kurtz, Harold. 'The Lansdowne Letter', *History Today*, XVIII (Feb. 1968), 85–92.

1114 Lammers, Donald N. 'From Whitehall after Munich: the Foreign Office and the future course of British policy', *Hist. J.*, XVI (no. 4, 1973), 831–56.

1115 Larew, Karl G. 'Great Britain and the Greco–Turkish War, 1921–1922', *Historian*, XXXV (Feb. 1973), 256–70.

1116 Leutze, James. 'The secret of the Churchill–Roosevelt correspondence, September 1939–May 1940', *Contemporary History*, X (July 1975), 465–91.

1117 Louis, William Roger. 'Great Britain and the African Peace Settlement of 1919', *AHR*, LXXI (Apr. 1966), 875–92.

1118 —— 'The United Kingdom and the beginning of the Mandates System, 1919–1922', *International Organization*, XXIII (1969), 73–96. Based on Cabinet Office and Foreign Office papers.

1119 Lowe, Cedric J. 'Britain and Italian intervention, 1914–1915', *Hist. J.*, XII (no. 3, 1969), 533–48.

1120 —— 'The failure of British policy in the Balkans, 1914–16', *Canadian Journal of History*, IV (Mar. 1969), 73–100.

1121 Lukowitz, David C. 'British pacifists and appeasement: The Peace Pledge Union', *JCH*, IX (no. 1, 1974), 115–27.

1122 Marder, Arthur J. 'The royal navy and the Ethiopian crisis of 1935–36', *AHR*, LXXV (June 1970), 1327–56.

1123 —— 'The influence of history on sea power: the Royal Navy and the lessons of 1914–1918', *Pacific Historical Review*, XLI (Nov. 1972), 413–43.

1124 Nevakivi, Jukka. 'Lord Kitchener and the partition of the Ottoman Empire, 1915–1916'. In K. Bourne and Donald Cameron Watt (eds.). *Studies in international history*. 1967, pp. 316–29.

1125 Ovendale, R. 'Britain, the U.S.A. and the European Cold War, 1945–8', *History*, LXVII (June 1982), 217–36.

1126 Parker, E. A. C. 'Great Britain, France and the Ethiopian crisis, 1935–1936', *EHR*, LXXXIX (Apr. 1974), 293–332.

1127 —— 'Britain, France and Scandinavia, 1929–40,' *History* LXI (Oct. 1976), 369–87.

1128 Penson, Lillian M. 'Obligations by treaty: their place in British foreign policy, 1898–1914'. In A. O. Sarkissian (ed.). *Studies in diplomatic history and historiography in honour of G. P. Gooch*. 1961, pp. 76–89.

1129 Pugh, Michael. 'Pacifism and politics in Britain, 1931–1935', *Hist. J.*, XXIII (no. 3, 1980), 641–56.

1130 Raffo, Peter. 'The Anglo–American preliminary negotiations for a League of Nations'. *JCH*, IX (Oct. 1974), 153–76.

1131 Renzi, William A. 'Great Britain, Russia and the Straits, 1914–1915', *JMH*, XLII (Mar. 1970), 1–20.

1132 Robbins, Keith G. 'Konrad Henlein, the Sudeten question and British foreign policy', *Hist. J.*, XII (no. 4, 1969), 674–97.

1133 Robertson, James C. 'The Hoare–Laval Plan', *JCH*, X (July 1975), 433–64.
1134 Rock, William. 'British appeasement (1930s): need for revision', *South Atlantic Quarterly*, LXXVIII (summer 1979), 290–301.
1135 Rothwell, Victor H. 'Mesopotamia in British war aims, 1914–1918', *Hist. J.*, XIII (no. 2, 1970), 273–94.
1136 Sainsbury, Keith. 'British policy and German unity at the end of the Second World War', *EHR*, XCIII (Oct. 1979), 786–804.
1137 Sharp, Alan J. 'The Foreign Office in eclipse, 1919–1922', *History*, LXI (1976), 198–218.
1138 Siracusa, Joseph M. 'The night Stalin and Churchill divided Europe: the view from Washington', *Review of Politics*, XLIII (July 1981), 381–409.
1139 Smith, C. Jay, Jr. 'Great Britain and the 1914–1915 Straits agreement with Russia: the British promise of November 1914', *AHR*, LXX (July 1965), 1015–34.
1140 Steiner, Zara and M. L. Dockrill. 'The Foreign Office reforms, 1919–1921', *Hist. J.*, XVII (no. 1, 1974), 131–56.
1141 Stromberg, Roland N. 'Uncertainties and obscurities about the League of Nations', *JHI*, XXXIII (Jan–Mar. 1972), 139–54. Includes discussion, 1915–1918, of a league or society of nations.
1142 Sweet, David W. 'The Baltic in British diplomacy before the First World War', *Hist. J.*, XIII (no. 3, 1970), 451–90.
1143 Taylor, Alan J. P. 'The war aims of the Allies in the First World War'. In his *Politics in wartime*. 1964, pp. 93–122. First published in Richard Pares and A. J. P. Taylor (eds.). *Essays presented to Sir Lewis Namier*. 1956, pp. 475–505.
1144 Toscano, Mario. 'Eden's mission to Rome on the eve of the Italo–Ethiopian conflict'. In A. O. Sarkissian (ed.), *Studies in diplomatic history and historiography in honour of G. P. Gooch*. 1961, pp. 126–52.
1145 Verete, Mayir. 'The Balfour Declaration and its makers'. In Elie Kedourie and Sylvia Haim. *Palestine and Israel in the 19th and 20th centuries*. 1982, pp. 60–88.
1146 Warman, Roberta M. 'The erosion of Foreign Office influence in the making of foreign policy, 1916–1918', *Hist. J.*, XV (no. 1, 1972), 133–59.
1147 Watt, Donald Cameron. 'The Anglo–German agreement of 1935: an interim judgment', *JMH*, XXVIII (June 1956), 155–75.
1148 —— 'Appeasement: the rise of a revisionist school?', *Political Quarterly*, XXXVI (no. 2, 1965), 191–213. Summarizes the controversy in a manner useful to the general student.
1149 Webster, Charles. 'Munich reconsidered: a survey of British policy', *International Affairs*, XXXVII (Apr. 1961), 137–53.
1150 Weinroth, Howard. 'The British Radicals and the balance of power, 1902–1914', *Hist. J.*, XIII (no. 4, 1970), 653–82.
1151 —— 'British Radicals and the Agadir Crisis', *European Studies Review*, III (Jan. 1973), 39–61.
1152 Wells, Samuel F., Jr. 'British strategic withdrawal from the western hemisphere, 1904–1906', *Canadian Historical Review*, XLIX (Dec. 1968), 335–56.
1153 Williams, Berl J. 'The strategic background to the Anglo–Russian Entente of August 1907, *Hist. J.*, IX (no. 3, 1966), 360–73.
1154 Wilson, Keith. 'The Agadir crisis, the Mansion House speech, and the double-edgedness of agreements', *Hist. J.*, XV (no. 3, 1972), 513–32.
1155 Winkler, Henry R. 'The emergence of a Labour foreign policy in Great Britain, 1918–1929', *JMH*, XXVIII (Sept. 1956), 247–58. See also (992).
1156 Woodward, David R. 'David Lloyd George, a negotiated peace with Germany, and the Kuhlmann peace kite of September, 1917', *Canadian Journal of History*, VI (Mar. 1971), 75–93.
1157 —— 'The British Government and Japanese intervention in Russia during World War I', *JMH*, XXXXVI (Dec. 1974), 663–85.
1158 Young, Harry F. 'The misunderstanding of August 1, 1914', *JMH*, XLVIII (Dec. 1976), 644–64.

VII. SOCIAL HISTORY

1. Printed sources

1159 Asquith, Margot. *An autobiography*. New York, 1920, 2 vols. Continued by *More Memories*. 1933.

1160 Beveridge, William. *Social insurance and allied services*. New York, 1942. This is the 'Beveridge Plan.' See also his *Power and influence*. 1953. Autobiographical.

1161 Boyd-Orr, John, Baron. *Food, health and income: report on a survey of adequacy of diet in relation to income*. 2nd ed., 1937. First issued in 1936. See also Boyd-Orr's autobiography, *As I recall*. 1966.

1162 Bragg, Melvyn. *Speak for England: an essay on England, 1900–1975*. 1976. Based on interviews with inhabitants of Wigton, Cumberland.

1163 Cooper, Lady Diana. *The rainbow comes and goes*. 1958. Continued by *The light of common day*. 1959. Autobiographies.

1164 Fleming Report. *The public schools and the general educational system*. H.M.S.O., 1944. Report of a committee, appointed by the president of the Board of Education.

1165 Gosden, Peter H. J. H. (ed.). *How they were taught: an anthology of contemporary accounts of learning and teaching in England, 1880–1950*. New York, 1969.

1166 Hay, J. R. *The development of the welfare state in Britain, 1880–1975*. Largely documents.

1167 Hilton, John. *Rich man, poor man*. 1944. Concerning the 'unequal distribution of wealth'. Foreward by William H. Beveridge.

1168 Jones, Kathleen (ed.). *The year book of social policy in Britain, 1971–*. 1972–. An annual publication, discussing the issues of the year covered; the latest volume is for 1984 (1985).

1169 Laver, James. *Edwardian promenade*. Boston, Mass., 1958. Selections from contemporary material.

1170 Lester, Muriel. *It occurred to me*. 1937. Autobiographical account of the life of a social and religious worker.

1171 Lubbock, Percy. *Earlham*. 1963. Fascinating account of country life of upper classes in early 1900s. First published in 1922.

1172 Lunn, Arnold. *Memory to memory*. 1956. Autobiography of a well-known mountaineer.

1173 *Mass-observation*. See Charles Madge and Tom Harrison. *Mass-observation*. 1937. An introduction to the series. Publications include: *Puzzled people: a study in popular attitudes to religion, ethics, progress and politics in a London borough*. 1947. And *The pub and the people: a work-town study*. Welwyn-Garden City, 1970.

1174 Masterman, Charles F. G. *England after war: a study*. New York, 1923. A contemporary view, widely read.

1175 —— *The condition of England*. Ed. James T. Boulton. 1960. First published in 1909. A significant analysis of Edwardian society.

1176 [Mitchell, Hannah]. *The hard way up: the autobiography of Hannah Mitchell, suffragette and rebel*. Ed. Geoffrey Mitchell. 1968.

1177 Morrell, Lady Ottoline. *Memoirs of Lady Ottoline Morrell: a study in friendship, 1873–1915*. Ed. Robert Gathorne-Hardy. New York, 1964. Continued by *Ottoline at Garsington*. 1974. Memoirs carried to 1918 with later comment by Lady Ottoline.

1178 Newsholme, Arthur. *The last thirty years in public health: recollections and reflections on my official and post-official life*. 1936. Newsholme was principal medical officer with the Local Government board, 1908–19.

1179 [Newsom Report]. *The Public Schools Commission first report*. 1966. Concerns 'independent day schools and direct grant grammar schools'. See also *The Public Schools Commission second report* (known as the 'Donnison Report'). 1970, 3 vols.

1180 O'Neill, William L. *The woman movement: feminism in the United States and England*. 1969. Documents with commentary on period 1838–1929.

1181 Padley, Richard and Margaret Cole (eds.). *Evacuation survey: a report to the Fabian Society*. 1940.
1182 Pankhurst, E. Sylvia. *The suffragette movement: an intimate account of persons and ideals*. 1931.
1183 Pike, E. Royston (ed.). *'Busy times': human documents of the age of the Forsytes*. 1969.
1184 [Plowden Report]. *Children and their primary schools: a report of the central advisory council for education (England)*. 1967, 2 vols. Lady Plowden was chairman of the council.
1185 Priestley, John B. *English journey*. 1934. An account of a journey in autumn of 1933.
1186 —— *Britain speaks*. New York, 1940. English ed., *Postscripts*. 1940. Broadcasts, May–September, 1940.
1187 Read, Donald (ed.). *Documents from Edwardian England, 1901–1915*. 1973.
1188 Reith, John Charles Walsham, Baron. *Into the wind*. 1949. Autobiography of the Director General of the BBC, 1927–38.
1189 Rowntree, B. Seebohm and George R. Lavers. *English life and leisure: a social study*. 1951. Case histories.
1190 *Royal commission on population*. Cmd. Report 7695. 1949. Reprinted, 1953.
1191 [Shadwell, Arthur]. 'The socialist movement in Great Britain', *The Times*, 7–19 Jan. 1909. An important comment.
1192 Swanwick, Helena M. L. *I have been young*. 1935. Autobiography.
1193 Tawney, Richard H. *The acquisitive society*. 1921. First published (1920) as *The sickness of an acquisitive society*. A celebrated tract of the times.
1194 Titmuss, Richard M. *Poverty and population: a factual study of contemporary social waste*. 1938.

2. Surveys

1195 Bedarida, François. *A social history of England, 1851–1975*. 1979. Informative and convincing.
1196 Carr-Saunders, Alexander M., D. Caradog Jones, and Claus A. Moser. *A survey of social conditions in England and Wales as illustrated by statistics*. 3rd ed., Oxford, 1958.
1197 Dent, H. C. *1870–1970: a century of growth in English education*. 1970.
1198 Fraser, Derek. *The evolution of the British welfare state; a history of social policy since the Industrial Revolution*. 1973.
1199 Gilbert, Bentley B. *The evolution of national insurance in Great Britain: the origins of the Welfare State*. 1966. The standard work. His investigation was continued in *British social policy, 1914–1939*. 1970.
1200 Glynn, Sean and John Oxburrow. *Interwar Britain: a social and economic history*. 1976.
1201 Graves, Robert and Alan Hodge. *The long week-end: a social history of Great Britain, 1918–1939*. 1940. Written with knowledge and spirit.
1202 Halsey, Albert H. *Change in British society*. 2nd ed., Oxford, 1981.
1203 Hearnshaw, Fossey J. C. (ed.). *Edwardian England*, A.D. *1900–1910*. 1933. As seen by scholars fifty years ago.
1204 Hopkins, Harry. *The new look: a social history of the forties and fifties in Britain*. 1963.
1205 Johns, Edward A. *The social structure of modern Britain*. 2nd ed., 1972. An excellent introduction.
1206 Macqueen-Pope, Walter J. *Twenty shillings in the pound*. 1948. Popular account of life in Edwardian Britain.
1207 Marwick, Arthur J. B. *Britain in the century of total war: war, peace and social change, 1914–67*. 1963.
1208 —— *British society since 1945*. 1982.
1209 Montgomery, John. *The twenties: an informal social history*. 1957. See also Montgomery's *The fifties*. 1965.
1210 Muggeridge, Malcolm. *The sun never sets: the story of England in the nineteen-thirties*. New York, 1940. English ed., *The thirties: 1930–1940 in Great Britain*. 1940.

1211 Nowell-Smith, Simon (ed.). *Edwardian England, 1901–1914*. 1964. Well informed articles, presented in popular style.

1212 Ogilvie, Vivian. *Our times: a social history, 1912–1952*. 1953.

1213 Read, Donald. *Edwardian England, 1901–1915: society and politics*. 1972. One of the best books on the period. Cf. Read, ed., *Edwardian England*, a series of essays that are lectures (revised) before the Historical Association.

1214 Roebuck, Janet. *The making of modern English society from 1850*. 1973. Includes an excellent bibliography.

1215 Ryder, Judith and Harold Silver. *Modern English society: history and structure, 1850–1970*. 3rd ed., 1985.

1216 Stevenson, John. *British society, 1914–1945*. New York, 1984.

1217 Thompson, Paul Richard. *The Edwardians: the remaking of British society*. 1975. Based on oral evidence.

3. Monographs

1218 Abbott, Albert. *Education for industry and commerce in England*. 1933. Extensive and reliable survey of technical education before 1933.

1219 Abrams, Mark. *The population of Great Britain: current trends and future problems*. 1945.

1220 Atkinson, Anthony B. *Poverty in Britain and the reform of social security*. Cambridge, 1969.

1221 Bagley, John J. and A. J. Bagley. *The state and education in England and Wales, 1833–1968*. 1969. Brief general treatment, well done.

1222 Banks, Olive. *Parity and prestige in English secondary education: a study in educational psychology*. 1955.

1223 Barker, Theodore and Michael Drake (eds.). *Population and society, 1850–1980*. New York, 1982.

1224 Beckerman, Wilfred and Stephen Clark. *Economics and politics: poverty and social security in Britain since 1961*. New York, 1982.

1225 Benjamin, Bernard. *The population census*. 1970. Sponsored by the Social Science Research Council; a brief, useful analysis.

1226 Bernbaum, Gerald. *Social change and the schools, 1918–1944*. 1967.

1227 Betts, Ernest. *The film business: a history of British cinema, 1896–1972*. 1973. The best account.

1228 Blyth, William A. L. *English primary education: a sociological description*. 1965, 2 vols. Vol. I provides historical background.

1229 Blythe, Ronald. *Akenfeld: portrait of an English village*. New York, 1969. Absorbing sociological study.

1230 Bogdanor, Vernon and Robert Skidelsky (eds.). *Age of affluence, 1951–1964*. 1970. Essays by various writers.

1231 Bonham-Carter, Victor. *Dartington Hall, the history of an experiment* 1958. A story of economic and social rehabilitation as well as of an educational enterprise.

1232 Booker, Christopher. *The neophiliacs*. 1969. Its theme is 'the psychic epidemic' of the fifties and sixties.

1233 Bowley, Arthur L. and Margaret H. Hogg. *Has poverty diminished?* 1925. Based on a study made in 1924.

1234 Bowley, Marian. *Housing and the state, 1919–1944*. 1945. Still standard.

1235 Bramwell, Robert D. *Elementary school work, 1900–1925*. Durham, 1961.

1236 Braydon, Gail. *Women workers in the First World War: the British experience*. 1981.

1237 Briggs, Asa. *The history of broadcasting in the United Kingdom*. 1961–70, 3 vols.

1238 —— *The BBC: the first fifty years*. 1985. See also Briggs's *Governing the BBC*. 1979.

1239 Britain, Ian. *Fabianism and culture: a study in British socialism and the arts, c. 1884–1918*. 1982.

1240 Brittain, Vera. *Lady into woman: a history of women from Victoria to Elizabeth II*. 1953.

1241 Brockington, C. Fraser. *A short history of public health*. 2nd ed., 1966.

1242 Brooke, Iris. *English costume, 1900–1950*. 1951.

1243 Buchanan, Colin. *Mixed blessing: the motor in Britain.* 1958.
1244 —— *The state of Britain.* 1972. The Chichele lectures at Oxford in 1971; a neat summary of the history of planning measures.
1245 Burnett, John. *A social history of housing, 1815–1976.* 1980.
1246 Calder, Angus. *The people's war: Britain, 1939–45.* 1969. Informative though not always reliable.
1247 Coates, R. D. *Teachers' unions and interest group politics: a study in the behaviour of organized teachers in England and Wales.* Cambridge, 1972. Detailed examination of the sixties.
1248 Cole, George D. H. and Margaret I. *The condition of Britain.* 1937. A well-known study; tables are particularly useful.
1249 Cole, Margaret I. (ed.). *The Webbs and their work.* 1949. Essays; critical analysis.
1250 Cunnington, C. Willett. *English women's clothing in the present century.* 1952. Well illustrated; an excellent work.
1251 Curtis, Stanley J. *Education in Britain since 1900.* 1952.
1252 Dent, Harold Collett. *Growth in English education, 1946–1952.* 1954. The best work on these important years.
1253 Douglas, Roy. *Land, people and politics: a history of the land question in the United Kingdom, 1878–1952.* 1976.
1254 Dunleavy, Patrick. *The politics of mass housing in Britain, 1945–1975: a study of corporate power and professional influence in the welfare state.* 1981.
1255 Eckstein, Harry. *The English health service: its origins, structure and achievement.* Cambridge, Mass., 1958.
1256 Ferguson, Sheila and Hilde Fitzgerald. *Studies in the social services.* 1954. Successor to R. M. Titmuss. *Problems of social policy.* 1950.
1257 Fiegehen, Guy C. *Poverty and progress in Britain, 1953–73.* 1977.
1258 Field, Frank. *Inequality in Britain: freedom, welfare and the state.* 1981.
1259 Ford, Percy. *Social theory and social practice: an exploration of experience.* Shannon, 1968. Efforts in the nineteenth and twentieth centuries at social planning as found in parliamentary reports.
1260 Gemmill, Paul. *Britain's search for health: the first twelve years of the National Health Service.* Philadelphia, Pa., 1962.
1261 George, V. *Social security: Beveridge and after.* 1968. Detailed analysis of income maintenance.
1262 Gittins, Diana. *Fair sex: family size and structure in Britain, 1900–39.* 1982.
1263 Glass, David V. *Population policies and movements in Europe.* 1940. Includes an extensive and suggestive analysis of experience in England and Wales, with useful references.
1264 —— (ed.). *Social mobility in Britain.* Glencoe, Ill., 1954. Fourteen articles by various authors.
1265 Gosden, Peter H. J. H. *The education system since 1944.* 1983.
1266 Gosling, John and Dennis Craig. *The great train robbery.* 1964. Popular account of a well-known event, 8 August 1963.
1267 Graves, John. *Policy and progress in secondary education, 1902–1942.* 1943.
1268 Hall, M. Penelope. *The social services of modern England.* 10th ed., 1983.
1269 Harris, Richard W. *National health service in Great Britain, 1911–1946.* 1946.
1270 Hay, J. Roy. *The origins of the Liberal welfare reforms, 1906–1914.* 1975.
1271 Hiro, Dilip. *Black British white British.* 1971. Thorough but not as reliable as (1306, 1314).
1272 Hoggart, Richard. *The uses of literacy: aspects of working-class life, with special reference to publications and entertainments.* 1957.
1273 Holmes, Colin. *Anti-Semitism in British society, 1876–1939.* 1979.
1274 Hurwitz, S. J. *State intervention in Great Britain: a study of economic and social response, 1914–1919.* 1949.
1275 Isaac, Julius. *British post-war migration.* Cambridge, 1954.
1276 Jenkins, Inez. *History of the women's Institute Movement of England and Wales.* 1953.
1277 Judge, Harry. *A generation of schooling: English secondary schools since 1944.* 1984.
1278 Kazamias, Andreas M. *Politics, society and secondary education in England.* Philadelphia, Pa., 1966.

SOCIAL HISTORY

1279 Kingsford, Peter. *The hunger marchers in Britain, 1920–1940*. Atlantic Highlands, N.J., 1982.
1280 Klein, Viola. *Britain's married women workers*. 1965. An historical and sociological study; includes statistical data.
1281 Lambert, Angela. *Unquiet souls: the Indian summer of the British aristocracy, 1880–1918*. 1984.
1282 Law, Christopher. *British regional development since World War I*. 1981.
1283 Lees-Milne, James. *Britain's heritage: a record of the national Trust*. 2nd ed., 1948.
1284 Lester-Smith, W. O. *Education in Great Britain*. 5th ed., 1967.
1285 Lewis, Jane. *Women in England, 1870–1950: sexual divisions and social change*. Bloomington, Ind. 1984.
1286 Lewis, Roy and Angus Maude. *The English middle classes*. 1949.
1287 Lindsey, Almont. *Socialized medicine in England and Wales: the National Health Service, 1948–1961*. Chapel Hill, N.C., 1962. Continued in R. G. S. Brown. *The changing National Health Service*. 1973.
1288 Low, Rachel. *The history of the British film*. 1948–71, 4 vols.
1289 Lowndes, George A. N. *The silent social revolution: an account of the expansion of public education in England and Wales, 1895–1965*. 2nd ed., 1969. One of best surveys.
1290 McGregor, Oliver R. *Divorce in England: a centenary study*. 1957. Scholarly.
1291 Macintyre, Stuart. *A proletarian science: Marxism in Britain, 1917–1933*. 1980.
1292 Marsh, David Charles. *The welfare state*. 1970. A good introduction.
1293 Marshall, Thomas. *Social policy in the twentieth century*. 2nd ed., 1967.
1294 Marwick, Arthur J. B. *The deluge: British society and the First World War*. 1965. See also his 'Impact of the First World War on British society', *JCH*, 3 (Jan. 1968), 51–63.
1295 —— *Women at war, 1914–1918*. 1977.
1296 Mendelsohn, Ronald. *Social security in the British Commonwealth: Great Britain, Canada, Australia, New Zealand*. 1954. Useful comparative study.
1297 Merrett, Stephen. *State housing in Britain*. Boston, 1979.
1298 Mitchell, David J. *Women on the warpath: the story of the women of the First World War*. 1966.
1299 —— *The fighting Pankhursts: a study in tenacity*. 1967. Concerns Emmeline, Christabel, Sylvia, and Adela Pankhurst.
1300 Moore, John. *Portrait of Elmbury*. 1945. Between the wars; Elmbury is really Tewkesbury.
1301 Mosley, Leonard. *Backs to the wall: London under fire, 1939–45*. 1971. Popular.
1302 Murphy, James. *Church, state and schools in Britain, 1890–1970*. 1971.
1303 Newton, Kenneth. *The sociology of British communism*. 1969. In a historical context.
1304 Parkin, Frank. *Middle class radicalism: the social bases of the British campaign for nuclear disarmament*. Manchester, 1968.
1305 Parkinson, Michael. *The Labour Party and the organization of secondary education, 1918–1965*. 1970.
1306 Patterson, Sheila. *Immigration and race relations in Britain, 1960–1967*. 1969. The best treatment of this problem.
1307 Pelling, Henry. *Britain and the Second World War*. 1970. Good brief account. Cf. Norman Longmate. *The way we lived then: a history of every-day life during the Second World War*. 1971.
1308 Playne, Caroline E. *Society at war, 1914–1916*. 1931. Continued by her *Britain holds on, 1917–1918*. 1933.
1309 Prain, Eric (ed.). *The Oxford and Cambridge Golfing Society, 1898–1948*. 1949. Chapters by various authors.
1310 Reisman, David A. *Richard Titmuss: Welfare and society*. 1977.
1311 Roberts, K., F. G. Cook, S. C. Clarke, and Elizabeth Semenoff. *The fragmentary class structure*. Atlantic Highlands, N.J., 1978.
1312 Robson, William A. *Welfare state and welfare society: illusion and reality*. 1976.
1313 Rodgers, Brian. *The battle against poverty*. 1968–9, 2 vols.
1314 Rose, Eliot J. B., et al. *Colour and citizenship: a report on British race relations*. 1969. An excellent analysis in a historical setting.

1315 Ross, James Stirling. *The National Health Service in Great Britain: an historical and descriptive study*. 1952.
1316 Rubenstein, David and Brian Simon. *The evolution of the comprehensive school, 1926–1966*. 1969.
1317 Runciman, Walter G. *Relative deprivation and social justice: a study of attitudes to social inequality in twentieth-century England*. Berkeley, Calif., 1966.
1318 Saran, Rene. *Policy-making in secondary education: a case study*. Oxford, 1973. A study of a large urbanized county in south of England, 1944–64.
1319 Selleck, Richard J. W. *English primary education and the progressives, 1914–1939*. 1972.
1320 Sherington, Geoffrey. *English education, social change and war*. 1911–20. 1981.
1321 Simon, Brian. *Studies in the History of Education*. Vol. II, *Education and the labour movement, 1870–1920*. 1960. Vol. III, *The politics of educational reform, 1920–1940*, 1974.
1322 Sissons, Michael and Philip French (eds.). *Age of austerity*. 1963. Essays on postwar Britain by writers too young to vote in 1945.
1323 Springhall, John. *Youth, empire and society: British youth movements, 1883–1940*. Hamden, Conn., 1977.
1324 Stocks, Mary. *The Workers' Educational Association: the first fifty years*. 1953.
1325 Strachey, Ray. *'The Cause': a short history of the women's movement in Great Britain*. 1928.
1326 Thane, P. (ed.). *The origins of British social policy*. 1978.
1327 Titmuss, Richard. *Income distribution and social change*. 1962. In a historical context.
1328 —— *Essays on the 'Welfare State'*. 2nd ed., 1963. Lectures and essays, some of them reprints, by a leading social scientist.
1329 Townsend, Peter. *Poverty in the United Kingdom*. 1979. Based on a national survey, 1968–9.
1330 —— and Nicholas Bosanquet. *Labour and inequality: a study in social policy, 1964–70*. 1972. Published by the Fabian Society.
1331 Vaizey, John. *The costs of education*. 1958.
1332 Waller, Robert J. *The Dykeries transformed: the social and political development of a twentieth century coalfield*. 1983.
1333 Walvin, James. *The people's game: a social history of British football*. 1975.
1334 Watkin, Brian. *The National Health Service: the first phase: 1948–1974 and after*. 1978.
1335 Weiler, Peter. *The New Liberalism: liberal social theory in Great Britain, 1889–1914*. New York, 1982.
1336 Widgery, David. *Health in danger: the crisis in the National Health Service*. 1979. Developments in the seventies.
1337 Wilson, Elizabeth. *Only halfway to paradise: women in post-war Britain, 1945–1968*. 1981.
1338 Worsfield, W. Basil. *The war and social reform*. 1919. 'An endeavour to trace the influence of the war as a reforming agency'.

4. Biographies

1339 Boardman, Philip. *Patrick Geddes: maker of the future*. Chapel Hill, N.C., 1944. Boardman was a sociologist and town planner.
1340 Briggs, Asa. *Social thought and social action: a study of the work of Seebohm Rowntree, 1871–1954*. 1961.
1341 Harris, Jose. *William Beveridge: a biography*. Oxford, 1977.
1342 Hillcourt, William. *Baden-Powell: the two lives of a hero*. 1964. 'Life Number two' was with the Boy Scout movement.
1343 Mansbridge, Albert. *Margaret McMillan, prophet and pioneer: her life and work*. 1932.
1344 Stocks, Mary. *Eleanor Rathbone: a biography*. 1949. Useful examination of the life of a social worker and Member of Parliament.
1345 Tsuzuki, Chushichi. *Edward Carpenter, 1884–1929; prophet of Human Fellowship*. 1980.
1346 Wood, Alan. *Mr. Rank: a study of J. Arthur Rank and British films*. 1952.

5. Articles

1347 Abrams, Philip. 'The failure of social reform: 1918–1920', *PP*, XXIV (Apr. 1963), 43–64.
1348 Akenson, D. H. 'Patterns of English educational change: the Fisher and the Butler Acts', *History of Education Quarterly*, XI (summer 1971), 143–56.
1349 Becker, Arthur Peter. 'Housing in England and Wales during the business depression of the 1930s', *EcHR*, 2nd ser., III (1950–1), 321–41.
1350 Bonnor, John. 'The four Labour cabinets', *Sociological Review*, new ser., VI (July 1958), 37–48. A study of social origins, education, and occupation.
1351 Bowley, Marian. 'The housing statistics of Great Britain', *Journal of the Royal Statistical Society*, CXIII (1950), 396–411. On the period 1861–1938.
1352 Briggs, Asa. 'The welfare state in historical perspective', *Archives Européenes de Sociologie*, II (no. 2, 1961), 221–58. An excellent commentary.
1353 Cronin, James E. 'Politics, class structure and the enduring weakness of British social democracy', *Journal of Social History*, XVI (spring 1983), 123–42.
1354 Dean, D. W. 'The difficulties of a Labour educational policy: the failure of the Trevelyan Bill, 1929–1931', *BJES*, XVII (Oct. 1969), 286–300.
1355 —— 'H. A. L. Fisher, reconstruction and the development of the 1918 Education Act' , *BJES*, XVIII (Oct. 1970), 259–76.
1356 —— 'Conservativism and the national education system 1922–40', *JCH*, VI (no. 2, 1971), 150–65.
1357 Dingle, A. E. 'Drink and working-class living standards in Britain, 1870–1914', *EcHR*, 2nd ser., XXV (no. 4, 1972), 608–21.
1358 Eaglesham, Eric. 'Implementing the Education Act of 1902', *BJES*, X (1961–2), 153–75.
1359 Friedlander, D. and R. J. Roshier. 'A study of internal migration in England and Wales: Part I', *Population Studies*, XIX (Mar. 1956), 239–79. On the period 1851–1951.
1360 Gillis, John R. 'Conformity and rebellion: contrasting styles of English and German youth, 1900–1933', *History of Education Quarterly*, XIII (fall 1973), 249–60.
1361 Greenwood, Major. 'British loss of life in the wars of 1794–1815 and in 1914–1918', *Journal of the Royal Statistical Society*, CV (pt. I, 1942), 1–16.
1362 Harbury, C. D. and P. C. McMahon. 'Inheritance and the characteristics of top wealth leavers in Britain', *EJ*, LXXXIII (Sept. 1973), 810–33.
1363 Jenkins, E. W. 'The Thomson Committee and the Board of Education 1916–1922', *BJES*, XXI (Feb. 1973), 76–87. Concerning the position of natural science in the educational system.
1364 Kennedy, Thomas C. 'Public opinion and the conscientious objector, 1915–1919', *JBS*, XII (May 1973), 105–19.
1365 Krausz, Ernest. 'Factors of social mobility in British minority groups', *BJS*, XXIII (Sept. 1972), 275–86.
1366 MacDougall, G. D. A. 'Inter-war population changes in town and country', *Journal of the Royal Statistical Society*, CIII (1940), 30–60.
1367 McGregor, Oliver. 'The Morton Commission: a social and historical commentary', *BJS*, VII (1956), 171–93. Concerning the report of the Royal Commission on Marriage and Divorce (1956).
1368 McKibbin, R. I. 'Social class and social observation in Edwardian England', *TRHS*, XXVIII (1978), 175–99.
1369 Mason, Francis M. 'Charles Masterman and National Health Insurance', *Albion*, X (spring 1978), 54–75.
1370 Middleton, Nigel. 'Lord Butler and the Education Act of 1944', *BJES*, XX (June 1972), 178–91.
1371 Morgan, John S. 'The break-up of the poor law in Britain, 1907–47: an historical footnote', *Canadian Journal of Economics and Political Science*, XIV (May 1948), 209–19. An analysis of social legislation.
1372 Pierce, Rachel M. 'Marriage in the fifties', *Sociological Review*, new ser.,

II (July 1963), 215–40. Based on inquiry into changing marriage habits.

1373 Reid, F. 'Socialist Sunday Schools in Great Britain, 1892–1939', *IRSH*, XI (pt. 1, 1966), 18–46.

1374 Rogers, Alan. 'Churches and children–a study in the controversy over the 1902 Education Act', *BJES*, VIII (Nov. 1959), 29–51.

1375 Rubinstein, W. D. 'Wealth, élites and the class structure of modern Britain, *PP*, LXXVI (Aug. 1977), 99–126.

1376 Smith, Harold L. 'The problem of "equal pay for equal work" in Great Britain during World War II', *JMH*, LIII (Dec. 1981), 652–72.

1377 —— 'The womenpower problem in Britain during the Second World War', *Hist. J.*, XXVII (no. 4, 1984), 925–45.

1378 Usherwood, Stephen. 'The B.B.C. and the General Strike', *History Today,* XXII (Dec. 1972), 858–65.

1379 Waites, B. A. 'The effect of the First World War on class and status in England, 1910–1920', *JCH*, II (Jan. 1976), 27–48.

1380 Wheeler, Robert F. 'Organized sport and organized labour: The Workers' Sport movement', *JCH*, XIII (no. 2, 1978), 191–210.

1381 Whitfield, George. 'The grammar schools through half a century', *BJES*, V (May 1957), 101–18. By a headmaster of Hampton Grammar School.

1382 Wilkinson, Paul. 'English youth movements, 1908–30', *JCH*, IV (Apr. 1969), 3–23.

1383 Willatts, E. C. and Marion G. C. Newson. 'The geographical pattern of population changes in England and Wales, 1921–1951', *GJ*, CXIX (Dec. 1953), 431–54.

1384 Wilson, J. 'British Israelism', *Sociological Review*, new ser., XVI (Mar. 1968), 41–57. As an organized element.

1385 Winter, J. M. 'Military fitness and civilian health during the First World War', *JCH*, XV (April 1980), 211–44. See also 'Some aspects of the demographic consequences of the First World War in Britain', *Population Studies*, XXX (Nov. 1976), 539–52.

VIII. ECONOMIC HISTORY

1. Printed sources

1386 Beveridge, William H. *Unemployment: a problem of industry.* 2nd. ed., 1910. Based on lectures at Oxford in 1908.

1387 —— *Full employment in a free society.* New York, 1945. Reflects Keynesian influence; includes an appendix on economic fluctuations.

1388 Chiozza Money, Leo G. *Riches and poverty.* 1905. A classic statement.

1389 Keynes, John Maynard. *Collected writings.* Ed. Donald E. Moggridge et al., 1971–. In progress. By 1979, 29 vols. had been published by the Royal Economic Society.

1390 Lane, Peter (ed.). *Documents on British economic and social policy.* II, *1870–1939*, 1968. III, *1945–1967*, 1969. An excellent collection.

1391 Macmillan, Harold. *The middle way: a study of the problem of economic and social progress in a free and democratic society.* 1938. Revealing on both author and subject.

1392 Mantoux, Etienne. *The Carthaginian Peace, or the economic consequences of Mr. Keynes.* 1946. An answer to John Maynard Keynes's *The economic consequences of the peace*, in (1389).

1393 Markham, Violet R. *Return passage.* 1953. Autobiography of a leading member of the Unemployment Assistance Board created in 1934.

1394 Munby, Denys Lawrence (ed.). *Inland transport statistics, Great Britain, 1900–1970.* Vol. I, Oxford, 1978.

1395 *The National Plan.* 1965. Drafted by the British National Economic Development Council and presented to Parliament, September, 1965.

1396 *Oxford pamphlets, 1914–1915.* N.d. War-time statements on the economy.

1397 Pearson, Arthur J. *Man of the rail.* 1967. A personal account by a practitioner of technical journalism.
1398 Robbins, Lionel Charles, Baron. *Autobiography of an economist.* 1971.
1399 Robens, Alfred, Baron. *Ten year stint.* 1972. By the chairman of the National Coal Board, 1960–71.
1400 Rolt, Lionel T. C. *Landscape with machines: an autobiography.* 1971. By a noted author of railroad history.
1401 *Royal Commission on trade unions and employer's associations, 1965–1968: report presented . . . June 1968.* 1968. Cmnd 3623. Known as the 'Donovan Report'. See (1665).
1402 Salter, Arthur. *Recovery: the second effort.* 1932. By a noted scholar and statesman.
1403 Sturt, George. *The journals of George Sturt, 1890–1927.* Ed. Eric D. Mackerness. 1967, 2 vols. Sturt (1863–1927) was associated with the wheelwright craft and industry.

2. Surveys

1404 Abrams, Mark. *The condition of the British people, 1911–1945: a study prepared for the Fabian Society.* 1946. Statistical.
1405 Aldcroft, Derek Howard. *The inter-war economy, 1919–1939.* 1970. Probably the best work on the period.
1406 —— and Harry W. Richardson. *The British economy, 1870–1939.* 1969. An introduction to central themes and problems with invaluable bibliography.
1407 Alford, B. W. E. *Depression and recovery? British economic growth, 1918–1939.* 1972.
1408 Ashworth, William. *An economic history of England, 1870–1939.* 1960. The best starting point.
1409 Bagwell, Philip S. and G. E. Mingay. *Britain and America, 1850–1939: a study of economic change.* 1970.
1410 Drummond, Ian. *Imperial economic policy, 1917–1939: studies in expansion and protection.* 1974.
1411 Dunning, John H. and C. J. Thomas. *British industry: change and development in the twentieth century.* 1961.
1412 Floud, Roderick and Donald McCloskey. *The economic history of Britain since 1700.* II, *1860–1970s.* 1981.
1413 Hobsbawm, Eric J. *Industry and empire: the making of modern English society.* II, *1750 to the present day.* 1968.
1414 Johnson, Walford, et al. *A short economic and social history of twentieth-century Britain.* 1967. Excellent brief account.
1415 Kirby, M. W. *Decline of British economic power since 1970.* 1981.
1416 Lenman, Bruce. *An economic history of modern Scotland, 1660–1976.* 1977. More than one-third concerns the twentieth century.
1417 Leruez, Jacques. *Economic planning & politics in Britain.* New York, 1975. Deals with 1945–74.
1418 Lewis, W. Arthur. *Economic survey, 1919–1939.* 1949. Good introduction to international aspects.
1419 Mathews, Robert Charles Oliver, Charles H. Feinstein, and J. C. Odling-Smee. *British economic growth, 1856–1973.* 1982.
1420 Phillips, G. A. and R. T. Maddock. *The growth of the British economy, 1918–1968.* 1973.
1421 Pollard, Sidney. *The development of the British economy, 1914–1967.* 3rd ed., 1983. Standard.
1422 Smith, Wilfred. *An economic geography of Great Britain.* 2nd ed., 1953. Part I is historical.
1423 Wright, J. F. *Britain in the age of economic management: an economic history since 1939.* New York, 1979.
1424 Youngson, Alexander. *Britain's economic growth, 1920–1966.* 1967. An extension of his *The British Economy, 1920–1957.* 1960.

3. Monographs

1425 Abel, Deryck. *A history of British tariffs, 1923–1942.* 1945.
1426 Aldcroft, Derek Howard. *British railways in transition: the economic problems of Britain's railways since 1914.* 1968.
1427 —— *British transport since 1914: an economic history.* 1975.
1428 Alexander, Kenneth J. W. and C. L. Jenkins. *Fairfields: a study of industrial change.* 1970. Study of the ship building industry.
1429 Allen, Cecil J. *Locomotive practice and performance in the twentieth century.* Cambridge, 1949.
1430 Allen, George C. *British industries and their organization.* 4th ed., 1959.
1431 —— *The structure of industry in Britain: a study in economic change.* 1961. On 1900–60.
1432 Anderson, Adelaide Mary. *Women in the factory.* New York, 1922. Concerning the Woman Inspectorate of Factories and Workshops, 1893–1921.
1433 Anderson, John R. L. *East of Suez: a study of Britain's greatest trading enterprise.* 1969. Story of British petroleum from 1909.
1434 Andrews, Irene Osgood. *Economic effects of the war upon women and children in Great Britain.* New York, 1918.
1435 Andrews, Philip W. S. and Elizabeth Brunner. *Capital development in steel: a study of the United Steel Companies Ltd.* Oxford, 1951.
1436 Arndt, Heinz W. *The economic lessons of the nineteen-thirties.* 1944.
1437 Baker, Stanley. *Milk to market: forty years of milk marketing.* 1973.
1438 Barker, T. C. and Michael Robbins. *A history of London transport.* II, 1974. Carries the story from 1900 to 1970.
1439 Beckerman, Wilfred (ed.). *The Labour Government's economic record: 1964–1970.* 1972. Various contributors.
1440 Benham, Frederic. *Great Britain under protection.* 1941. Good account of depression years.
1441 Berkovitch, Israel. *Coal on the switchback: the coal industry since nationalization.* 1977.
1442 Best, Robin H. and John T. Coppock. *The changing use of land in Britain.* 1962. See also (1616).
1443 Blank, Stephen. *Industry and government in Britain: the Federation of British Industry in politics, 1945–1965.* Lexington, Mass., 1973.
1444 Bonner, Arnold. *British co-operation: the history, principles and organization of the British co-operative movement.* Manchester, 1961.
1445 Bowley, Arthur L. *Prices and wages in the United Kingdom, 1914–20.* Oxford, 1921.
1446 —— *Some economic consequences of the Great War.* 1930.
1447 —— (ed.). *Studies in national income, 1924–1938.* 1942. A study sponsored by the National Institute of Economic and Social Research.
1448 Briggs, Asa. *Friends of the people: the centenary history of Lewis's.* 1956.
1449 *Britain in depression: a record of British industries since 1929.* 1935. See also *Britain in recover.* 1938. Contemporary attitudes; sponsored by the British Association for the Advancement of Science.
1450 Broadway, Frank. *State intervention in British industry, 1964–68.* Madison, N.J., 1969.
1451 Brown, Arthur Joseph. *The great inflation, 1939–1951.* 1955. Special concern for Britain.
1452 Burn, Duncan (ed.). *The structure of British industry: a symposium.* Cambridge, 1958, 2 vols. Essays on nineteen industries.
1453 Burns, Eveline M. *British unemployment programs, 1920–1938.* Washington, D.C., 1941.
1454 Buxton, Neil K. and Derek H. Alcroft (eds.). *British industry between the wars: instability and industrial development, 1919–1939.* 1979.
1455 Cairncross, Alexander K. (ed.). *The Scottish economy: a statistical account of Scottish life.* 1954. Twenty essays, considered 'authoritative', by various writers.
1456 —— [Alec] and Eichengreen, Barry. *Sterling in decline: the devaluations of 1931, 1949 and 1967.* Oxford, 1983.

1457 Camps, Miriam. *Britain and the European community, 1955–1963.* Princeton, N.J., 1964. Excellent on the 'Common Market'.

1458 Carter, Charles Frederick and Andrew D. Roy. *British economic statistics: a report.* Cambridge, 1954. A critical comment on their use.

1459 Cartter, Alan Murray. *The redistribution of income in postwar Britain: a study of the central Government fiscal program in 1948–49.* New Haven, Conn., 1955.

1460 Caves, Richard E., et al. *British economic prospects.* 1968. Examines the period, 1950–65. For its sequel see Cairncross, Alec (ed.). *Britain's economic prospects reconsidered.* Albany, N.Y., 1970.

1461 Chaloner, William Henry and Barrie M. Ratcliffe. *Trade and transport: Essays in economic history in honour of T. S. Wilan.* Manchester, 1977.

1462 Chapman, Agatha L. and Rose Knight. *Wages and salaries in the United Kingdom, 1920–1938.* Cambridge, 1953.

1463 Chester, Daniel Norman. (ed.). *Lessons of the British war economy.* Cambridge, 1951. Thirteen articles by various authors.

1464 —— *The nationalization of British industry, 1945–1951.* 1979.

1465 Church, Roy. *Herbert Austin: the British motor car industry to 1941.* 1979.

1466 Clark, Colin. *National income and outlay.* 1937. A revision and extension of his *The national income, 1924–1931.* 1932.

1467 —— *The conditions of economic progress.* 3rd ed., 1955. Presented in an historical context; a significant book.

1468 Cocks, Edward J. and Bernhardt Walters. *A history of the zinc smelting industry in Britain.* 1968.

1469 Coleman, Donald C. *Courtalds: an economic and social history.* 3 vols. – 1969, 1980. Vol. III takes the story to 1965.

1470 Corbett, John. *History of the Birmingham Trades Council, 1866–1966.* 1966.

1471 Cox, Andrew W. *Adversary politics and land: the conflict over land and the property policy in post-war Britain.* 1984.

1472 Croome, David R. and Harry G. Johnson. *Money in Britain, 1959–1969.* 1970. Papers to commemorate the tenth anniversary of the report of the Radcliffe Committee on the monetary and credit system, 1957–9.

1473 Deakin, Brian M. and T. Seward. *Productivity in transport: a study of employment, capital, output, productivity and technical change.* Cambridge, 1969.

1474 Dearle, Norman B. *The labour cost of the World War to Great Britain, 1914–1922.* 1940. 'A statistical analysis'.

1475 Denby Marshall, Chapman F. *Centenary history of the Liverpool and Manchester Railway.* 1930.

1476 —— *A history of the Southern Railway.* 2nd, enlarged, ed. by R. W. Kidner. 1963, 2 vols.

1477 Devons, Ely. *An introduction to British economic statistics.* Cambridge, 1956. Purpose: 'a general survey of the main British economic statistics'.

1478 Dickie, John P. *The coal problem – a survey: 1910–1936.* 1936.

1479 Dimock, Marshall E. *British public utilities and national development.* 1933. The story after 1918.

1480 Dobb, Maurice Herbert. *Studies in the development of capitalism.* 1947.

1481 Dorfman, Gerald A. *Wage politics in Britain, 1945–1967.* Ames, Iowa, 1973. The Government versus the Trades Union Congress.

1482 Dow, John C. R. *The management of the British economy, 1945–1960.* Cambridge, 1964.

1483 Drummond, Ian. *The floating pound and the sterling area, 1931–1939.* 1981.

1484 Feinstein, Charles H. *Domestic capital formation in the United Kingdom, 1920–1938.* Cambridge, 1965.

1485 —— *National income, expenditure and output of the United Kingdom, 1855–1965.* Cambridge, 1972.

1486 Fels, Allan. *The British Prices and Incomes Board.* Cambridge, 1972. A discussion of the role of the Board, 1965–70.

1487 Ferrier, Ronald W. *The history of the British Petroleum Company.* Vol. I, *The developing years, 1901–1932.* 1982.

1488 Flanders, Allan and Hugh A. Clegg. *The system of industrial relations in Great Britain: its history, law and institutions.* 1954.

1489 Floud, Roderick. *The British machine-tool industry, 1850–1914.* Cambridge, 1976.

1490 French, David. *British economic and strategic planning, 1905–1915.* 1982.

1491 Garnett, Ronald G. *A century of co-operative insurance.* 1968. The story of the co-operative insurance society, 1867–1967.

1492 Grant, Alexander T. K. *A study of the capital market in Britain from 1919 to 1936.* 2nd ed., 1967. Reprint, with new introduction of his *A study of the capital market in post-war Britain.* 1937.

1493 Greenleaf, Horace. *Britain's big four: the story of the London Midland and Scottish, London and North Eastern, Great Western, and Southern Railways.* 1948.

1494 Hannah, Leslie. *The rise of the corporate economy: the British experience.* 1976.

1495 —— *Electricity before nationalisation: a study of the electricity supply industry in Britain to 1948.* 1979.

1496 Haresnape, Brian. *Railway design since 1830.* 1968–9, 2 vols. Pictorial; vol. II is on 1914–69.

1497 Harlow, Chris. *Innovation and productivity under nationalisation: the first thirty years.* 1977. Aircraft, electricity, telephone, gas, coal.

1498 Harris, Jose. *Unemployment and politics: a study in English social policy, 1886–1914.* 1973. Exhaustive and meticulous.

1499 Harris, Nigel. *Competition and the corporate society: British Conservatives, the state and industry, 1945–1964.* 1972.

1500 Harrison, Anthony. *The framework of economic activity: the international economy and the rise of the state in the twentieth century.* 1967. Includes detailed discussion of the United Kingdom.

1501 Harrod, Roy F. *The British economy.* New York, 1963. Theories and principles.

1502 Hart, Peter E. *Studies in profit, business saving and investment in the United Kingdom, 1920–1962.* 1965–8, 2 vols.

1503 Harte, N. B. (ed.). *The study of economic history: collected inaugural lectures.* 1971.

1504 Hawtrey, Ralph G. *Incomes and money.* 1967. 'A criticism of British monetary policy since 1945' in a historical context.

1505 Haynes, William Warren. *Nationalization in practice: the British coal industry.* Boston, 1953. Balanced but with a bias for nationalization.

1506 Henderson, Hubert Douglas. *The inter-war years and other papers.* Ed. Henry Clay. Oxford, 1955.

1507 Hibbs, John. *The history of British bus services.* 1968.

1508 Higham, Robin. *Britain's imperial air routes, 1918 to 1939: the story of Britain's overseas airlines.* 1960.

1509 Hirst, Francis W. *The consequences of the war to Great Britain.* 1934.

1510 Hodson, Henry V. *Slump and recovery, 1929–1937: a survey of world economic affairs.* 1938. By an authority of the time.

1511 Holmes, Martin. *Political pressure and economic policy: the British government, 1970–74.* 1982.

1512 Holton, Bob. *British syndicalism, 1900–1914: myths and realities.* 1976.

1513 Hutchinson, Terence W. *Economics and economic policy in Britain, 1946–1966: some aspects of their interrelations.* 1968.

1514 Jenkins, Clive. *Power at the top: a critical survey of the nationalized industries.* 1959. On post-1945 developments.

1515 Jevons, H. Stanley. *The British coal trade.* 1915. Excellent on the industry before 1914.

1516 Johnson, Elizabeth S. and Harry G. *The shadow of Keynes: understanding Keynes, Cambridge and Keynesian economics.* Chicago. 1978.

1517 Jones, Jeffrey. *The state and the emergence of the oil industry.* 1981.

1518 Kahn, Alfred E. *Great Britain in the world economy.* New York, 1946. A study of 1919–39; excellent.

1519 Kelf-Cohen, Reuben. *Twenty years of nationalization: the British experience.* 1969.

1520 Kenen, Peter B. *British monetary policy and the balance of payments, 1951–1957.* Cambridge, Mass., 1960.

1521 Keynes, Milo (ed.). *Essays on John Maynard Keynes.* 1975.

1522 Kidd, Howard C. *A new era for British railways.* 1929. Study of the Railway Act, 1921.

ECONOMIC HISTORY

1523 Kirby, M. W. *The British coal mining industry, 1870–1946: a political and economic history*. 1977.

1524 —— *The decline of British economic power since 1970*. 1981.

1525 Klapper, Charles F. *The golden age of tramways*. 1961.

1526 Lipson, Ephraim. *A planned economy or free enterprise: the lessons of history*. 2nd ed., 1946. A careful inquiry.

1527 Lipton, Michael. *Assessing economic performance*. 1968. 'British economic development, 1950–1965, in the light of economic theory and the principles of economic planning'.

1528 Loveday, Arthur. *Britain and world trade*. 1931. Essays on postwar period; Loveday was head of the Economic Intelligence Service of the League of Nations Secretariat.

1529 Lydall, Harold F. *British incomes and savings*. Oxford, 1955. Based on a survey in 1952.

1530 McCloskey, Donald N. *Economic maturity and entrepreneurial decline: British iron and steel, 1870–1913*. Cambridge, Mass. 1973.

1531 MacDermot, Edward Terrence, et al. *History of the Great Western Railway*. Rev. ed., 1964–7, 3 vols.

1532 Mallett, Bernard. *British budgets, 1887–88 to 1912–13, 1913–14 to 1920–21, 1921–22 to 1932–33*. 1913–33, 3 vols. Each budget is analysed.

1533 Mess, Henry Adolphis. *Factory legislation and its administration, 1891–1924*. 1926.

1534 Middlemas, Keith. *Politics in industrial society: the experience of the British system since 1911*. 1979.

1535 Miliband, Ralph. *Capitalist democracy in Britain*. 1982. 'Political system' since 1867, but largely twentieth century.

1536 Milward, Alan S. *War, economy and society, 1939–1945*. Berkeley, Calif., 1977.

1537 Mitchell, Joan. *The National Board for Prices and Incomes*. 1972. An account of the board, 1965–71.

1538 Moggridge, Donald E. *British monetary policy, 1924–1931: the Norman conquest of $4.86*. 1972.

1539 Morgan, E. Victor and William A. Thomas. *The Stock Exchange: its history and functions*. 2nd ed., 1969.

1540 Morton, Walter A. *British finance, 1930–1940*. Madison, Wis., 1943.

1541 Munby, Denys Lawrence. *Inland transport: Great Britain, 1900–1970*. Vol. I, 1978.

1542 Nock, Oswald S. *The Great Western Railway in the twentieth century*. 1964. See also his *The Great Northern Railway*. 1958.

1543 Olson, Mancur, Jr. *The economics of the wartime shortage: a history of British food supplies in the Napoleonic War and in World Wars I and II*. Durham, N.C., 1963.

1544 Paish, Frank W. *The post war financial problem and other essays*. 1950. Articles originally written in the thirties and forties.

1545 —— *Studies in an inflationary economy: the United Kingdom, 1948–1961*. 1962. Articles and papers.

1546 Peden, G. C. *British rearmament and the treasury: 1932–1939*. Edinburgh, 1979.

1547 Pigou, A. C. *Aspects of British economic history, 1918–1925*. 1947.

1548 Pinder, John. *Britain and the Common Market*. 1961.

1549 Pinto-Duschinsky, Michael. *British political finance, 1830–1980*. Washington, D.C., 1981.

1550 Pollard, Sidney. *The wasting of the British economy: British economic policy from 1945 to the present*. 1982.

1551 Prest, Alan R. and A. A. Adams. *Consumers' expenditures in the United Kingdom, 1900–1919*. Cambridge, 1954.

1552 Pryke, Richard. *The nationalised industries: policies and performances since 1968*. Oxford, 1981.

1553 Reader, William Joseph. *Imperial chemical industries: a history*. I, *The forerunners, 1870–1926*. 1970. II, *The first quarter century, 1926–1952*. 1975.

1554 Reid, Graham, et al. *The nationalized fuel industries*. 1973.

1555 Richardson, Harry W. *Economic recovery in Britain, 1932–9*. 1967.

1556 —— and Derek H. Aldcroft. *Building in the British economy between the wars.* 1968.

1557 —— and C. C. O'Gallagher. *The British motor industry, 1896–1939.* Hamden, Conn., 1977.

1558 Robbins, Lionel. *The great depression.* 1934. World context.

1559 Robson, Robert. *The cotton industry in Britain.* 1957.

1560 Robson, William A. *Nationalised industry and public ownership.* 1960.

1561 —— (ed.). *Public enterprise: developments in social ownership and control in Great Britain.* 1937. Essays by various writers analysing public boards and commissions.

1562 Rosenberg, Nathan. *Economic planning in the British building industry, 1945–49.* 1960.

1563 Roseveare, Henry. *The Treasury: evolution of a British institution.* New York, 1969.

1564 Rostas, Laszlo. *Comparative productivity in British and American industry.* Cambridge, 1948.

1565 Sanderson, J. Michael. *The universities and British industry, 1850–1970.* 1972.

1566 Savage, Christopher I. *An economic history of transport.* 1959. A survey.

1567 Sayers, Richard S. *The Bank of England, 1891–1944.* Cambridge, 1976, 3 vols.

1568 Scott, John D. *Vickers: a history.* 1962. Excellent study of armament manufacture.

1569 Seers, Dudley George. *The levelling of incomes since 1938.* Oxford, 1951.

1570 Self, Henry and Elizabeth M. Watson. *Electricity supply in Great Britain: its development and organization.* 1952.

1571 Shonfield, Andrew. *Modern capitalism: the changing balance of public and private power.* 1965. Examination of postwar period.

1572 Simmons, Jack. *The railways of Britain: an historical introduction.* 1961. Includes an excellent bibliography.

1573 Skidelsky, Robert Jacob (ed.). *The end of the Keynesian era: essays on the disintegration of the Keynesian political economy.* 1977.

1574 Snyder, Rixford Kinney. *The tariff problem in Great Britain, 1918–1923.* Stanford, Calif., 1944.

1575 Stamp, Lawrence Dudley. *The land of Britain: its use and misuse.* 2nd ed., 1950.

1576 Stark, Thomas. *The distribution of personal income in the United Kingdom, 1949–1963.* Cambridge, 1972.

1577 Stewart, Michael. *Keynes and after.* 1967. A discussion of unemployment and 'full employment' since 1918. A 'popular' account is found in his *The Jekyll & Hyde years: politics and economic policy since 1964.* 1978.

1578 Stone, Richard and D. A. Rowe. *The measure of consumers' expenditure and behaviour in the United Kingdom, 1920–1938.* Cambridge, 1954–66, 2 vols. A massive study.

1579 Strange, Susan. *Sterling and British policy: a political study of an international currency in decline.* 1971. The thesis that the changing status of Sterling was the root cause of economic difficulty in the sixties.

1580 Sturmey, Stanley. *British shipping and world competition.* 1962. Comprehensive treatment for the twentieth century.

1581 Supple, Barry. *The Royal Exchange Assurance: a history of British insurance, 1720–1970.* Cambridge, 1970. Significant section on twentieth century.

1582 Sykes, Alan. *Tariff reform in British politics, 1903–1913.* Oxford, 1979.

1583 Thomas, David St. John and J. Allan Patmore (eds.). *A regional history of the railways of Great Britain.* The series now includes: I, David St. John Thomas. *The west country.* 4th ed., 1973. II, H. P. White. *Southern England.* 3rd ed., 1972. III, H. P. White. *Greater London.* 1963. IV, K. Hoole. *Northeast England.* 1965. V, D. I. Gordon. *The eastern counties.* Newton Abbot, 1968. VI, John Thomas. *Scotland: The lowlands and the borders.* Newton Abbot, 1971. VII Rex Christiansen. *The west midlands.* Newton Abbot, 1973. VIII, David Joy. *South and west Yorkshire: the industrial West Riding.* Newton Abbot, 1975.

1584 Thompson, A. W. J. and L. C. Hunter. *The nationalized transport industries.* 1973. Thorough and of general interest.

1585 Tomlinson, William Weaver. *Tomlinson's North Eastern Railway: its rise and development*, new ed. with introd. by K. Hoole. Newton Abbot, 1967. Tomlinson's book, originally published in 1915, includes valuable statistics and other information for 1900–14.

1586 Townshend-Rose, H. *The British coal industry*. 1951. On its nationalization.

1587 Vaizey, John. *The brewing industry, 1886–1951*. 1960.

1588 —— *The history of British steel*. 1974. For the general reader.

1589 Walker, Gilbert. *Economic planning by programme and control in Great Britain*. 1957. Developments after 1945.

1590 Webb, Sidney and Beatrice Webb. *The consumers' co-operative movement*. 1921.

1591 Wells, Sidney J. *British export performance: a comparative study*. Cambridge, 1964. A study of the fifties.

1592 Wigham, Eric. *The power to manage: a history of the Engineering Employers' Federation*. 1973.

1593 Williams, Trevor I. *A history of the British gas industry*. 1981.

1594 Wilson, Charles H. *The history of Unilever: a study in economic growth and social change*. 1954–68, 3 vols.

1595 Wilson, Geoffrey. *London United Tramways: a history – 1894 to 1933*. 1971.

1596 Winton, J. R. *Lloyd's Bank, 1918–1969*. 1982.

1597 Worswick, George D. N. and Peter H. Ady (eds.). *The British economy, 1945–1950*. Oxford, 1952. 'Studies of economic development and policies' by various writers; valuable bibliography.

1598 —— *The British economy in the nineteen-fifties*. 1962. Fourteen essays by various authors.

4. Biographies

1599 Andrews, Philip W. S. and Elizabeth Brunner. *The life of Lord Nuffield*. 1959.

1600 Bolitho, Hector. *Alfred Mond, First Lord Melchett*. 1933.

1601 Boyle, Andrew. *Montagu Norman: a biography*. 1967. See comment by Theodore Gregory. 'Lord Norman: a new interpretation', *Lloyds Bank Review*, LXXXVIII (Apr. 1968), 31–51.

1602 Clay, Henry. *Lord Norman*. 1957.

1603 Harrod, Roy F. *The life of John Maynard Keynes*. 1951.

1604 Hession, Charles H. *John Maynard Keynes*. 1984.

1605 Jones, J. Harry. *Josiah Stamp, public servant: the life of the First Baron Stamp of Shortlands*. 1964.

1606 Pound, Reginald. *Selfridge: a biography*. 1960.

1607 Skidelsky, Robert Jacob Alexander. *John Maynard Keynes: hopes betrayed, 1883–1920*. 1983. An interesting comparison with (1603, 1604).

1608 Vernon, Anne. *A Quaker businessman: the life of Joseph Rowntree, 1836–1925*. 1958.

5. Articles

1609 Aldcroft, Derek H. 'Railways and economic growth', *JTH*, new ser., I (no. 4, 1973), 238–48.

1610 —— 'A new chapter in transport history: the twentieth century revolution', *JTH*, new ser., III (Feb. 1976), 217–39.

1611 Atkin, John. 'Official regulation of British overseas investment, 1914–1931', *EcHR*, XXIII (no. 2, 1970), 324–35.

1612 Bacon, F. W., et al. 'The growth of pension rights and their impact on the national economy', *Journal of the Institute of Actuaries*, LXXX (1954), 141–266.

1613 Baxter, J. L. 'Long-term unemployment in Great Britain, 1953–1971', *Bulletin, Oxford University Institute of Economics and Statistics*, XXXIV (Nov. 1972), 329–44.

1614 Beckerman, Wilfred, et al. 'The National Plan: a discussion before the Royal Statistical Society . . . Nov. 24, 1965', *Journal of the Royal Statistical Society*, ser. A, CXXIX (1966), 1–24. See also (1662).

1615 Bell, R. and E. W. Arkle. 'The London & North Eastern Railway', *JTH*, V (May 1962), 133–45. On the period 1922–48.

1616 Best, Robin H. 'Recent changes and future prospects of land use in England and Wales', *GJ*, CXXXI (Mar. 1965), 1–12. Extends (1442).

1617 Booth, A. E. and A. W. Coats. 'The market for economists in Britain, 1944–75', *EJ* LXXXVIII (Sept. 1978), 436–54.

1618 Bosanquet, Nicholas and Guy Standing. 'Government and unemployment, 1966–1970: a study of policy and evidence', *British Journal of Industrial Relations*, X (July 1972), 180–92.

1619 Capie, Forrest. 'The British tariff and industrial protection in the 1930s', *EcHR*, 2nd ser., XXXI (no. 3, 1978), 399–409.

1620 Chang, Tse Chun. 'The British balance of payments, 1924–1938', *EJ*, LVII (Dec. 1947), 475–503.

1621 Coats, A. W. 'Political economy and the tariff reform campaign of 1903', *Journal of Law and Economics*, XI (Apr. 1968), 181–229.

1622 —— and S. E. Coats. 'The changing social composition of the Royal Economic Society, 1890–1960, and the professionalization of British economics', *BJS*, XXIV (June 1973), 165–87.

1623 Dewey, P. E. 'Food production and policy in the United Kingdom, 1914–1948', *TRHS*, 5th ser., XXX (1980), 71–89.

1624 Dowie, J. A. '1919–20 is in need of attention', *EHR*, 2nd ser., XXVIII (no. 3, 1975), 429–50.

1625 Fearon, Peter. 'The formative years of the British aircraft industry', *Business History Review*, XLIII (winter 1969), 476–95.

1626 Feinstein, Charles H. 'Production and productivity, 1920–1962', *London and Cambridge Bulletin*, No. 48 (1963).

1627 George, Kenneth D. 'The changing structure of competitive industry', *EJ*, LXXXII (Mar. 1972, suppl.), 353–68. On the years 1924–68; technical.

1628 Glenny, M. V. 'The Anglo–Soviet trade agreement, March 1921', *JCH*, V (no. 2, 1970), 63–82.

1629 Gowing, Margaret M. 'The organisation of manpower in Britain during the Second World War', *JCH*, VII (nos. 1–2, 1972), 147–67.

1630 Grant, W. P. and D. Marsh. 'The Confederation of British Industry', *PS*, XIX (1971), 403–15. Its history since formation in July 1965.

1631 Hahn, Frank and Robert C. O. Matthews. 'The theory of economic growth: a survey', *EJ*, LXXIV (Dec. 1964), 779–902.

1632 Irving, R. J. 'British railway investment and innovation, 1900–1914', *BH*, XIII (Jan. 1971), 39–63.

1633 Jack, Marion. 'The purchase of the British government's shares in the British Petroleum Company', *PP*, XXXIX (Apr. 1968), 139–68.

1634 Jefferys, James B. and Dorothy Walters. 'National income and expenditure of the United Kingdom, 1870–1952', *Income and Wealth*, 5th ser. (1955), 1–40.

1635 Kirby, M. W. 'Government intervention in industrial organization: coal mining in the nineteen thirties', *BH*, XV (July 1973), 160–73.

1636 Knapp, John and Kenneth Lomax. 'Britain's growth performance: the enigma of the 1950s', *Lloyds Bank Review*, No. 74 (Oct. 1964), 1–24.

1637 Knight, K. G. 'Strike and wage inflation in British manufacturing industry, 1950–1968', *Bulletin, Oxford University Institute of Economics and Statistics*, XXXIV (Aug. 1972), 281–94. Technical.

1638 Lauterbach, Albert T. 'Economic demobilization in Great Britain after the First World War', *Political Science Quarterly*, LVII (Sept. 1942), 376–93.

1639 Lee, K. M. 'The British Civil Service and the war economy: bureaucratic conceptions of the "Lessons of History" in 1918 and 1945', *TRHS*, XXX (1980), 183–96.

1640 Lowe, Rodney. 'The erosion of state intervention in Britain, 1917–24', *EHR*, 2nd ser., XXXI (no. 2, 1978), 370–86.

1641 MacDonald, C. A. 'Economic appeasement and the German "moderates" 1937–1939. An introductory essay', *PP*, LVI (Aug. 1972), 105–35.

1642 McDonald, G. W. and Howard F. Gospel. 'The Mond–Turner talks, 1927–1933: a study in industrial cooperation', *Hist. J.*, XVI (no. 4, 1973), 807–29.

1643 Matthews, Robert C. O. 'Some aspects of post-war growth in the British economy in relation to historical experience', *Transactions of the Manchester Statistical Society* (1964), 3–25. Favorable comment; somewhat technical.

1644 Mishan, Edward J. 'A survey of welfare economics, 1939–51', *EJ*, LXX (June 1960), 197–265.

1645 Moore, Barry and John Rhodes. 'Evaluating the effects of British regional economic policy', *EJ*, LXXXIII (Mar. 1973), 87–110. A study of 1950–71.

1646 Nicholson, R. J. 'Capital stock, employment and output in British industry, 1948–64', *YBESR*, XVIII (Nov. 1966), 65–85.

1647 Pollard, Sidney. 'British and world shipbuilding, 1890–1914: a study in comparative costs', *JEcH*, XVII (no. 3, 1957), 426–44.

1648 —— (ed.). *The gold standard and employment policies between the wars.* 1970. Reprints of articles by Edward Nevin, K. J. Hancock, L. J. Hume, Sidney Pollard, and others.

1649 Quin-Harkin, A. J. 'Imperial airways, 1924–40', *JTH*, I (Nov. 1954), 197–215.

1650 Richardson, Harry W. 'The new industries between the wars', *Oxford Economic Papers*, XIII (Oct. 1961), 360–84.

1651 —— 'The basis of economic recovery in the nineteen-thirties: a review and a new interpretation, *EcHR*, 2nd ser., XV (no. 2, 1962), 344–63.

1652 Ridley, T. M. 'Industrial production in the United Kingdom, 1900–1953', *Economica*, new ser., XXII (Feb. 1955), 1–11.

1653 Robinson, Austin. 'John Maynard Keynes: economist, author, statesman', *EJ*, LXXXII (June 1972), 531–46.

1654 Robinson, Olive. 'Representation of the white-collar worker: the Bank Staff Associations in Britain', *British Journal of Industrial Relations*, VII (Mar. 1969), 19–41.

1655 Sanderson, J. Michael. 'The University of London and industrial progress', *JCH*, VII (July–Oct. 1972), 243–62.

1656 Saul, Samuel B. 'The American impact on British industry, 1895–1914', *BH*, III (Dec. 1960), 19–38.

1657 —— 'The motor industry in Britain to 1914', *BH*, V (Dec. 1962), 22–44.

1658 —— 'The machine tool industry in Britain to 1914', *BH*, X (Jan. 1968), 22–43.

1659 Sayers, Richard S. 'The springs of technical progress in Britain, 1919–39', *EJ*, LX (June 1950), 275–91. 'Classic' article.

1660 Sleeman, John F. 'The British tramway industry: the growth and decline of a public utility', *Manchester School of Economic and Social Studies*, X (1939), 157–74.

1661 Stolper, Wolfgang Frederick. 'British monetary policy and the housing boom', *Quarterly Journal of Economics*, LVI (Nov. 1941), pt. 2.

1662 Surrey, M. J. C. 'The National Plan in retrospect', *Bulletin of the Oxford Institute of Economics and Statistics*, XXXIV (Aug. 1972), 249–68. See also (1614).

1663 Tawney, Richard H. 'The abolition of economic controls, 1918–1921', *EcHR*, XIII (1943), 1–30.

1664 Thomas, Mark. 'Rearmament and economic recovery in the late 1930s', *EcHR*, XXXVI (Nov. 1983), 552–79.

1665 Turner, Herbert A. 'The Donovan Report', *EJ*, LXXIX (Mar. 1969), 1–10. See (1401).

1666 Usher, Abbot Payson, 'Sir John Howard Clapham and the empirical reaction in economic history', *JEcH*, XI (no. 2, 1951), 148–53. A critique of Clapham's *The study of economic history.* Cambridge, 1929.

1667 Wadsworth, J. E. (ed.). *The banks and the monetary system in the U.K., 1959–1970.* 1973. Reprint of articles in *Midland Bank Review.*

1668 Watt, D. C. 'Britain and North Sea oil: policies past and present', *Political Quarterly*, XLVII (1976), 377–97.

1669 Williams, David. 'London and the 1931 financial crisis', *EcHR*, 2nd ser., XV (no. 3, 1963), 513–28.

1670 Zebel, Sydney H. 'Joseph Chamberlain and the genesis of tariff reform', *JBS*, VII (Nov. 1967), 131–57. Informative.

IX. LABOUR HISTORY

For general guidance in this section, the reader should consult the Preface.

1. Printed sources

1641 Arnot, R. Page. *The General Strike, May 1926: its origin and history.* Reprint, 1967. Originally published by the Labour Research Department, 1926. Useful documentary account, with comment.

1672 Askwith, George Ranken, 1st Baron. *Industrial problems and disputes.* 1920. By a noted industrial conciliator, 1911–19.

1673 Beales, H. Lancelot and R. S. Lambert (eds.). *Memoirs of the unemployed.* 1934.

1674 Brown, William J. *So far....* 1943. Autobiography of a journalist, trade union advisor, and Labour M.P.

1675 Citrine, Walter McLennan, Baron. *An autobiography.* 1964–7, 2 vols. By the general-secretary of the T.U.C., 1926–46.

1676 Coates, Ken and Anthony Tophan. *Industrial democracy in Great Britain.* 1968. A book of readings.

1677 Gallacher, William. *Revolt on the Clyde: an autobiography.* 1936. Communist politics. See also *The last memoirs of Willie Gallacher.* 1966.

1678 *The General Strike: the British Gazette and the British Worker.* Reprints of issues for 5–13 May 1926 of the Government paper and the Trade Union Congress paper.

1679 Glasgow, George. *General strikes and road transport.* 1926.

1680 Gleason, Arthur. *What the workers want: a study of British labour.* New York, 1920.

1681 Greenwood, Walter. *Love on the dole.* New ed., 1955.

1682 Hannington, Wal. *Unemployed struggles, 1919–1936: my life and struggles amongst the unemployed.* 1936. See also his *Ten lean years: an examination of the record of the National Government in the field of unemployment.* 1940.

1683 Harrison, Norman. *Once a miner.* 1954. Personal experience in the 1940s.

1684 Kirkwood, David. *My life of revolt.* 1935. Clydeside.

1685 Labour Party. *The war aims of the British people.* [1918]. Adopted by the Joint Conference of the Labour Party and the Parliamentary Committee of the Trades Union Congress, 28 Dec. 1917.

1686 Labour Representation Committee. *Conference on labour representation held... on Tuesday, the 27th February, 1900....* [London, 1900].

1687 Leeson, Robert A. *Strike: a live history, 1887–1971.* 1973. 'Recollections of some 80 people in some 180 strikes.'

1688 [Mann, Tom]. *Tom Mann's Memoirs.* 1923. Reprinted, 1967.

1689 *Men without work: a report made to the Pilgrim Trust.* Cambridge, 1938. A social analysis of the unemployed in the thirties.

1690 Pugh, Sir Arthur. *Men of steel: by one of them. A chronicle of eighty-eight years of trade unionism in the British iron and steel industry.* 1951.

1691 *Report of the Annual Trades Union Congress.* 1901–. Manchester, 1901–.

1692 Robertson, Norman and Kenneth I. Sams. *British trade unionism: select documents.* Oxford, 1972, 2 vols. Useful.

1693 Smillie, Robert. *My life for labour.* 1924.

1694 [Stewart, Robert]. *Breaking the fetters: the memoirs of Bob Stewart.* 1967. A story, carried to about 1930, by an activist in Scottish trade unionism and communism.

1695 Thomas, J. H. *My story.* 1937. Useful for General Strike of 1926.

1696 Thorne, Will. *My life's battles.* [1925]. By a trade union official.

2. Surveys

1697 Birch, Lionel (ed.). *The history of the T.U.C., 1868–1968.* 1968. Remarkable photography with brief, interesting comment.

1698 Bowley, A. L. *Wages and income in the United Kingdom since 1860*. Cambridge, 1937. Incorporates earlier studies.
1699 Charles, Rodger. *Development of industrial relations in Britain, 1911–1939*. 1973.
1700 Clegg, Hugh Armstrong. *A history of British trade unions since 1889*. 2 vols. – 1964, 1985. Vol. II is on 1911–33.
1701 Cronin, James E. *Industrial conflict in modern Britain*. 1979.
1702 —— *Labour and society in Britain, 1918–1979*. New York, 1984.
1703 Hawkins, Kevin. *British industrial relations, 1945–75*. 1976.
1704 Hinton, James. *Labour & socialism: a history of the British labour movement, 1867–1974*. Amherst, Mass., 1983.
1705 Hutt, Allen. *Post-war history of the British working-class*. 1938.
1706 —— *British trade unionism: a short history*. 1975.
1707 Lovell, John Christopher and B. C. Roberts. *A short history of the T.U.C.* 1968. Brief, reliable.
1708 Martin, Ross M. *TUC: the growth of a pressure group, eighteen eighty- six to nineteen seventy-six*. New York, 1980.
1709 Mason, Arthur. *The General Strike in the northeast*. Hull, 1970.
1710 Meacham, Standish. *A life apart: the English working class – 1890–1914*. Cambridge, Mass., 1977.
1711 Mitchell, Arthur. *Labour in Irish politics, 1890–1930*. 1974.
1712 Muller, William D. *The 'Kept Men'?: the first century of trade union representation in the British House of Commons, 1874–1975*. 1977.
1713 Orton, William Aylott. *Labour in transition: a survey of British industrial history since 1914*. 1921.
1714 Roberts, B. C. *The Trades Union Congress, 1868–1921*. 1958.
1715 Soldon, Norbert G. *Women in British trade unions, 1874–1976*. 1978.
1716 Wrigley, C. J. (ed.). *A history of British industrial relations*. 1982.

3. Monographs

1717 Allen, Victor L. *Trade union leadership, based on a study of Arthur Deakin*. 1957. On period after 1940, in detail. See also Allen's *Trade unions and the government*. 1960.
1718 Amulree, William Warrender Mackenzie, 1st Baron. *Industrial arbitration in Great Britain*. 1929. Excellent account, representative of its time.
1719 Anderson, Adelaide Mary. *Women in the factory*. New York, 1922. Story of the Woman Inspectorate of Factories and Workshops, 1893–1921.
1720 Arnot, R. Page. *The miners: a history of the Miners' Federation of Great Britain*. 1949–61, 3 vols.
1721 —— *A history of the Scottish miners from the earliest times*. 1955.
1722 Bagwell, Philip S. *The Railwaymen: the history of the National Union of Railwaymen*. 1963. Biased.
1723 Bain, George Sayers. *The growth of white collar unionism*. Oxford, 1970.
1724 Barnes, Denis and Eileen Reed. *Government and trade unions: the British experience, 1964–1979*. 1982.
1725 Briggs, Asa and John Saville (eds.). *Essays in labour history, 1886–1923*. 1971. *Essays in labour history, 1918–1939*. 1977. These twenty essays, written by specialists, are indispensable.
1726 Brown, Kenneth. *Labour and unemployment, 1900–1914*. Totowa, N.J., 1971.
1727 —— (ed.). *Essays in anti-labour history: responses to the rise of labour in Britain*. 1974.
1728 Bundock, Clement J. *The National Union of Journalists: a jubilee history*. Oxford, 1957.
1729 —— *The story of the National Union of Printing, Bookbinding and Paper Workers*. Oxford, 1959.
1730 Burns, Emile. *The General Strike, May 1926: trades councils in action*. Labour Research Department, 1926.
1731 Burridge, T. D. *British labour and Hitler's war*. 1976.
1732 Calhoun, Daniel Fairchild. *The united front: the TUC and the Russians, 1923–1928*. New York, 1976.

1733 Chapman, S. D. (ed.). *The history of working-class housing: a symposium.* Newton Abbot, 1971. Case studies from several urban industrial areas.

1734 Clarke, R. O., et al. *Workers' participation in management in Britain.* 1973. A study carried out at London School of Economics.

1735 Clegg, Hugh A. *General Union in a changing society – a short history of National Union of General and Municipal Workers, 1889–1964.* Oxford, 1964.

1736 —— *The system of industrial relations in Great Britain.* 2nd ed., 1972.

1737 Clinton, Alan. *The trade union rank and file: Trades Councils in Britain, 1900–40.* Manchester, 1977.

1738 Crook, W. H. *The general strike: a study of Labor's tragic weapon in theory and practice.* Chapel Hill, N.C., 1931.

1739 Dorfman, Gerald Allen. *Wage politics in Britain, 1945–67: Government vs. the TUC.* Ames, Iowa, 1973.

1740 —— *Government versus Trade Unionism in British politics since 1968.* Stanford, Calif., 1979.

1741 —— *British trade unionism against the Trades Union Congress.* Stanford, Calif., 1983. Emphasizes the 'weakness and therefore the ineffectiveness of the TUC'.

1742 Durcan, J. W., et al. *Strikes in post-war Britain: a study of stoppages of work due to industrial disputes, 1946–73.* 1983.

1743 Edwards, Ness. *History of the South Wales Miners' Federation.* 1938. Largely from personal knowledge.

1744 Farman, Christopher. *The General Strike, May 1926.* 1972. Well balanced and well documented.

1745 Flanagan, Desmond. *1869–1969: a centenary story of the Cooperative Union of Great Britain and Ireland.* Manchester, 1969.

1746 Fyrth, H. J. and Henry Collins. *The foundry workers: a trade union history.* Manchester, 1959.

1747 Gilson, Mary Barnett. *Unemployment insurance in Great Britain.* 1931. Concerning the post–World War I period to 1930.

1748 Goldstein, Joseph. *The government of a British trade union.* Glencoe, Ill., [1952]. A study of the Transport and General Workers Union.

1749 Grant, Wynford and David Marsh. *The Confederation of British Industry.* 1977.

1750 Graubard, Stephen Richards. *British labour and the Russian Revolution, 1917–1924.* 1956.

1751 Gregory, Roy. *The miners and British politics, 1906–1914.* Oxford, 1968.

1752 Griffin, Alan R. *The miners of Nottinghamshire, 1914–1944: a history of the Nottinghamshire Miners' Union.* 1962.

1753 Gupta, Partha Sarathi. *Imperialism and the British labour movement, 1914–64.* New York, 1975.

1754 Harrison, Martin. *Trade unions and the Labour Party since 1945.* 1960. A careful treatment of a difficult problem.

1755 Hawkins, Kevin H. *British industrial relations, 1945–75.* 1976.

1756 Hill, Arthur C. C., Jr. and Isador Lubin. *The British attack on unemployment.* 1934. A Brookings Institute book; the atmosphere of the thirties.

1757 Hinton, James. *The first shop stewards' movement.* 1974. During World War I. See also (1780).

1758 —— *Labour and socialism.* Brighton, 1983.

1759 Hobsbawn, Eric J. *Workers: world of labor.* New York, 1984. Essays. An earlier collection was published in 1964.

1760 Howell, David. *British workers and the Independent Labour Party, 1888–1906.* 1983.

1761 Hutt, Allen. *The condition of the working class in Britain.* 1933. A Marxist view of the 'ills of society in Britain'.

1762 Hyman, Richard. *The Workers' Union.* Oxford, 1971. On period 1898–1929.

1763 Jacobs, Julius (ed.). *London Trades Council, 1860–1950.* 1950.

1764 Jefferys, James Bovington. *Trade unions in a Labour Britain.* 1947.

1765 Kellogg, Paul U. and Arthur Gleason. *British labor and the war: reconstructors for a new world.* New York, 1919.

1766 Knowles, Kenneth Guy Jack Charles. *Strikes: a study in industrial conflict with special reference to British experience between 1911 and 1947.* Oxford, 1952.

LABOUR HISTORY

1767 Lovell, John Christopher. *British trade unions, 1875–1933.* 1977.
1768 McCarthy, William E. J. *The closed shop in Britain.* Berkeley, Calif., 1964.
1769 MacDonald, Duncan F. *The state and the trade unions.* 2nd ed., 1976.
1770 Martin, David E. and David E. Rubenstein. *Ideology & the Labour movement: Essays presented to John Saville.* 1979.
1771 Martin, Roderick. *Communism and the British trade unions, 1924–1933: a study of the National Minority Movement.* Oxford, 1969.
1772 Milne-Bailey, Walter A. *Trade unions and the state.* 1934.
1773 Murray, John. *The General Strike of 1926: a history.* 1951.
1774 Nordlinger, Eric. *The working class Tories.* Berkeley, Calif., 1967.
1775 Panitch, Leo. *Social democracy and industrial militancy: the Labour Party, the trade unions and incomes policy, 1945–1947.* Cambridge, 1976.
1776 Phelps Brown, Ernest H. *The growth of British industrial relations: a study from the standpoint of 1906–1914.* 1959. Significant interpretation.
1777 Phillips, Gordon Ashton. *The General Strike: the politics of industrial conflict.* New York, 1976.
1778 Pimlott, Ben. *Labour and the left in the 1930s.* 1977.
1779 —— and C. Cook (eds.). *Trade unions in British politics.* 1982. Essays.
1780 Pribicevic, Branko. *The shop stewards' movement and workers control, 1910–1922.* Oxford, 1959. See also (1757).
1781 Price, Richard. *An imperial war and the British working class: working class attitudes and reactions to the Boer War, 1899–1902.* 1972.
1782 —— *Masters, unions and men.* Cambridge, 1980.
1783 Prochaska, Alice. *History of the General Federation of Trade Unions, 1899–1980.* 1982.
1784 Renshaw, Patrick. *The General Strike.* 1975. Published as *Nine days that shook Britain: the 1926 General Strike.* 1976.
1785 Richter, Irving. *Political purpose in trade unions.* 1973.
1786 Roberts, Benjamin C. *National wages policy in war and peace.* 1958. Includes examination of the economy, 1939–51.
1787 —— *Trade union government and administration in Great Britain.* 1956.
1788 Rogow, Arnold A. *The Labour Government and British industry, 1945–1951.* Oxford, 1955.
1789 Routh, Guy C. *Occupation and pay in Great Britain, 1906–1960.* 1965.
1790 Sharp, Ian G. *Industrial conciliation and arbitration in Great Britain.* 1950.
1791 Simpson, Bill. *Labour, the unions and the party: a study of the trade unions and the British labour movement.* 1973.
1792 Spoor, Alec. *White-collar union: sixty years of NALGO.* 1967. A study of the National Association of Local Government Officers, founded in 1905.
1793 Symons, Julian. *The General Strike: a historical portrait.* 1957. Careful study with accounts by participants.
1794 Tillyard, Frank and F. N. Ball. *Unemployment insurance in Great Britain, 1911–1948.* 1949.
1795 Turner, Herbert A. *Trade union growth, structure and policy: a comparative study of the cotton unions.* 1962. Sociological approach.
1796 ——, Garfield Clack, and Geoffrey Roberts. *Labour relations in the motor industry: a study of industrial unrest and an international comparison.* 1907.
1797 Van der Slice, Austin. *International labor, diplomacy and peace, 1914–1919.* Philadelphia, Pa., 1941.
1798 Weiner, Herbert E. *British labor and public ownership.* Washington, D.C., 1960. Treated historically throughout the twentieth century.
1799 Wigham, Eric. *Strikes and the government, 1893–1974.* 1976.
1800 Williams, Francis. *Magnificent journey: the rise of the trade unions.* 1954. Popular; very readable.
1801 Winter, Jay (ed.). *The working class in modern English history: essays in honour of Henry Pelling.* Cambridge, 1983.
1802 Wrigley, Chris. *David Lloyd George and the British Labour movement: peace and war.* New York, 1976.
1803 Young, Agnes F. *Social services in British industry.* 1968.

4. Biographies

1804 Brockway, Fenner. *Socialism over sixty years: the life of Jewett of Bradford (1864–1944)*. 1946.
1805 Goodman, Geoffrey. *The awkward warrior, Frank Cousins: His life and times*. 1979.
1806 Kent, William. *John Burns: Labour's lost leader*. 1950.
1807 Larkin, Emmet. *James Larkin: Irish labour leader, 1876–1947*. Cambridge, Mass., 1965.
1808 Lawson, Jack. *The man in the cap: the life of Herbert Smith*. 1941. Smith was president of the Miners' Federation, 1921–9.
1809 Morgan, Kenneth O. *Keir Hardie: radical and socialist*. 1975. Better than Emrys Hughes, *Keir Hardie*. 1956.
1810 Schneer, Jonathan. *Ben Tillett: portrait of a labour leader*. 1982.
1811 Silver, Erie. *Victor Feather: TUC*. 1973.

5. Articles

1812 Alderman, Geoffrey. 'The railway companies and the growth of trade unionism in the late nineteenth and early twentieth centuries', *Hist. J.*, XIV (no. 1, 1971), 129–52.
1813 Allen, Victor L. 'The reorganization of the Trades Union Congress, 1918–1927', *BJS*, XI (Mar. 1960), 24–43.
1814 Anderson, Alan. 'The labour laws and the Cabinet Legislative Committee of 1926–27', *Bulletin, Society for the Study of Labour History*, XXIII (Autumn 1971), 37–54.
1815 Bain, George Sayers and Robert Price. 'Union growth and employment trends in the United Kingdom, 1964–1970', *British Journal of Industrial Relations*, X (Nov. 1972), 366–81.
1816 Barker, Bernard. 'Anatomy of Reformism: the social and political ideas of the Labour leadership in Yorkshire', *IRSH*, XVIII (pt. 1, 1973), 1–27.
1817 Baxter, R. 'The working class and labour politics', *PS*, XX (no. 1, 1972), 97–107.
1818 Chaloner, W. H. 'The British miners and the coal industry between the wars', *History Today*, XIV (June 1964), 418–26.
1819 Clegg, H. A. 'Some consequences of the General Strike', *Transactions of the Manchester Statistical Society, 1954–4*, pp. 1–29.
1820 Clinton, Alan. 'Trade councils during the First World War', *IRSH*, XV (pt. 2, 1970), 202–34.
1821 Craig, J., et al. 'Humberside: employment, unemployment and migration: the evolution of industrial structure, 1951–66', *YBESR*, XXII (Nov. 1970), 123–42.
1822 Epstein, Leon D. 'British class consciousness and the Labour Party', *JBS*, II (May 1962), 136–60.
1823 Galambos, P. and E. W. Evans. 'Work stoppages in the United Kingdom, 1951–64; a quantitative study', *Bulletin, Oxford University Institute of Economics and Statistics*, XXVIII (no. 1, 1966), 33–62. Continued in their 'Work stoppages in the United Kingdom, 1965–70; a quantitative study', *Bulletin of Economic Research*, XXV (May 1973), 22–42.
1824 Glynn, Sean and Alan Booth. 'Unemployment in interwar Britain: a case for relearning the lessons of the 1930s?', *EcHR*, XXXVI (no. 3, 1983), 329–48.
1825 Hart, Peter E. and Ernest H. Phelps Brown. 'The sizes of trade unions: a study in the laws of aggregation', *EJ*, LXVII (Mar. 1957), 1–15.
1826 Hines, A. G. 'Wage inflation in the United Kingdom, 1948–62: a disaggregated study', *EJ*, LXXIX (Mar. 1969), 66–89.
1827 Lowe, Rodney. 'The failure of consensus in Britain: the National Industrial Conference, 1919–1921', *Hist. J.*, XXI (no. 3, 1976), 649–75.
1828 —— 'Hours of labour: negotiating industrial legislation in Britain, 1919–39', *EcHR*, XXXV (May 1982), 254–71.

1829 Macintyre, Stuart. 'British labour, Marxism and working class apathy in the nineteen twenties', *Hist. J.*, XX (no. 2, 1977), 479–96.
1830 McKibbin, Ross. 'Economic policy of the second Labour Government, 1929–1931', *PP*, LXVIII (Aug. 1975), 95–123.
1831 Marwick, Arthur. 'James Maxton: his place in Scottish labour history', *SHR*, XLIII (Apr. 1964), 25–43.
1832 Mason, A. 'The Government and the General Strike, 1920', *IRSH*, XIV (1969), 1–21. Uses Cabinet papers.
1833 Matthews, Robert C. O. 'Why has Britain had full employment since the war?', *EJ*, LXXVIII (Sept. 1968), 555–69.
1834 Middlemas, Keith. 'Unemployment: the past and future of a political problem', *Political Quarterly*, LI (Oct.–Dec. 1980), 464–80.
1835 Mogridge, Basil. 'Militancy and inter-union rivalries in British shipping, 1911–1929', *IRSH*, VI (1961), 375–412.
1836 Parker, R. A. C. 'British rearmament, 1936–9: Treasury, trade unions and skilled labour', *EHR*, XCVI (Apr. 1981), 306–43.
1837 Pencavel, John H. 'An investigation into industrial strike activity in Britain', *Economica*, new ser., XXXVII (Apr. 1970), 239–56. A study of the period 1950–67.
1838 Phillips, G. A. 'The triple industrial alliance in 1914', *EcHR*, 2nd ser., XXIIII (no. 1, 1970), 55–67. Discounts possibility of a general strike in 1914.
1839 Reid, Alastair and Steven Tolliday. 'The General Strike, 1926', *Hist. J.*, XX (no. 4, 1977), 1001–12. Reviews five books.
1840 Renshaw, Patrick. 'Black Friday, 1921', *History Today*, XXI (June 1971), 416–25.
1841 Scargill, Arthur. 'The new unionism', *New Left Review*, XCII (Aug.–Sept. 1975), 3–33.
1842 Silver, Michael. 'Recent British strike trends: a factual analysis', *British Journal of Industrial Relations*, XI (Mar. 1973), 66–104. A study of the period 1959–71.
1843 Sires, Ronald V. 'Labor unrest in England, 1910–1914', *JEcH*, XV (no. 3, 1955), 246–66.
1844 Slaughter, C. 'The strike of Yorkshire mineworkers in May, 1955', *Sociological Review*, new ser. VI (Dec. 1958), 241–59.
1845 Smith, J. H. and T. E. Chester. 'The distribution of power in nationalized industries', *BJS*, II (Sept. 1951), 275–93.
1846 Stubbs, J. O. 'Lord Milner and patriotic labour, 1914–1918', *EHR*, LXXXVII (Oct. 1972), 717–54. A study of Milner and the British Workers League.
1847 Thomas, Brinley. 'The movement of labour into south-east England, 1920–32', *Economica*, new ser., I (May 1934), 220–41.
1848 —— 'The influx of labour into the midlands, 1920–37', *Economica*, new ser., V (Nov. 1938), 410–34.
1849 Williams, J. E. 'The political activities of a trade union, 1906–1914', *IRSH*, II (pt. 1, 1957), 1–21. In Derbyshire.
1850 Zeitlin, Jonathan. 'The emergence of shop steward organization and job control in the British car industry', *History Workshop*, No. 10 (autumn 1980), 119–38. Detailed bibliography with comments.

X. URBAN HISTORY

1. Printed sources

1851 Abercrombie, Patrick. *Greater London plan, 1944*. 1945. A master plan for 'renewal and dispersal'; complements the County of London plan. See (1853).
1852 Booth, Charles. *Life and labour of the people in London*. 1902–3, 17 vols. A study of poverty, industry, religious, and social influences. See (1854) for a later survey.
1853 Forshaw, John H. and Patrick Abercrombie. *County of London plan prepared for the London County Council*. 1944. Like (1851), a celebrated wartime report.

1854 *New survey of London life and labour*. 1930–5, 9 vols. Prepared by the London School of Economics and Political Science; various authors.

1855 Roberts, Robert. *The classic slum: Salford life in the first quarter of the century*. Manchester, 1971. A combination of 'personal reminiscence' and 'research'.

1856 Rowntree, B. Seebohm. *Poverty: a study in town life*. 1901. A classic study of York, based upon a house-to-house canvas. See also his *Poverty and progress*. 1941. This was based on a survey of York made in 1936. See also (1189) and (1857).

1857 —— and George R. Lavers. *Poverty and the welfare state: a third social survey of York dealing only with economic questions*. 1951. For a more recent assessment see Charles Edward Russell. *Social problems of the north*. 1980.

2. Surveys

1858 Abercrombie, Patrick. *Town and country planning*. 3rd ed., rev. by D. Rigby Childs. 1959. A very useful survey.

1859 Finer, Herman. *English local government*. 4th ed., 1950. Standard.

1860 Griffith, Ernest S. *The modern development of city government in the United Kingdom and the United States*. 1927, 2 vols.

1861 Parker, Theodore Cardwell and Michael Robbins. *A history of London transport, passenger travel and the development of the metropolis*. 2 vols. – 1963, 1974. Vol. II is on the twentieth century to 1970.

3. Monographs

1862 Aldridge, Meryl. *British new towns: a program without a policy*. 1979.

1863 Barker, Brian. *Labour in London: a study in municipal achievement*. 1946. London politics.

1864 Bealey, Frank, J. Blondell, and W. P. McCann. *Constituency politics: a study of Newcastle-under-Lyme*. 1965.

1865 Buchanan Report. *Traffic in towns: a study of the long term problems of traffic in urban areas. Reports of the steering group and working group appointed by the minister of transport*. 1963.

1866 Burns, Wilfred. *New towns for old: the technique of urban renewal*. 1963. Post-1945 developments.

1867 Coppock, J. T. and Hugh C. Prince (eds.). *Greater London*. 1964. Essays.

1868 Corbett, John. *History of the Birmingham Trades Council, 1866–1966*. 1966.

1869 Creese, Walter L. *The search for environment. The garden city: before and after*. 1966.

1870 Cullingworth, John B. *Town and country planning in England and Wales, an introduction*. 1964.

1871 Donnison, David V., et al. *Social policy and administration: studies in the development of social services at the local level*. 1965.

1872 Dyos, H. J. *Exploring the urban past: essays in urban history*. Ed. David Connadine and David Reeder. 1982.

1873 Evans, Hazel (ed.). *New towns: the British experience*. 1973.

1874 Farnie, D. A. *Manchester ship canal & the rise of the port of Manchester, 1894–1975*. Manchester, 1980.

1875 Foley, Donald L. *Controlling London's growth: planning the Great Wen, 1940–1960*. Berkeley, Calif., 1963. Continued by his *Governing the London region: reorganization and planning in the 1960s*. Berkeley, Calif., 1972.

1876 Freeman, T. W. *The conurbations of Great Britain*. 2nd ed., Manchester, 1966.

1877 —— *Geography and regional administration. England and Wales, 1830–1968*. 1968. Attention 'to local government units as areas'.

1878 Garside, William R. *The Durham miners, 1919–1960*. 1971. Thorough.

1879 Gill, Conrad and Asa Briggs. *History of Birmingham*. II, *Borough and City, 1865–1938*. 1952. III, Anthony Sutcliffe and Roger Smith. *Birmingham, 1939–1970*. 1974.

1880 Hall, Peter, et al. *The containment of urban England*. 1973, 2 vols. A judgment on town planning since 1940.

1881 Hawson, H. Keeble. *Sheffield: the growth of a city, 1893–1926*. Sheffield, 1968.

1882 Hyde, Francis E. *Liverpool and the Mersey: an economic history of a port, 1700–1970.* 1971.
1883 Jones, D. Caradog (ed.). *The social survey of Merseyside.* Liverpool, 1934. Based on a survey, 1929–32.
1884 Lloyd, David Wharton. *The making of English towns.* 1984.
1885 Lovell, John. *Stevedores and dockers: a study of trade unionism in the Port of London, 1870–1914.* 1969.
1886 MacInnes, Charles M. *Bristol at war.* London, 1962. On World War II.
1887 Maclure, Stuart. *One hundred years of London education, 1870–1970.* 1970.
1888 Martin, John E. *Greater London: an industrial geography.* 1966. Much attention to the past.
1889 Mellish, Michael. *The docks after Devlin: a study of the effects of the recommendations of the Devlin Committee on industrial relations in the London docks.* 1973. Studies pursued at the London School of Economics.
1890 Osborn, Frederic J. and Arnold Whittick. *The new towns: the answer to Megalopolis.* Rev. ed., 1969. Developments since 1939.
1891 Pimlott, John A. R. *Toynbee Hall: fifty years of social progress, 1884–1934.* 1935.
1892 Pollard, Sidney. *A history of labour in Sheffield.* Liverpool, 1959. A pioneer work.
1893 Rhodes, Gerald. *The government of London: the struggle for reform.* 1970. Contemporary problems in historical context.
1894 Richardson, Kenneth and Elizabeth Harris. *Twentieth-century Coventry.* 1972.
1895 Robson, William A. *Government and misgovernment of London.* 1939.
1896 Rodgers, Barbara N. and June Stevenson. *A new portrait of social work: a study of the social services in a northern town from Younghusband to Seebohm.* 1973. See also Barbara N. Rodgers and Julia Dixon. *Portrait of social work: a study of social services in a northern town.* Oxford, 1960.
1897 Sansom, William. *Westminster at war.* 1947. One of the best accounts of the *Blitz* in London.
1898 Simmons, Jack. *Leicester past and present.* II, *Modern city, 1860–1974.* 1974.
1899 Thompson, Francis M. L. *Hampstead: building a borough, 1650–1964.* 1974. An 'emphasis . . . on the process of the creation of the urban environment'.
1900 Waller, P. J. *Democracy and sectarianism: a political and social history of Liverpool, 1868–1939.* Liverpool, 1981.
1901 Whiting, R. C. *The view from Cowley: the impact of industrialization upon Oxford, 1918–1939.* 1983.
1902 Young, Ken and Patricia Garside. *Metropolitan London: politics and urban change, 1837–1981.* New York, 1982.

4. Biographies

1903 Stocks, Mary. *Ernest Simon of Manchester.* Manchester, 1963. Biography of an industrialist and public servant.

5. Articles

1904 Bealey, Frank and David J. Bartholomew. 'The local election in Newcastle-under-Lyme, May 1958', *BJS*, XIII (Sept., Dec., 1962), 273–85, 350–68. Based on a survey of opinion and voting intention five days before the election.
1905 Benjamin, Bernard. 'The urban background to public health changes in England and Wales, 1900–1950', *Population Studies*, XVII (1963–4), 225–48.
1906 Bowley, Marian E. A. 'Local authorities and housing subsidies since 1919', *Manchester School of Economic and Social Studies*, XII (1941), 57–79.
1907 Cherry, Gordon E. 'Influences on the development of town planning in Britain', *JCH*, IV (July 1969), 43–58.
1908 Clarke, Peter F. 'British politics and Blackburn politics, 1900–1910', *Hist. J.*, XII (no. 2, 1969), 302–27.
1909 Connor, L. R. 'Urban housing in England and Wales', *Journal of the Royal*

Statistical Society, XCIX (1936), 1–66. 'A discussion of housing reform from a statistical point of view'.

1910 Fraser, Derek. 'The urban history masqueraded: recent trends in the study of English urban development', *Hist. J.*, XXVII (Mar. 1984), 253–64. Comment on seven studies.

1911 Jenkins, Simon. 'Decline and fall of London town', *Encounter*, XXXV (Oct. 1970), 77–84. Changes during World War II and after.

1912 Murphy, Lawrence R. 'Rebuilding Britain: the government's role in housing and town planning, 1945–57', *Historian*, XXXII (May 1970), 410–27.

1913 Stedman, M. B. and P. A. Wood. 'Urban renewal in Birmingham: an interim report', *Geography*, L (1965), 1–17. Developments since 1945.

1914 Walker, Gilbert. 'The growth of population in Birmingham and the Black Country between the wars', *University of Birmingham Historical Journal*, I (1947–8), 158–79.

1915 Wise, M. J. 'The Birmingham Black Country in its regional setting', *Geography*, LVII (Apr. 1972), 89–104.

1916 Wright, H. Myles. 'The first ten years: post-war planning and development in England', *Town Planning Review*, XXVI (July 1955), 73–92.

XI. AGRICULTURAL HISTORY

1. Printed sources

1917 Bensusan, Semuel L. *Latter-day rural England 1927*. 1928. Based on a four-month visit to agricultural counties.

1918 Ernle, Rowland Edmund Prothero, Lord. *Whippingham to Westminster*, 1938. Reminiscences of a leading agriculturalist.

1919 Ministry of Agriculture, Fisheries and Food. *A century of agricultural statistics, Great Britain, 1866–1966*. 1968.

1920 Pratt, Edwin, A. *The transition in agriculture*. 1906. As it looked early in the century.

1921 Thompson, Flora. *Lark Rise to Candleford: a trilogy*. 1945. On rural society.

2. Surveys

1922 Ernle, Rowland Edmund Prothero, Lord. *English farming, past and present. With introductions by George E. Fussell and Oliver R. McGregor*. 6th ed., 1961.

1923 Green, Frederick E. *A history of the English agricultural labourer, 1870–1920*. 1920.

1924 Harvey, Nigel. *The farming kingdom*. 1955. On transformation in twentieth century.

1925 Russell, E. John. *A history of agricultural science in Great Britain, 1620–1954*. 1966. More than half is devoted to the twentieth century.

1926 Symon, J. A. *Scottish farming past and present*. Edinburgh, 1959.

1927 Trow-Smith, Robert. *English husbandry, from the earliest times to the present day*. 1951.

1928 Whetham, Edith Holt. *Agrarian History of England and Wales*. Vol. VIII (1914–39). 1978. See also her *British farming, 1939–49*. 1952.

3. Monographs

1929 *Agriculture in the twentieth century*. Oxford, 1939. Essays by various specialists to be presented to Sir Daniel Hall.

1930 Astor, Waldorf, 2nd Viscount and B. Seebohm Rowntree. *British agriculture: the principles of future policy*. 1939. Useful for the interwar years.

1931 Bateson, Frederick W. (ed.). *Towards a socialist agriculture: studies by a group of Fabians*. 1946.

1932 Groves, Reg. *Sharpen the sickle! The history of the Farm Workers' Union*. 1949.

1933 Hall, Alfred Daniel. *Agriculture after the war*. 1916. A plan for reorganization developed more fully in his *Reconstruction and the land*. 1941.

1934 Hurd, Archibald R. *A farmer in Whitehall: Britain's farming revolution, 1939–1950.* 1951.

1935 Jones, Eric L. *Seasons and prices: the role of the weather in English agricultural history.* 1964.

1936 Layton, Walter T. and Geoffrey Crowther. *An introduction to the study of prices.* 1935.

1937 Levy, Hermann. *Large and small holdings: a study of English agricultural economics.* 1911.

1938 Mejer, Eugeniusz. *Agricultural labour in England and Wales.* Sutton Bonington, 1949–51, 2 pts.

1939 Murray, Keith A. H. *Agriculture.* 1955. During World War II, with useful introduction for 1914–39.

1940 Ojala, Eric M. *Agriculture and economic progress.* 1952. Comparative study of the U.K., Sweden, and USA, based on a statistical inquiry.

1941 Orwin, Charles S. and William R. Peel. *The tenure of agricultural land.* 2nd ed., Cambridge, 1926.

1942 Perry, P. V. *British farming in the great depression, 1870–1914: an historical geography.* Newton Abbot, 1974. Excellent bibliography.

1943 Robertson Scott, J. W. *The story of the Women's Institute movement in England and Wales and Scotland.* Idbury, Kingham, Oxon., 1925.

1944 Savage, William G. *Rural housing.* 1915.

1945 Saville, John. *Rural depopulation in England and Wales, 1851–1951.* 1957.

1946 Self, Peter and Herbert J. Storing. *The state and the farmer.* 1962. On the post-1945 period.

1947 Sutherland, Douglas. *The landowners.* 1968.

1948 Williams, H. T. (ed.). *Principles for British agricultural policy.* 1960. Report of a committee of experts representing agricultural science, sociology, economics, and human nutrition; includes useful historical section.

4. Biographies

1949 Ashby, Mabel K. *Joseph Ashby of Tysoe, 1859–1919: a study of English village life.* Cambridge, 1961. In Warwickshire.

1950 Dale, Harold E. *Daniel Hall, pioneer in scientific agriculture.* 1956.

5. Articles

1951 Chew, Hilary C. 'Changes in land use and stock over England and Wales, 1939 to 1951', *GJ*, CXXII (Dec. 1956), 466–70.

1952 Coppock, John T. 'The changing arable in England and Wales in 1870–1956', *Tijdschrift voor Economische en sociale Geografie.* L (no. 6–7, 1959), 121–30.

1953 Ernle, Rowland Edmund Prothero, Lord. 'The food campaign of 1916–18', *Journal of the Royal Agricultural Society of England*, LXXXII (1922), 1–48.

1954 Hallett, Graham. 'The economic position of British agriculture', *EJ*, LXIX (Sept. 1959), 522–40. On the early fifties.

1955 Kirk, J. H. 'The output of British agriculture during the war', *Journal of the Proceedings of the Agricultural Economics Society*, VII (June 1946), 30–45.

1956 Orton, C. R. 'The development of stratified sampling methods for the agricultural census of England and Wales', *Journal of the Royal Statistical Society*, ser. A, CXXXV (1972), 307–35.

1957 Orwin, Charles S. 'Commodity prices and farming policy', *Journal of the Royal Agricultural Society of England*, LXXXIII (1922), 3–14. On fortunes of agriculture in early twentieth century.

1958 Perren, R. 'The North American beef and cattle trade with Great Britain, 1870–1914', *EcHR*, ser. 2, XXIV (no. 3, 1971), 430–44.

1959 Voelcker, J. Augustus. 'Woburn and its work, 1876–1921', *Journal of the Royal Agricultural Society of England*, LXXXIV (1923), 110–66.

1960 Whetham, Edith H. 'The mechanisation of British farming, 1910–1945', *Journal of Agricultural Economics*, XXXI (Sept. 1960), 317–31.

1961 —— et al. *A record of agricultural policy, 1947–1952, 1952–1954, 1954–1956,*

1956–1958, 1958–1960. Cambridge, 1952–. Occasional Papers, Cambridge University School of Agriculture.

XII. SCIENCE AND TECHNOLOGY

1. Printed sources

1962 Badash, Lawrence (ed.). *Rutherford and Boltwood: letters on radioactivity*. 1969. During the years 1904–24.

1963 Brabazon, John Theodore Cuthbert Moore, 1st Baron. *The Brabazon story*. 1966.

1964 Brock, William H. (ed.). *H. E. Armstrong and the teaching of science, 1880–1930*. Cambridge, 1973. Essays.

1965 Crowther, James Gerald. *The social relations of science*. New York, 1941.

1966 Eddington, Arthur S. *The mathematical theory of relativity*. 2nd ed., 1924.

1967 —— *The nature of the physical world*. 1928.

1968 Haldane, J. S. *The sciences and philosophy*. 1929. Gifford Lectures, Glasgow, 1927–8.

1969 Holliday, Leslie (ed.). *The integration of technologies*. 1966. A group of essays 'searching for the common ground between different technologies'.

1970 Hutton, Robert S. *Recollections of a technologist*. 1964. By an authority in metallurgy.

1971 Huxley, Julian. *Memories I; Memories II*. 1970, 1973. Autobiography of a celebrated biologist.

1972 Jeans, James Hopwood. *Astronomy and cosmogony*. 1928. 'Attempts to describe the present position of cosmogony and...associated problems of astronomy'.

1973 —— *The universe around us*. 1929. 'A brief account, written in simple language, of the methods and results of modern astronomical research'.

1974 Royal Society. *Notes and records of the Royal Society of London*. Vol. I, 1938–. Semiannual. Notes of society's activities and publications.

1975 Russell, Bertrand. *Our knowledge of the external world as a field for scientific method in philosophy*. 1914.

1976 —— *The ABC of atoms*. 1923.

1977 Whitehead, Alfred North. *Science and the modern world*. 1926.

1978 Zuckerman, Solly. *Scientists and war: the impact of science on military and civil affairs*. 1966.

1979 —— *From apes to warlords: autobiography*. 1978.

2. Surveys

1980 Cardwell, Donald S. L. *Organisation of science in England: a retrospect*. 2nd ed., Melbourne, 1957.

1981 Crombie, Alistair C. (ed.). *Scientific change: historical studies in the intellectual, social and technical conditions for scientific discovery and technical invention, from antiquity to the present*. 1963. A symposium on the history of science at Oxford, 9–15 July 1961.

1982 Crowther, James Gerald. *Discoveries and inventions of the 20th century*. 5th ed., 1966.

1983 Dampier[-Whetham], William Cecil. *A history of science and its relations with philosophy and religion*. 4th ed., Cambridge, 1948. Reprinted with a postscript by I. Bernard Cohen. Cambridge, 1966.

1984 Dingle, Herbert (ed.). *A century of science, 1851–1951*. 1951.

1985 Dunsheath, Percy (ed.). *A century of technology, 1851–1951*. New York, [1951].

1986 Fyrth, Hubert J. and Maurice Goldsmith. *Science, history and technology*. Book 2, pt. 2, *The age of uncertainty: the 1880s to the 1940s. Book 2, pt. 3, The age of choice: the 1940s to the 1960s*. 1969.

1987 Harre, H. Romano (ed.). *Scientific thought, 1900–1960: a selective survey*. 1969. Essays on twelve areas.

1988 Mason, Stephen F. *Main currents of scientific thought: a history of the sciences.* New York, 1953.
1989 Singer, Charles and E. Ashworth Underwood. *A short history of medicine.* 2nd ed., 1962. A good reference work.
1990 Williams, Trevor I. *A short history of twentieth century technology, c. 1910–c. 1950.* New York, 1982. An international study with Britain coming out well.

3. Monographs

1991 Ahrons, Ernest L. *The British steam railway locomotive, 1825–1925.* 1927. Continued in Oswald S. Nock. *The British steam railway locomotive, 1925–65.* 1966.
1992 Allibone, T. E. *Rutherford, the father of nuclear energy.* Manchester. 1973. The Rutherford lecture at Manchester U., 1972.
1993 Baker, W. J. *A history of the Marconi Company.* 1970.
1994 Birks, John B. (ed.). *Rutherford at Manchester.* 1962. Commemorative essays together with correspondence and scientific papers of the noted physicist.
1995 Burstall, Aubrey F. *A history of mechanical engineering.* 1963.
1996 Clair, Colin. *A history of printing in Britain.* 1965.
1997 Clark, Ronald W. *The birth of the bomb: the untold story of Britain's part in the weapon that changed the world.* 1961.
1998 Crowther, James Gerald. *The Cavendish Laboratory, 1875–1974.* 1974.
1999 —— and R. Whiddington. *Science at war.* 1947. Excellent for the lay reader.
2000 Dronamraju, K. R. (ed.). *Haldane and modern biology.* Baltimore, Md., 1968.
2001 Dunsheath, Percy A. *A history of electrical engineering.* 1962.
2002 Fletcher, Harold R. *The story of the Royal Horticultural Society, 1804–1968.* 1969.
2003 Freeman, T. W. *One hundred years of geography.* 1961. 'Written with a basis of British geography'.
2004 Gale, Walter K. V. *The British iron and steel industry: a technical history.* Newton Abbot, 1967.
2005 Gibbs-Smith, Charles H. *The aeroplane: an historical survey of its origins and development.* 1960. Excellent on Britain's role.
2006 Gowing, Margaret M. *Britain and atomic energy, 1939–1945.* 1965.
2007 —— *Independence and deterrence: Britain and atomic energy, 1945–52.* 1974, 2 vols.
2008 Hall, Alfred Rupert. *The Cambridge Philosophical Society: a history, 1819–1969.* Cambridge, 1969.
2009 Hardie, David W. F. and J. Davidson Pratt. *A history of the modern British chemical industry.* 1966. Of general interest.
2010 Hearnshaw, Leslie S. *A short history of British psychology, 1840–1940.* New York, 1964.
2011 Hilken, Thomas J. N. *Engineering at Cambridge University, 1783–1965.* 1967.
2012 Honigsbaum, Frank. *The division in British medicine: a history of the separation of general practice from hospital care, 1911–1968.* 1979.
2013 Hunt, Thomas (ed.). *The Medical Society of London, 1773–1973.* 1972.
2014 Kidner, R. W. *A short history of mechanical traction and travel.* 1946–7, 6 pts. Pts. 5 and 6 concern locomotives and carriages in twentieth century.
2015 Lock, Robert Heath. *Recent progress in the study of variation, heredity and evolution.* 4th ed., 1916.
2016 Nayler, Joseph L. and Ernest Ower. *Aviation: its technical development.* 1965.
2017 Newsholme, Arthur. *The story of modern preventive medicine.* 1929.
2018 Nock, Oswald S. *The locomotives of Sir Nigel Gresley.* 1945. Concerning 'the most notable English locomotive engineer' of his time. See also Nock's *The locomotives of R. E. L. Maunsell, 1911–1937.* Bristol, 1954.
2019 —— *Steam locomotives: the unfinished story of steam locomotives and steam locomotive men on the railways of Great Britain.* 1957.
2020 North, John D. *The measure of the universe: a history of modern cosmology.* 1965.
2021 Payne, George Louis. *Britain's scientific and technological manpower.* 1960. Important chapters on expansion of technological education and research after World War II.

2022 Penrose, Harald. *British aviation: the pioneer years, 1903–1914.* 1967. Continued by his *British aviation: the Great War and armistice, 1915–1919.* New York, 1969. Also, *British aviation: the adventuring years, 1920–1929.* 1973.
2023 *Perkin centenary: 100 years of synthetic dyestuffs.* 1958. Includes the 'life and work of Professor W. H. Perkin' (1838–1907) and developments thereafter.
2024 Rolt, Lionel T. C. *Tools for the job: a short history of machine tools.* 1965.
2025 Rose, Hilary and Steven. *Science and society.* 1969. Interrelations of science, technology, and society in the twentieth century.
2026 Rowe, A. P. *One story of radar.* Cambridge, 1948. Concerns the governmental department, The Telecommunications Research Establishment, from 1934 to 1945.
2027 Rutherford, Ernest, Baron. *The newer alchemy.* Cambridge, 1937. 'A brief account of modern work on the transmutation of the elements'.
2028 Searle, Geoffrey Russell. *Eugenics and politics in Britain, 1900–1914.* Leyden, 1976.
2029 Shorter, Alfred H. *Paper making in the British Isles: a historical and geographical study.* Newton Abbot, 1971. A standard work.
2030 Snow, Charles Percy, Baron. *Science and government.* Cambridge, 1961. Lectures on Henry Tizard, F. A. Lindemann, and World War II.
2031 Swazey, Judith P. *Reflexes and motor integration: Sherrington's concept of integrative action.* Cambridge, Mass., 1969. Sherrington (1859–1932) was a leader in neurophysiology.
2032 Vaughan, Paul. *Doctors' Commons: a short history of the British Medical Association.* 1959.
2033 Webb, Brian. *The British internal combustion locomotive, 1894–1940.* Newton Abbot, 1973.
2034 Whittaker, Edmund. *A history of the theories of æther and electricity.* II, *The modern theories, 1900–1926.* 1953.
2035 Wilson, William. *A hundred years of physics.* 1950.

4. Biographies

2036 Armytage, Walter H. G. *Sir Richard Gregory: his life and work.* 1957. Gregory was a scientific journalist, editor of *Nature*, 1919–39.
2037 Bickel, Lennard. *Rise up to life: a biography of Howard Walter Florey who gave penicillin to the world.* 1972.
2038 Birkenhead, Frederick W. F. Smith, 2nd Earl of. *The Prof. in two worlds: the official life of F. A. Lindemann, Viscount Cherwell.* 1961. Lindemann was a close adviser of Churchill.
2039 Clark, Ronald William. *Tizard.* 1965. Concerning Sir Henry Tizard and radar.
2040 —— *J. B. S.: the life and work of J. B. S. Haldane.* 1968.
2041 —— *Sir Edward Appleton.* 1971. Biography of a noted physicist.
2042 Crowther, James Gerald. *British scientists of the twentieth century.* 1952. Essays on J. J. Thomson, Ernest Rutherford, J. H. Jeans, A. S. Eddington, F. G. Hopkins, and William Bateson.
2043 —— *Statesmen of science.* 1965. Includes R. B. Haldane, H. T. Tizard, and F. A. Lindemann. 1965.
2044 Eve, A. S. *Rutherford: being the life and letters of the Rt. Hon. Lord Rutherford, O.M.* Cambridge, 1939.
2045 Granit, Ragnar. *Charles Scott Sherrington: an appraisal.* 1966.
2046 Grosskirth, Phyllis. *Havelock Ellis: a biography.* New York, 1980.
2047 Gunther, Albert E. *Robert T. Gunther: a pioneer in the history of science, 1869–1940.* 1967.
2048 Harrod, Roy F. *The Prof.: a personal memoir of Lord Cherwell.* 1959.
2049 Heilbron, John L. *H. G. J. Moseley: the life and letters of an English physicist, 1887–1915.* 1973.
2050 Kilmister, Clive W. *Men of physics: Sir Arthur Eddington.* Oxford, 1966. Includes extracts from Eddington's writing.
2051 Lockyer, T. Mary and Winifred L. *Life and work of Sir Norman Lockyer.* 1928.
2052 Pogson, Beryl. *Maurice Nicoll: a portrait.* 1961. Of a well-known psychiatrist.

2053 Thomson, George P. *J. J. Thomson and the Cavendish Laboratory in his day*. 1964. Published in the United States as *J. J. Thomson, discoverer of the electron*. New York, 1966. For Thomson's association with the Cavendish Laboratory, see James Gerald Crowther. *The Cavendish laboratory, 1874–1974*. 1974.

5. Articles

2054 Clark, D. H. 'Administrative psychiatry, 1942–1962', *British Journal of Psychiatry*, CIX (Mar. 1963), 178–201.
2055 Crone, G. R. 'British geography in the twentieth century', *GJ*, CXXX (June 1964), 197–220.
2056 De Beer, Gavin. 'Mendel, Darwin, and Fisher (1865–1965)', *Notes and Records of the Royal Society of London*, XIX, (Dec. 1964), 192–226.
2057 Filner, Robert E. 'The Social Relations of Science Movement (SRS) and J. B. S. Haldane'. *Science and Society*, XLI (fall 1977), 303–16.
2058 Fleure, H. J. 'Sixty years of geography and education: a retrospect of the Geographical Association'. *Geography*, XXXVIII (Nov. 1953), 231–65. On the period 1890–1950.
2059 Goldberg, Alfred. 'The atomic origins of the British nuclear deterrent'. *International Affairs*, XL (July 1964), 409–29.
2060 Goldberg, Stanley. 'In defense of ether: the British response to Einstein's special theory of relativity, 1905–1911'. In Russell McCormmach (ed.). *Historical studies in the physical sciences*, II, Philadelphia, Pa., 1970.
2061 Lamb, H. H. 'Britain's changing climate'. *GJ*, CXXXIII (Dec. 1967), 445–68.
2062 McCormmach, Russell. 'J. J. Thomson and the structure of light', *British Journal of the History of Science*, III (1966–7), 362–87.
2063 McKie, Douglas. 'Science and technology'. In G. N. Clark et al. (eds.). *New Cambridge Modern History*, XII (2nd ed., 1968), pp. 87–111.
2064 *The Newcomen Society for the Study of the History of Engineering and Technology: transactions*. 1920–1)–. Some 40 vols. have been published, covering the story to 1968. Valuable for information on 'the lives and works of men who have laid the foundations of our present industries'.
2065 Venables, P. F. R. 'The emergence of colleges of advanced technology in Britain', *The year book of education, 1959*. New York, 1959, pp. 224–36. On developments after 1944.
2066 Waters, D. W. 'Seamen, scientists, historians and strategy', *British Journal for the History of Science*, XIII (pt. 3, no. 45), 189–210.

XIII. MILITARY AND NAVAL HISTORY

For guidance to the literature of this topic the advanced student is at once referred to (17–18, 26, 28). Indispensable for the two World Wars are the 'Official Histories', published by H.M.S.O.; the major categories with key items are listed in (2144–5).

1. Printed sources

2067 Bell, Julian (ed.). *We did not fight: 1914–1918 experiences of war resisters*. 1935.
2068 Blake, Robert (ed.). *The private papers of Douglas Haig, 1914–1919*. 1952. A selection. See also (2178).
2069 Carrington, Charles E. *Soldier from the war returning*. 1964. Sensitive account of life at the front during World War I.
2070 Churchill, Winston Spencer. *The Second World War*. Boston, Mass., 1948–53, 6 vols.
2071 Flower, Desmond and James Reeves (eds.). *The war, 1939–1945*. 1960. Documentary.
2072 Fremantle, Sydney R. *My naval career, 1880–1928*. 1949. One of the more useful naval memoirs.
2073 Glubb, John. *Into battle: a soldier's diary of the great war*. 1978.

2074 Graham, John W. *Conscription and conscience*. with a preface by Clifford Allen. 1971. Originally published in 1922.

2075 Graves, Robert. *Goodbye to all that*. New York, 1930. One of the finest autobiographical books on World War I. Another, on 1916–17, is Siegfried Sassoon. *Memoirs of an infantry officer*. New York, 1930.

2076 Ismay, Hastings Lionel, 1st Baron. *The memoirs of General the lord Ismay*. 1960. Ismay was deputy secretary (military) to the War Cabinet, 1940–5, and chief of staff to the minister of defence (Churchill), 1940–5.

2077 Jellicoe, John Rushworth, 1st Earl. *The Grand Fleet, 1914–1916*. New York, 1919. See also Alfred Temple Patterson (ed.). *The Jellicoe papers: selections from the private and official correspondence of Admiral of the Fleet Earl Jellicoe of Scapa*. 1966–8, 2 vols. Patterson's biography, *Jellicoe* (1969) is standard.

2078 Liddell Hart, Basil Henry. *The memoirs of Captain Liddell Hart*. 1965–6, 2 vols. Especially useful for years between the wars.

2079 *The Keyes Papers: selections from the private and official correspondence of Admiral of the Fleet Baron Keyes of Zeebrugge*. Ed. Paul G. Halpern. 1979–80, 2 vols.

2080 Macmillan, Harold. *War diaries: politics and war in the Mediterranean, January 1943–May 1945*. 1984.

2081 Marder, Arthur J. (ed.). *Fear God and dreadnought: the correspondence of Admiral of the Fleet Lord Fisher of Kilverstone*. 1952–9, 3 vols.

2082 Montague, Charles. *Disenchantment*. New York, 1922. A classic account of conditions at the front in World War I.

2083 Montgomery, Bernard Law, 1st Viscount. *The memoirs of Field-Marshal the Viscount Montgomery of Alamein, K.G.* Cleveland, Ohio, 1958.

2084 Pownall, Henry. *Chief of staff: the diaries of Lieutenant-General Sir Henry Pownall*. I, *1933–1940*. Ed. Brian Bond. 1973.

2085 Robertson, William Robert. *Soldiers and statesmen, 1914–1918*. 1926. See also his *From private to field-marshal*. 1921. The first volume is vital for an analysis of strategy. See also Victor Bonham-Carter. *Soldier true: the life and times of Field-Marshal Sir William Robertson . . . 1860–1933*. 1963.

2086 Slim, William. *Defeat into victory*. 1965. Probably the best account of the Burma campaign, written by the general in command. On treatment of Wingate, cf. Christopher Sykes. *Orde Wingate*. 1959.

2087 Tedder, Arthur, Lord. *With prejudice*. This account by the air chief marshal rings true, as does Arthur Harris. *Bomber offensive*. New York, 1947.

2088 Wemyss, Victoria. *The life and letters of Lord Wemyss, Admiral of the Fleet*. 1935. Important selections from diaries and correspondence.

2089 Wilson, Henry Maitland, Baron. *Eight years overseas, 1939–1947*. By the supreme allied commander in the Mediterranean, 1943–4.

2. Surveys

2090 Bartlett, Vernon, et al. (eds.). *The war of 1939*. N.d., 10 vols. Popular.

2091 Calvocoressi, Peter and Guy Wint. *Total war: causes and courses of the Second World War*. 1972. Good narrative based on printed sources.

2092 Collier, Basil. *A short history of the Second World War*. New York, 1967. Good writing and good history.

2093 Cruttwell, C. R. M. F. *A history of the Great War, 1914–1918*. Oxford, 1936. Highly regarded.

2094 Fuller, J. F. C. *The Second World War*. 1948. As seen immediately after.

2095 Kemp, Peter (ed.). *History of the Royal Navy*. 1969. Popular.

2096 Liddell Hart, Basil Henry. *A history of the First World War, 1914–1918*. 2nd ed., 1934. First published as *The real war, 1914–1918*. 1930. Often called a classic.

2097 —— *History of the Second World War*. 1970.

2098 Robbins, Keith. *The First World War*. 1984. With excellent bibliography.

2099 Schofield, B. B. *British sea power: naval policy in the twentieth century*. 1967.

2100 Stokesbury, James L. *A short history of World War I*. New York, 1981. See also his *A short history of World War II*. New York, 1980.

2101 Woodward, Ernest Llewellyn. *Great Britain and the war of 1914–1918*. 1967. Excellent general account.

3. Monographs

2102 Barker, Arthur J. *Suez: the seven day war.* 1964. The 1956 war.

2103 —— *Dunkirk: the great escape.* 1977.

2104 Barker, Rachel. *Conscience, government and war: conscientious objection in Great Britain, 1939–45.* 1982.

2105 Beckett, Ian and John Gooch (eds.). *Politicians and defence: studies in the formulation of British defence policy, 1945–1970.* Dover, N.H., 1983. Essays.

2106 Bennett, Geoffrey. *Naval battles of the First World War.* 1968. Well told; no documentation.

2107 Bond, Brian. *Liddell Hart: a study of his military thought.* 1977.

2108 —— *British military policy between the two world wars.* Oxford, 1980.

2109 Bryant, Arthur. *The turn of the tide, 1939–1943: a study based on the diaries and autobiographical notes of Field Marshal the Viscount Alanbrooke* .... 1957. Continued in Bryant's *Triumph in the West.* New York, 1959. Significant; also controversial.

2110 Carnegie Endowment for International Peace Series. *Economic and social history of the World War. British series.* Ed. James T. Shotwell. New Haven, Conn., 1921–40, 25 vols. For a complete listing of titles see (18, 26, 28).

2111 Cruickshank, Charles. *Deception in World War II.* Oxford, 1979. Psychological warfare.

2112 Davin, Daniel M. *Crete* (New Zealand Official History), Oxford, 1953.

2113 Dean, Maurice. *The Royal Air Force and two world wars.* 1979.

2114 Dennis, Peter. *Decision by default: peacetime conscription and British defence, 1919–39.* 1972.

2115 Doughty, Martin. *Merchant shipping and war: a study of defence planning in twentieth century Britain.* Atlantic Highlands, N.J., 1983.

2116 Driver, Christopher. *The disarmers: a study in protest.* 1964. The CND movement.

2117 Dunlop, John K. *The development of the British army, 1899–1914.* 1938. See also Nicholas D'Ombrain. *War machinery and high policy: defense administration in peace-time Britain, 1902–1914.* 1973.

2118 Fleming, Peter. *Invasion, 1940.* 1957. Published in USA as *The sea lion.*

2119 Fraser, David. *And we shall shock them: British army in the Second World War.* 1983.

2120 Freedman, Lawrence. *Britain and nuclear weapons.* 1981.

2121 Glubb, John. *Into battle.* 1978.

2122 Gooch, John. *The plans of war: the General Staff and British military strategy, c. 1900–1916.* 1974.

2123 Hastings, Max. *Bomber command.* 1979. Controversial but important.

2124 Higham, Robin. *Armed forces in peace time: Britain, 1918–1940, a case study.* 1962.

2125 Hinsley, F. H., et al. *British Intelligence in the Second World War: its influence on strategy and operations.* Vol. I, *1939–Summer 1941.* New York, 1979. Vol. II, *Mid 1941–mid 1943.* New York, 1981. Vol. III, Pt. I: *June 1943–June 1944.* New York, 1984. The basis for any examination of this complicated matter. See also Richard Langhorne. *Diplomacy and intelligence during the Second World War: essays in honour of F. H. Hinsley.* 1985.

2126 Hough, Richard. *The great war at sea, 1914–1918.* 1983.

2127 Howard, Michael Eliot. *The theory and practice of war: essays presented to Captain B. H. Liddell Hart on his seventieth birthday.* 1965.

2128 —— *The Mediterranean strategy in the Second World War.* 1968. A brilliant critique.

2129 —— *The continental commitment: the dilemma of British defense policy in the era of the two world wars.* 1972.

2130 Hyde, H. Montgomery. *British air policy between the wars, 1918–1939.* 1976.

2131 James, Robert Rhodes. *Gallipoli.* 1965. The best account. Consult for further study: John Masefield. *Gallipoli.* 1916.

2132 Jones, Reginald Victor. *The wizard war: British scientific intelligence, 1939–1945.* 1978.

2133 Jordan, Gerald (ed.). *Naval warfare in the twentieth century, 1900–1945: essays in honor of Arthur Marder.* 1977.
2134 Kemp, Peter K. *The key to victory: the triumph of British sea power in World War II.* Boston, 1958.
2135 Kennedy, Paul M. *The rise and fall of English naval mastery.* 1976.
2136 Longmate, Norman. *The bombers: the RAF offensive against Germany, 1939–1945.* London, 1983.
2137 Marder, Arthur Jacob. *From the dreadnought to Scapa Flow: the Royal Navy in the Fisher era, 1904–1919.* 1961–70, 5 vols.
2138 —— *From the Dardanelles to Oran: Studies of the Royal Navy in war and peace, 1915–1940.* 1974. Essays.
2139 —— *Operation Menace: the Dakar expedition and the Dudley North Affair.* Oxford, 1976.
2140 —— *Old friends, new enemies: Royal Navy and the Imperial Japanese Navy.* 1981.
2141 Mason, Francis K. *Battle over Britain.* New York, 1969. Another absorbing account is Basil Collier. *The Battle of Britain.* 1962.
2142 Morris, A. J. Anthony. *The scaremongers: the advocacy of war and rearmament, 1896–1914.* Boston, 1984.
2143 Neidpath, James. *The Singapore naval base & the defence of Britain's eastern empire, 1919–1941.* Oxford, 1981.
2144 Official Histories: First World War, 1914–18 (series)

Military operations

East Africa. Vol. I, August 1914–September 1916 (incomplete). By Charles Hordern. 1941.

Egypt and Palestine. By George MacMunn and Cyril B. Falls. 1928–30, 2 vols.

France and Belgium. By James E. Edmonds. 1922–49, 14 vols.

Italy, 1915–1919. By James E. Edmonds et al. 1949.

Macedonia. By Cyril Falls. 1933–5, 2 vols.

Mesopotamia. By Frederick J. Moberly. 1923–7, 4 vols.

Togoland and the Cameroons, 1914–16. By Frederick J. Moberly. 1931.

Order of battle divisions

Medical

Naval operations

Corbett, Julian S. and Henry Newbolt. *History of the Great War: Naval operations.* 1920–31, 5 vols. Vol. III (including the Battle of Jutland), rev. ed., 1940.

Air operations

Raleigh, Walter Alexander and H. A. Jones. *The war in the air.* Oxford, 1922–37, 6 vols.

2145 Official Histories: Second World War, 1939–45 (series) *United Kingdom Military Series.* James R. M. Butler (ed.).

Grand strategy

I. *1933 to September 1939: rearmament policy.* By N. H. Gibbs. 1976.

II. *September 1939–June 1941.* By James R. M. Butler. 1957.

III. *June 1941–August 1942.* By J. M. A. Gwyer and James R. M. Butler. 1964.

IV. *August 1942–August 1943.* By Michael Howard. 1972.

V–VI. *August 1943–August 1945.* By John Ehrman. 1956.

Campaigns

The campaign in Norway. By T. K. Derry. 1952.

France and Flanders, 1939–40. By L. F. Ellis. 1953.

The Royal Air Force, 1939–45. By Denis Richards and Hilary St. G. Saunders. 1953–4, 3 vols.

The war at sea, 1939–45. By Stephen W. Roskill. 1954–61, 3 vols. in 4.

The Mediterranean and Middle East. By Ian Stanley, Ord Playfair, C. J. C. Molony, et al. 1954–73, 5 vols.

The defence of the United Kingdom. By Basil Collier. 1957.

The war against Japan. By Woodburn Kirby et al. 1957–69, 5 vols.

The strategic air offensive. By Charles Webster and Noble Frankland. 1961, 4 vols.

Victory in the west. By L. F. Ellis et al. 2 vols. – 1962, 1968.
United Kingdom Civil Series. William Keith Hancock (ed.).
Introductory. This includes *Statistical digest of the war* (Central Statistical Office). 1951.
General Series
War Production Series
United Kingdom Medical Series. Arthur S. MacNalty (ed.).

2146 Padfield, Peter. *The great naval race: the Anglo–German naval rivalry, 1900–1914.* 1974. For an earlier treatment, still very useful, see (2158).

2147 Pakenham, Thomas. *The Boer war.* New York, 1979. Cf. Byron Farwell. *The great Anglo–Boer war.* New York, 1976.

2148 Rae, John. *Conscience and politics: the British government and the conscientious objector to military service, 1916–1919.* 1970. Cf. David Boulton. *Objection overruled.* 1967.

2149 Rosecrance, R. N. *Defence of the realm: British strategy in the nuclear epoch.* New York, 1968. Concerns the years 1946–57. For a more comprehensive treatment see Andrew J. Pierre. *Nuclear politics: the British experience with an independent strategic force, 1939–1970.* 1972.

2150 Roskill, Stephen Wentworth. *Naval policy between the wars.* I, *1919–1929.* 1968. II, *1930–1939.* 1976.

2151 —— *Churchill and the admirals.* 1977.

2152 Shay, Robert Paul. *The British rearmament in the thirties: politics and profits.* Princeton, N.J., 1977.

2153 Smith, Malcolm. *British air strategy between the wars.* Oxford, 1984.

2154 Thorne, Christopher G. *Allies of a kind: the United States, Britain and the war against Japan, 1941–1945.* 1978.

2155 Turner, Ernest S. *The phoney war on the home front.* 1961.

2156 Warwick, Peter and S. B. Spies (eds.). *The South African War: the Anglo–Boer War, 1899–1902.* 1980. Essays.

2157 Woodward, David R. *Lloyd George and the generals.* 1983.

2158 Woodward, Ernest Llewellyn. *Great Britain and the German navy.* Oxford, 1935.

2159 Wright, Robert. *Dowding and the Battle of Britain.* 1969.

4. Biographies

2160 Callwell, C. E. *Field Marshal Sir Henry Wilson: his life and diaries.* 1927, 2 vols. Wilson was chief of the Imperial Staff 1918–22. Especially useful for strategic problems. Cf. John Terraine. *The western front, 1914–1918.* 1964.

2161 Cassar, George H. *Kitchener: architect of victory.* 1977. Attempt at rehabilitation.

2162 Chalmers, William S. *The life and letters of David, Earl Beatty.* 1951. Beatty, commander-in-chief of the Grand Fleet, 1916–19, was a key figure in the Battle of Jutland.

2163 Colville, John R. *Man of valour: the life of Field-Marshal, the Viscount Gort.* 1972.

2164 Connell, John [John Henry Robertson]. *Auchinleck.* 1959. See also Philip Warner. *Auchinleck, the lonely soldier.* 1981.

2165 —— *Wavell, soldier and scholar to June 1941.* 1964.

2166 Fraser, David. *Alanbrooke.* New York, 1982. Excellent biography of the chief of General Staff, 1941–6.

2167 Hamilton, Nigel. *Monty: the making of a general, 1887–1942.* 1981. *Monty, master of the battlefield, 1942–1944.* 1983. See also Ronald Lewin. *Montgomery as military commander.* 1971.

2168 Hannah, W. H. *Bobs: Kipling's general: life of Field Marshal Earl Roberts of Kandahar, V.C.* 1972.

2169 Holmes, Richard. *The little field marshal: Sir John French.* 1982. First satisfactory biography.

2170 Hunt, Barry D. *Sailor-scholar: Admiral Sir Herbert Richmond, 1871–1946.* 1982.

2171 Lewin, Ronald. *Slim: the standard bearer.* 1976.

2172 —— *Field Marshall Lord Wavell, commander-in-chief and viceroy, 1939–1947.* 1976.

2173 MacKay, Ruddock F. *Fisher of Kilverstone*. Oxford, 1974. Excellent.
2174 Marder, Arthur J. *Portrait of an admiral: the life and papers of Sir Herbert Richmond*. 1952.
2175 Marlowe, John. *Late Victorian: the life of Sir Arnold Talbot Wilson*. 1967.
2176 Nicolson, Nigel. *Alex: the life of Field Marshal Earl Alexander of Tunis*. 1973.
2177 Roskill, Stephen Wentworth. *Admiral of the Fleet Earl Beatty: the last naval hero*. 1981.
2178 Terraine, John. *Douglas Haig, the educated soldier*. 1963. Other biographies include: John Charteris. *Field Marshal Earl Haig*. New York, 1929. Duff Cooper. *Haig*. 2 vols., 1935–6.

5. Articles

2179 Adams, R. J. Q. 'Delivering the goods: reappraising the Ministry of Munitions: 1915–1916', *Albion*, VII (fall 1975), 232–44.
2180 Dunbabin, J. P. D. 'British rearmament in the 1930s: a chronology and review', *Hist. J.*, XVIII (Sept. 1975), 587–609.
2181 Gollin, Alfred. 'The mystery of Lord Haldane and early British military aviation', *Albion*, XI (spring 1979), 5–65.
2182 Henderson, W. O. 'The conquest of the German colonies, 1914–18', *History*, new ser., XXVII (Sept. 1942), 124–39.
2183 Howard, Michael E. 'Lord Haldane and the territorial army'. In Howard's *Studies in war and peace*. 1970, pp. 83–98.
2184 Kennedy, P. M. 'The development of German naval operations plans against England, 1896–1914', *EHR*, LXXXIX (Jan. 1974), 48–76.
2185 Mead, Peter. 'Orde Wingate and the official historians', *JCH*, XIV (Jan. 1979), 55–82. See also Shelford, Bidwell. 'Wingate and the official historians: Our alternative view', *JCH*, XV (April 1980), 245–56.
2186 Parker, R. A. C. 'British rearmament, 1936–9', *EHR*, XCI (Oct. 1976), 306–44.
2187 Terraine, John. 'Twenty-five years of military history, 1945–1970', *Journal of the Royal United States Institute for Defence Studies*, CXVI (Dec. 1971), 13–23.
2188 Weinroth, Howard. 'Left-wing opposition to naval armaments in Britain before 1914', *JCH*, VI (no. 4, 1971), 93–120.
2189 Williams, T. Desmond. 'The historiography of World War II', *Historical Studies*, 1958, 33–49.

XIV. RELIGIOUS HISTORY

1. Printed sources

2190 Bayne, Stephen Fielding, Jr. *An Anglican turning point: documents and interpretations*. 1964. When Bayne was executive officer of the Anglican Communion, 1960–4.
2191 Bell, George K. A. (ed.). *Documents on Christian unity: a selection from the first and second series, 1920–30*. 1955. See also his *Documents on Christian unity, third series, 1930–1948*. 1948.
2192 Buchman, Frank N. D. *Remaking the world*. 1947. Speeches.
2193 *Conversations between the Church of England and the Methodist Church: a report to the Archbishops of Canterbury and York and the Conference of the Methodist Church*. 1963. Concerning union.
2194 [COPEC]. *Politics and citizenship, being the report presented to the Conference on Christian Politics and Citizenship at Birmingham, April 5–12, 1924*. 1925.
2195 Edwards, David L. (ed.). *The Honest to God debate. Some reactions to the book 'Honest to God'*. Philadelphia, Pa., 1963.
2196 Eliot, Thomas S. *Christianity and culture: the idea of a Christian society and notes towards the definition of culture*. New York, [1940]. A widely discussed book.
2197 Garbett, Cyril F. *In an age of revolution*. 1952. Concerning 1880–1950.

2198 Heenan, John C. *A crown of thorns: an autobiography, 1951–1963*. 1974. By the Archbishop of Westminster. See also his *Not the whole truth*. 1971.
2199 Henson, Herbert Hensley. *Retrospect of an unimportant life*. 1942–50, 3 vols. Autobiography of the Bishop of Durham.
2200 Inge, William Ralph. *Outspoken essays*. 1919. See also *Outspoken essays, second series*. 1923. For commentary on Inge's thought, see Helm, Robert M. *The gloomy dean: the thought of William Ralph Inge*. 1962.
2201 —— *Diary of a dean: St. Paul's, 1911–1934*. New York, 1950.
2202 Lambeth Conference. *Conference of bishops of the Anglican communion: holden at Lambeth Palace ... 1908. Encyclical letter from the bishops, with the resolutions and reports*. 1908.
2203 —— *The reports of the 1920, 1930 and 1948 conferences ....* 1948.
2204 —— *Lambeth Conference 1948: the encyclical letter from the bishops; together with resolutions and reports*. 1948. A notable conference.
2205 Lewis, Clive S. *The Screwtape letters*. 1942. A lay churchman on a theological theme. See also *Letters of C. S. Lewis*. New York, 1966. During the years 1915–63.
2206 [Lindsay, Alexander D., Baron (ed.)]. *Christianity and the present moral unrest*. 1926. By various writers; inspired by COPEC. See (2194).
2207 *Malvern, 1941. The life of the church and the order of society; being the proceedings of the Archbishop of York's Conference*. 1941.
2208 [Oldham, Joseph H.]. *The churches survey their task. The report of the conference at Oxford, July 1937 on church, community and state*. With an introduction by J. H. Oldham. 1937.
2209 Orchard, William E. *From faith to faith: an autobiography of religious development*. New York, 1933. Orchard was minister at the King's Weigh House, London.
2210 Pickering, William S. F. (ed.). *Anglican–Methodist relations: some institutional factors*. Papers presented to the Study Commission on Institutionalism, Commission on Faith and Order, World Council of Churches. 1961. Pertaining to the search for unity.
2211 Reckitt, Maurice B. *As it happened: an autobiography*. 1941.
2212 Robinson, John A. T. *Honest to God*. 1964. See (2195).
2213 Smethurst, Arthur F. (ed.). *Acts of the convocations of Canterbury and York together with certain other resolutions, passed since the reform of the convocations in 1921*. 1948.
2214 Southcott, Ernest W. *The parish comes alive*. New York, 1957. Evangelism in a parish over a period of twelve years.
2215 Temple, Frederick S. (ed.). *William Temple: some Lambeth letters*. 1963. 'Of a busy war-time archbishop, 1942–4'.
2216 Temple, William. *Christianity and the social order*. New York, 1942. When Temple was Archbishop of York.
2217 Underhill, Evelyn. *Mysticism: a study in the nature and development of man's spiritual consciousness*. 7th ed., 1918. Important book by a noted religious writer. See also her *The life of the spirit and the life of today*. 1922.
2218 Weatherhead, Leslie D. *The Christian agnostic*. 1965. The minister (1936–60) of the City Temple, London, analyses his own faith.

2. Surveys

2219 Cowling, Maurice. *Religion and public doctrine in modern England*. 1981. Examines the 'role of religion in English public thought'.
2220 Davies, Horton. *Worship and theology in England*, V, *The ecumenical century, 1900–1965*. Princeton, N.J., 1965. Masterful treatment.
2221 Davies, Rupert Eric. *Methodism*. 1963. Brief survey.
2222 —— and Gordon Rupp (eds.). *History of the Methodist Church in Great Britain*. 1965–84, 4 vols.
2223 Headlam, Arthur C. *The Church of England*. 2nd ed., 1925.
2224 Jones, Robert Tudur. *Congregationalism in England, 1622–1962*. 1962.
2225 Lloyd, Roger. *The Church of England, 1900–1965*. 1966. Rev. ed. of his *Church of England in the twentieth century*. 1946–50, 2 vols.

2226 Mathew, David. *Catholicism in England.* 3rd ed., 1955.
2227 Moorman, John R. H. *A history of the church of England.* Rev. ed., 1973.
2228 Neill, Stephen Charles. *Anglicanism.* 1958.
2229 Ramsey, Arthur Michael. *An era in Anglican theory from Gore to Temple: the development of Anglican theology between Lux Mundi and the Second World War, 1889–1939.* New York, 1960.
2230 Spinks, G. Stephens, et al. *Religion in Britain since 1900.* 1952.
2231 Underwood, Alfred C. *A history of the English Baptists.* 1947.
2232 Welsby, Paul A. *A history of the Church of England, 1945–1980.* New York, 1984.

3. Monographs

2233 *The City Temple in the City of London.* Published by the City Temple Church Council on the occasion of the reopening and rededication. 1958.
2234 Clark, Walter Houston. *The Oxford Group: its history and significance.* New York, 1951. A critical study of Moral Rearmament.
2235 Clarke, W. K. Lowther. *A hundred years of hymns ancient and modern.* 1961.
2236 Cowling, Maurice. *Religion and public doctrine in modern England.* 1980–5, 2 vols.
2237 Crossman, Richard H. S. (ed.). *Oxford and the Groups.* Oxford, 1934. Essays.
2238 Currie, Robert. *Methodism divided: a study in the sociology of ecumenicalism.* 1968.
2239 Davies, Horton. *Varieties of English preaching, 1900–1960.* 1963.
2240 Driberg, Tom. *The mystery of moral rearmament: a study of Frank Buchman and his movement.* 1964.
2241 Edwards, David L. *Religion and change.* 1969.
2242 Edwards, Maldwyn. *Methodism and England: a study of Methodism in its social and political aspects, 1850–1932.* 1943.
2243 Freeman, Ruth. *Quakers and peace.* 1947. Excellent summary of role of Quakers.
2244 Goodall, Norman. *A history of the London Missionary Society, 1895–1945.* 1954.
2245 —— *Ecumenical progress: a decade of change in the ecumenical movement, 1961–71.* 1972.
2246 Hickey, John. *Urban Catholics: urban Catholicism in England and Wales from 1829 to the present day.* 1967.
2247 Kaye, Elaine. *The history of the King's Weigh House.* 1968. An Anglican church becomes Congregational.
2248 Koss, Stephen. *Nonconformity in modern British politics.* 1975.
2249 Langford, Thomas A. *In search of foundations: English theology, 1900–1920.* Nashville, Tenn., 1969.
2250 Lebzelter, Gisela C. *Political anti-semitism in England, 1918–1939.* 1978.
2251 Lewis, John, et al. (eds.). *Christianity and the social revolution.* New York, 1936. Various authors challenge the 'traditional attitudes of Christianity towards . . . radical social change'.
2252 Marrin, Albert. *The last crusade: the Church of England in the First World War.* Durham, N.C., 1974. A scholarly study, relying largely on printed sources.
2253 Mozley, John Kenneth. *Some tendencies in British theology, from the publication of 'Lux Mundi' to the present day.* 1951.
2254 Neill, Stephen Charles. *Towards Church union, 1937–1952.* 1952. On this question, there are, after 1952, summaries twice annually by J. R. Nelson in the *Ecumenical Review.*
2255 —— *The interpretation of the New Testament, 1861–1961.* 1964. Based on the Firth Lectures at Nottingham in 1962.
2256 —— *A history of Christian missions.* 1965.
2257 Norman, E. R. *Church and society in England, 1770–1970: a historical study.* New York, 1976.
2258 Oliver, John. *The church and social order: social thought in the Church of England, 1918–1939.* 1968. A significant book with useful bibliography.
2259 Page, Robert J. *New directions in Anglican theology: a survey from Temple to Robinson.* New York, 1965.
2260 Payne, Ernest A. *The Baptist Union: a short history.* 1959.

2261 Reckitt, Maurice B. (ed.). *Prospect for Christianity: essays in Catholic social reconstruction*. 1945.

2262 —— (ed.). *For Christ and the people: studies of four socialist priests and prophets of the Church of England between 1870 and 1930*. 1968. Analyses of Thomas Hancock, Steward Headlam, Charles Marson, and Conrad Noel.

2263 Rouse, Ruth and Stephen Charles Neill (eds.) *A history of the ecumenical movement, 1517–1948*. 2nd ed., Philadelphia, Pa., 1968. A standard work. Continued by Harold E. Fey (ed.). *Ecumenical advance: a history of the ecumenical movement*, II, *1948–1968*. Philadelphia, Pa., 1970.

2264 Sacks, Benjamin. *The religious issue in the state schools of England and Wales, 1902–1914*. Albuquerque, N. Mex., 1961.

2265 Thompson, Kenneth A. *Bureaucracy and church reform: the organizational response of the Church of England to social change, 1800–1965*. Oxford, 1970. Half of the treatment concerns the twentieth century.

2266 Vidler, Alec R. *20th century defenders of the faith*. 1965.

2267 Warren, Max. *The missionary movement from Britain in modern history*. 1979.

2268 Wasserstein, Bernard. *Britain and the Jews of Europe, 1939–45*. 1979.

2269 Wearmouth, Robert F. *The social and political influence of Methodism in the twentieth century*. 1957. An admirable study.

2270 Wiggins, Arch A. *The history of the Salvation Army*, V, *1904–1914*. 1968. F. C. Coutts. VI, *1914–1946*. 1973.

2271 Wilkinson, Alan. *The Church of England and the First World War*. 1978.

2272 Williams, Daniel Day. *What present-day theologians are thinking*. 3rd ed., rev., New York, 1967.

2273 Williams, Geoffrey. *Inside Buchmanism: an independent inquiry into the Oxford Group movement and Moral Rearmament*. 1955.

2274 Wilson, Roger C. *Quaker relief: an account of the relief work of the Society of Friends, 1940–1948*. 1952.

2275 Wood, Herbert George. *Living issues in religious thought from George Fox to Bertrand Russell*. Freeport, N.Y., 1966. First published in 1924; includes religious views of Russell, Bernard Shaw, and H. G. Wells.

2276 Young, Kenneth. *Chapel: the joyous days and prayerful nights of the non-conformists in their heyday, circa 1850–1930*. 1972.

4. Biographies

2277 Barnes, John. *Ahead of his age: Bishop Barnes of Birmingham*. 1979. His years as bishop: 1924–53.

2278 Bell, George K. A. *Randall Davidson, Archbishop of Canterbury*. 3rd ed., 1952.

2279 Carpenter, Spencer C. *Winnington-Ingram: the biography of Arthur Foley Winnington-Ingram, Bishop of London, 1901–1939*. 1949.

2280 —— *Duncan-Jones of Chichester*. 1956. A well-known dean.

2281 Chadwick, Owen. *Hensley Henson: a study in the friction between church and state*. 1983.

2282 Cropper, Margaret. *Evelyn Underhill*. 1958.

2283 Edwards, David L. *Leaders of the Church of England, 1828–1944*. 1971.

2284 —— *Ian Ramsey, Bishop of Durham: a memoir*. Oxford, 1973.

2285 Fletcher, Joseph. *William Temple: twentieth century Christian*. 1963. 'A portrait' of the Archbishop of Canterbury. See (2289).

2286 Fox, Adam. *Dean Inge*. 1960.

2287 Gordon, Anne Wolrige. *Peter Howard: life and letters*. 1969. Howard was a leader in Moral Rearmament.

2288 Heenan, John C. *Cardinal Hinsley*. 1944.

2289 Iremonger, Frederic A. *William Temple, Archbishop of Canterbury: his life and letters*. 1948. See (2285).

2290 Jasper, Ronald. *Arthur Cayley Headlam: life and letters of a bishop*. 1960. Headlam was Bishop of Gloucester, 1923–45.

2291 —— *George Bell, Bishop of Chichester*. 1967.

2292 Kemp, Eric Waldram. *Life and letters of Kenneth Escott Kirk, Bishop of Oxford, 1937–1954*. 1959.

2293 Lockhart, John G. *Cosmo Gordon Lang.* 1949. Biography of the Archbishop of Canterbury, 1929–42.
2294 McKay, Roy. *John Leonard Wilson, confessor for the faith.* 1973. Biography of the Bishop of Birmingham, 1953–69.
2295 Maitland, Christopher. *Dr. Leslie Weatherhead of the City Temple.* 1960.
2296 [Margaret], the Prioress of Whitby. *Archbishop Garbett: a memoir.* 1957. Garbett was Archbishop of York.
2297 Paget, Stephen. *Henry Scott Holland, memoir and letters.* 1921. Biography of a Regius Professor of Divinity at Oxford.
2298 Prestige, George L. *The life of Charles Gore, a great Englishman.* 1935. Gore was Bishop of Birmingham and Bishop of Oxford.
2299 Purcell, William. *Portrait of Soper: a biography of the Reverend the Lord Soper of Kingsway.* 1972.
2300 Reckitt, Maurice B. *P. E. T. Widdrington, a study in vocation and versatility.* 1961. Study of a key figure in the Anglo–Catholic movement.
2301 Roberts, Richard Ellis. *H. R. L. Sheppard: life and letters.* 1942. Study of a noted vicar of St. Martin's-in-the-Fields and dean of Canterbury. See also Carolyn Scott. *Dick Sheppard: a biography.* 1977.
2302 Smyth, Charles. *Cyril Foster Garbett, archbishop of York.* 1959.
2303 Tomkins, Oliver. *The life of Edward Woods.* 1957. Biography of the bishop of Lichfield, associated with the Life and Liberty Movement.
2304 Wakefield, Gordon S. *Robert Newton Flew, 1886–1962.* 1971. Biography of a leading Methodist.
2305 Weatherhead, Kingsley. *Leslie Weatherhead: a personal portrait.* 1975.
2306 Wood, Herbert George. *Henry T. Hodgkin, a memoir.* 1937. A study of a leader in the Fellowship of Reconciliation.
2307 Woods, Edward S. and Frederic MacNutt. *Theodore, Bishop of Winchester.* 1933. Biography of F. T. Woods.

5. Articles

2308 Brown, L. W., et al. 'Anglican–Methodist unity: a symposium', *Church Quarterly*, I (Oct. 1968), 98–136. Subject: the report of the Anglican–Methodist Unity Commission.
2309 Cannon, Charmian. 'The influence of religion on educational policy, 1902–1944', *BJES*, XII (May 1964), 143–60.
2310 Edwards, David L. '101 years of the Lambeth Conference', *Church Quarterly*, I (July 1968), 21–35.
2311 Finlay, John L. 'The religious response to Douglasism in England', *Journal of Religious History*, VI (Dec. 1971), 363–83. On Major C. H. Douglas and Social Credit.
2312 Fuller, Reginald H. 'Draft liturgy of 1953 in Anglican perspective', *Anglican Theological Review*, XLI (July 1959), 190–8.
2313 Hachey, Thomas E. 'The archbishop of Canterbury's visit to Palestine: an issue in Anglo–Vatican relations in 1931', *Church History*, XLI (June 1972), 198–207. Uses Foreign Office papers.
2314 Hill, Clifford. 'From church to sect: West Indian religious sect development in Britain', *Journal for the Scientific Study of Religion*, X (summer 1971), 114–23. Studies the period 1951–71.
2315 Langford, Thomas A. 'The theological methodology of John Oman and H. H. Farmer', *Religious Studies*, I (1965–6), 229–40.
2316 Miller, William and Gillian Raab. 'The religious alignment at English elections between 1918 and 1970', *PS*, XXV (June 1977), 227–51.
2317 Morgan, D. H. J. 'The social and educational background of Anglican bishops – continuities and changes', *BJS*, XX (Sept. 1969), 295–310.
2318 Nichols, James Hastings. 'Religion in Toynbee's history', *Journal of Religion*, XXVIII (Jan. 1948), 99–119.
2319 Pugh, D. R. 'The Church and education: Anglican attitudes, 1902', *Journal of Ecclesiastical History*, XXIII (July 1972), 219–32.
2320 Smith, Bardwell L. 'Liberal Catholicism: an Anglican perspective', *Anglican Theological Review*, LIV (July 1972), 175–93. On period 1889–1914.

XV. HISTORY OF THE FINE ARTS

1. Printed sources

2321 Beecham, Thomas. *A mingled chime: an autobiography.* New York, 1943.
2322 Dolmetsch, Mabel. *Personal recollections of Arnold Dolmetsch.* 1957. Concerning a noted musicologist.
2323 Fellowes, Edmund H. *Memories of an amateur musician.* 1946.
2324 Gill, Eric. *Autobiography.* 1940. Of a notable stone carver.
2325 Holst, Imogen. *The music of Gustav Holst.* 2nd ed., 1968.
2326 Howes, Frank Stewart. *The music of Ralph Vaughan Williams.* 1954.
2327 James, Philip (ed.). *Henry Moore on sculpture: a collection of the sculptor's writings and spoken words.* Rev. ed., New York, 1971.
2328 Jekyll, Gertrude. *Colour schemes for the flower garden.* 8th ed., 1936.
2329 —— and Christopher Hussey. *Garden ornament.* 2nd ed., 1927.
2330 —— and Lawrence Weaver. *Gardens for small country houses.* 6th ed., 1927.
2331 Rothenstein, John. *Brave day, hideous night. Summer's lease. Time's thievish progress.* 1965–70, 3 vols. Autobiography of the director of the Tate Gallery, 1938–64.
2332 Rothenstein, William. *Men and memories: recollections of William Rothenstein.* 1931–2, 2 vols., Vol. II embraces 1900–22.
2333 Scott, M. H. Baillie and A. Edgar Beresford. *Houses and Gardens.* 1939.
2334 Shewring, Walter (ed.). *Letters of Eric Gill.* 1947.
2335 Sickert, Walter. *A free house! Or the artist as craftsman.* Ed. Osbert Sitwell. 1947. The writings of Sickert.

2. Surveys

2336 Cooper, Martin (ed.). *The new Oxford history of music*, X, *The modern age, 1890–1960.* Oxford, 1974.
2337 Farr, Dennis. *Oxford History of English Art, 1870–1940.* 1979.
2338 Goodhart-Rendel, Harry S. *English architecture since the regency: an interpretation.* 1953.
2339 Hitchcock, Henry-Russell. *Architecture: nineteenth and twentieth centuries.* 3rd ed., 1968.
2340 Howes, Frank. *The English musical renaissance.* 1966. Nineteenth and twentieth centuries.
2341 MacKerness, Eric D. *A social history of English music.* 1964.
2342 Myers, Rollo H. *Twentieth century music.* 2nd ed., 1968.
2343 Richards, James M. *An introduction to modern architecture.* 1940.
2344 Walker, Ernest. *A history of music in England.* 3rd ed., rev. by J. A. Westrup. Oxford, 1952. Standard.
2345 Wilson, Albert E. *Edwardian theatre.* 1951.
2346 Young, Percy M. *A history of British music.* 1967.

3. Monographs

2347 The Arts Enquiry. *Music: a report on musical life in England sponsored by the Dartington Hall trustees.* 1949. PEP publication, see (98).
2348 Arundell, Dennis. *The story of Sadler's Wells, 1683–1964.* 1965.
2349 Barman, Christian. *An introduction to railway architecture.* 1950.
2350 Butler, Arthur S. G. *The architecture of Sir Edwin Lutyens.* 1950, 3 vols.
2351 Chadwick, George F. *The park and the town: public landscape in the 19th and 20th centuries.* New York, 1966. Excellent treatment, with emphasis on Britain.
2352 Clarke, Mary. *The Sadler's Wells ballet: a history and an appreciation.* 1955.
2353 Colles, Henry C. *The Royal College of Music: a jubilee record, 1883–1933.* 1933.
2354 Crowe, Sylvia. *Garden design.* 1958.
2355 Dannatt, Trevor. *Modern architecture in Britain: selected examples of recent building.* 1959.

2356 Dent, Edward J. *A theatre for everybody: the story of the Old Vic and Sadler's Wells.* 1945. A popular, well-informed treatment.
2357 Dickinson, Alan E. F. *Vaughan Williams.* 1963. A study of his compositions.
2358 Donaldson, Frances. *The British Council.* 1984.
2359 Elson, John and Nicholas Tomalin. *The history of the National Theatre.* 1978.
2360 Ferguson, John. *The arts in Britain in World War I, 1914–1918.* 1980.
2361 Gelatt, Roland. *The fabulous phonograph: the story of the gramophone from tin foil to high fidelity.* 1956.
2362 Godfrey, W. G. *The work of Ernest Newton, R.A.* 1923.
2363 Gregoriev, Sergi L. *The Diaghilev Ballet, 1909–1929.* 1953.
2364 Harris, John S. *Government patronage of the arts in Great Britain.* Chicago, 1970. After 1945.
2365 Hill, Ralph. *Music.* 1950. Developments after 1945.
2366 Hinchcliffe, Arnold P. *British Theatre, 1950–1970.* Oxford, 1974.
2367 Hitchcock, Henry Russell. *Architecture of H. H. Richardson and his times.* 2nd ed., 1966.
2368 Howarth, Thomas. *Charles Rennie Mackintosh and the modern movement.* 1952. Architecture.
2369 Itzin, Catherine. *Stages in the revolution: political theatre in Britain since 1968.* 1980.
2370 Jenkins, Hugh. *The culture gap: an experience of government and the arts.* 1979.
2371 Kaye, Barrington. *The development of the architectural profession in Britain: a sociological study.* 1960.
2372 Kemp, Thomas C. and John C. Trewin. *The Stratford Festival: a history of the Shakespeare Memorial Theatre.* Birmingham, 1953.
2373 Kennedy, Michael. *The works of Ralph Vaughan Williams.* 1964.
2374 —— *History of the Royal Manchester College of Music, 1893–1972.* Manchester, 1971.
2375 King, A. Hyatt. *Some British collectors of music; c. 1600–1960.* Cambridge, 1963.
2376 Melly, George. *Revolt into style: the pop arts in Britain.* 1970.
2377 Mitchell, Donald and Hans Keller (eds.). *Benjamin Britten: a commentary on his works from a group of specialists.* 1952.
2378 Nettel, Reginald. *The orchestra in England: a social history.* [1946].
2379 Newton, Ernest and W. G. Newton. *English domestic architecture,* VI. N.d.
2380 Pakenham, Simona. *Ralph Vaughan Williams: a discovery of his music.* 1957. Excellent for the average reader.
2381 Pevsner, Nikolaus (ed.). *The buildings of England.* Harmondsworth, 1951–74, 46 vols. By counties.
2382 —— *Pioneers of modern design: from William Morris to Walter Gropius.* 2nd ed., 1966. Well illustrated chapter on English architecture.
2383 Richards, James M. (ed.). *The bombed buildings of Britain.* 3rd ed., 1947. 'A record of architectural casualties, 1940–1'.
2384 Rosenthal, Harold. *Opera at Covent Garden: a short history.* 1967. Largely on twentieth century.
2385 Rothenstein, John. *British art since 1900: an anthology.* 1962.
2386 Royal Institute of British Architecture. *One hundred years of British architecture, 1851–1951.* 1951.
2387 Royal Society of Arts. *The post-war home: a series of lectures on its interior and equipment.* Foreword by Oliver Lyttleton. 1942. Lectures delivered during 1941–2.
2388 —— *A century of British progress, 1851–1951.* 1951. Six papers read before the Royal Society in 1951.
2389 Scholes, Percy A. *The mirror of music, 1844–1944: a century of musical life as reflected in the pages of the 'Musical Times'.* 1947, 2 vols. Packed with information.
2390 Service, Alistair. *Edwardian architecture and its origins.* 1975.
2391 Spence, Basil. *Phoenix at Coventry: the building of a cathedral.* 1962.
2392 Trewin, John C. *The theatre since 1900.* 1951.
2393 —— *The Birmingham Repertory Theatre, 1913–1963.* 1963.
2394 —— *Drama in Britain, 1951–1964.* 1965.
2395 Weaver, Lawrence. *Small country houses of today.* [1910].

2396 —— *Lutyens houses and gardens.* 1921. This is a new edition of Edwin L. Lutyens. *Houses and gardens.* 1913.
2397 Williamson, Audrey. *Ballet of 3 decades.* 1958. On period 1931–57.

4. Biographies

2398 Bailey, Cyril. *Hugh Percy Allen.* 1948. Biography of a musician and a musical statesman.
2399 Colles, Henry C. *Walford Davies: a biography.* 1942.
2400 Day, James. *Vaughan Williams.* 1961.
2401 Emmons, Robert. *The life and opinions of Walter Richard Sickert.* 1941.
2402 Fox Strangways, A. H. and Maud Karpeles. *Cecil Sharp.* 2nd ed., 1955. Biography of a collector and arranger of folk songs.
2403 Grierson, Mary. *Donald Francis Tovey: A biography based on letters.* 1952. Tovey was a leading musician and musicologist.
2404 Hall, Donald. *Henry Moore: the life and work of a great sculptor.* New York, 1966.
2405 Hassall, Christopher. *Edward Marsh, patron of the arts: a biography.* 1959.
2406 Hill, William Thompson. *Octavia Hill: pioneer of the National Trust and housing reformer.* 1956.
2407 Holroyd, Michael. *Augustus John: a biography.* 1974–5, 2 vols.
2408 Holst, Imogen. *Gustav Holst: a biography.* 2nd ed., 1969.
2409 Hussey, Christopher. *The life of Sir Edwin Lutyens.* 1950.
2410 Hutchings, Arthur. *Delius.* 1948.
2411 Kennedy, Michael. *Portrait of Elgar.* 1968.
2412 Kornwolf, James D. *M. H. Baillie Scott and the Arts and Crafts Movement: pioneers of modern design.* 1972.
2413 Laughton, Bruce. *Philip Wilson Steer, 1860–1942.* Oxford, 1971.
2414 Lilly, Marjorie. *Sickert: the painter and his circle.* 1971.
2415 Massingham, Betty. *Miss Jekyll, portrait of a great gardener.* 1966.
2416 Pound, Reginald. *Sir Henry Wood.* 1969.
2417 Powell, Dora M. *Edward Elgar: memories of a variation.* 3rd ed., 1949.
2418 Reid, Charles. *Thomas Beecham: an independent biography.* 1961.
2419 Rothenstein, John. *The life and death of Conder.* 1938. On Charles Conder, a painter.
2420 St. John, Christopher. *Ethel Smyth: a biography.* 1959.
2421 Speaight, Robert. *William Rothenstein: the portrait of an artist in his time.* 1962.
2422 —— *The life of Eric Gill.* 1966.
2423 Stroud, Dorothy. *Sir John Soame, architect.* 1984.
2424 Trewin, John C. *Benson and the Bensonians.* 1960. On Frank Benson (1858–1939), an actor.
2425 —— *Robert Donat: a biography.* 1968.
2426 —— *Peter Brock: a biography.* 1971.
2427 White, Eric Walter. *Benjamin Britten: his life and operas.* New ed., 1970.
2428 Whittick, Arnold. *Eric Mendelsohn.* 2nd ed., 1956. Chap. 6 concerns this architect's English phase, 1933–7.

5. Articles

2429 Antcliffe, Herbert. 'Problems of music and history', *Music & Letters,* IX (July 1928), 265–75.
2430 Foss, Hubert J. 'Elgar and his age', *Music & Letters,* XVI (Jan. 1935), 5–12.
2431 Fox Strangways, A. H. 'Ralph Vaughan Williams', *Music & Letters,* I (Apr. 1920), 78–86.
2432 King, A. Hyatt. 'The Forsytes and music', *Music & Letters,* XXIII (Jan. 1942), 24–36.
2433 Lethaby. 'William Richard Lethaby, 1857–1931, a symposium in honour of his centenary', *Journal of the Royal Institute of British Architects,* LIV (1957), 218–25.

2434 Lovell, Percy. 'The proposed National Opera House at Glastonbury, 1913–15', *Music & Letters*, L (Jan. 1969), 172–9.

XVI. INTELLECTUAL HISTORY

1. Printed sources

2435 Angell, Norman. *After all.* New York, 1951. Autobiography.

2436 Ayerst, David (ed.). *The Guardian omnibus, 1821–1971.* An anthology, largely of the twentieth century.

2437 Blatchford, Robert. *My eighty years.* 1931. By a talented journalist and ardent socialist.

2438 Blumenfeld, Ralph D. *R. D. B.'s diary, 1887–1914.* By editor of the *Daily Express*, 1904–1928.

2439 Blunt, Wilfrid Scawen. *My diaries, being a personal narrative of events, 1884–1914.* By a man of letters.

2440 Brittain, Vera. *Testament of youth: an autobiographical study of the years 1900–1925.* New York, 1933. Reprinted, 1980, with preface by Shirley Williams. See also her *Chronicle of youth; the war diary, 1913–1917.* 1981.

2441 Buchan, John, Baron Tweedsmuir. *Pilgrim's way.* Cambridge, Mass., 1940. Published in England as *Memory hold the door.* 1940. Autobiography of a noted author and governor-general of Canada.

2442 Collingwood, Robin G. *An autobiography.* 1938. Largely concerned with his studies in philosophy and history.

2443 Cornelius, David K. and Edwin St. Vincent (eds.). *Cultures in conflict: perspectives on the Snow–Leavis controversy.* Chicago, 1964.

2444 Coulton, George G. *Fourscore years: an autobiography.* 1944. By a leading historian and educator.

2445 Day Lewis, Cecil. *The mind in chains: socialism and the cultural revolution.* 1937. Essays on a revolutionary theme.

2446 Evans, Harold. *Downing Street Diary: the Macmillan years, 1957–1963.* 1981. Evans was editor of the *Sunday Times*, 1967–81, and editor of *The Times*, 1981–2.

2447 —— *Good times, bad times.* New York, 1984.

2448 Flexner, Abraham. *Universities: American – English – German.* 1930. An important book reflecting the ideas of its time.

2449 Gardiner, Alfred G. *Pillars of society.* 1913. See also his *Prophets, priests & kings.* 1914. Selections from *The Daily News.*

2450 Harris, Henry Wilson. *Life so far.* 1954. Autobiography of a journalist and politician.

2451 *Higher education . . . report of the committee . . . under the chairmanship of Lord Robbins . . . .* 1963. Cmnd 2154.

2452 Hirst, Francis W. *In the golden days.* 1947. Autobiography of the editor of the *Economist*, 1907–16.

2453 Hobhouse, Leonard T. *Democracy and reaction.* 1904. See also his *Liberalism.* 1911. These two works were widely read.

2454 Hobson, John A. *Imperialism: a study.* New York, 1902. Often considered Hobson's most influential book.

2455 —— *Crisis of Liberalism: new issues of democracy.* 1909. Reprinted, 1974. Ed. Peter F. Clarke.

2456 —— *Confessions of an economic heretic.* 1938. Autobiography of a noted economist and publicist.

2457 Holmes–Laski letters. *The correspondence of Mr. Justice Holmes and Harold J. Laski, 1916–1935.* Ed. Mark DeWolfe Howe. Cambridge, Mass., 1953, 2 vols.

2458 Jerrold, Douglas. *Georgian adventure.* New York, 1938. 'Memories' of an author and publisher.

2459 Joad, Cyril E. M. *Under the fifth rib: a belligerent autobiography.* 1932. By a writer, philosopher, and teacher.

2460 Lehmann, John. *I am my brother*. 1960. Autobiographical; on World War II years.

2461 Mallock, William H. *Social reform as related to realities and delusions: an examination of the increase and distribution of wealth from 1801 to 1910*. 1914. An influential book.

2462 Marsh, Edward. *A number of people: a book of reminiscences*. 1939.

2463 Martin, Kingsley. *Father figures: a first volume of autobiography, 1897–1931*. 1966. Continued by *Editor: a second volume of autobiography, 1931–1945*. 1968. By the editor of the *New Statesman and Nation*, 1930–60.

2464 Massingham, Harold J. (ed.). *H. W. M.: a selection from the writings of H. W. Massingham*. 1925. Introduced by essays from contributors to the *Nation*. See also (2614).

2465 Masterman, Charles F. G. *In peril of change*. 1905. See also (1174–5).

2466 Masterman, John Cecil. *On the chariot wheel: an autobiography*. 1975.

2467 [Moore, George Edward]. *The philosophy of G. E. Moore*. Ed. Paul Arthur Schilpp. *Library of Living Philosophers*, Vol. IV. Chicago, 1942. See also Moore's *Principia ethica*. 1909. This was widely read by intellectuals in the Edwardian period.

2468 Murray, Gilbert. *An unfinished autobiography with contributions by his friends*. Ed. Jean Smith and Arnold Toynbee. 1960.

2469 Nevinson, Henry W. *More changes, more chances*. 1925. Autobiography, 1903–14, of a distinguished essayist and war correspondent. Concluded to 1926 by his *Last chances, last changes*. 1928.

2470 Nicolson, Harold. *Diaries and letters*. Ed. Nigel Nicolson. 1966–8, 3 vols. On years 1930–62.

2471 [Orwell, George]. *Collected essays, journalism and letters of George Orwell*. Ed. Sonia Orwell and Ian Angus. New York, 1968, 4 vols.

2472 Oxford University. *Report of the Commission of Inquiry*. 1966, 2 vols. The commission was headed by Lord Franks.

2473 PEP [Political and Economic Planning]. *Report on the British press: a survey of its current operations and problems with special reference to national newspapers and their part in public affairs*. 1938.

2474 Rolph, C. H. *The life, letters and diaries of Kingsley Martin*. 1973.

2475 *Royal Commission on the press, 1947–1949: report presented to Parliament by command of His Majesty, June 1949*. Cmnd 7700.

2476 Russell, Bertrand. *Philosophy*. New York, 1927. Published in England as *An outline of philosophy*. 1927.

2477 —— *Autobiography of Bertrand Russell*. 1967–9, 3 vols.

2478 Selver, Paul. *Orage and the New Age circle: reminiscences and reflections*. 1959. See (2550).

2479 Shaw, George Bernard. *Bernard Shaw, collected letters*. II, *1898–1910*. 1972. III, *1911–1925*. 1985. Ed. Dan H. Laurence.

2480 Sitwell, Osbert. *Laughter in the next room*. Boston, 1948. Includes important reflections on society, 1918–40.

2481 Snow, Charles Percy, Baron. *The two cultures and the scientific revolution*. 1961. A discussion of the harmony (or lack of it) between letters and science is continued in *The two cultures and a second look*. 1964. See comment by F. R. Leavis. *Two cultures?: the significance of C. P. Snow*. 1962. See also (2443).

2482 Spender, John A. *Life, journalism and politics*. New York, n.d., 2 vols. Spender was editor of the *Westminster Gazette*, 1896–1922. See also (2613).

2483 Spender, Stephen. *World within world*. 1951. Autobiography of a poet; political as well as literary.

2484 Strachey, Lytton. *Eminent Victorians*. 1918. Tells us more about the twentieth century than the nineteenth.

2485 Webb, Beatrice. *The diary of Beatrice Webb*. Eds. Norman and Jeanne MacKenzie. Cambridge, Mass., 1982–5, 4 vols.

2486 Webb, Sidney and Beatrice Webb. *Letters....* Ed. Norman MacKenzie. 1978, 3 vols.

2487 Wells, Herbert G. *Mr. Britling sees it through*. 1916. This novel reflects Wells' own thoughts on World War I; a best-seller in Great Britain and the United States.

2488 —— *Experiment in autobiography.* New York, 1934.
2489 Whitehead, Alfred North and Bertrand Russell. *Principia mathematica.* 1910–13, 3 vols. One of the great works of the century.
2490 Williams, Francis. *Nothing so strange.* 1970. Autobiography of a journalist.
2491 Woodward, Ernest Llewellyn. *Short journey.* 1942. Memoirs (to 1939) of a historian.
2492 Woolf, Leonard. *Sowing.* 1960. *Growing.* 1961. *Beginning again.* 1964. *Downhill all the way.* 1967. *The journey not the arrival matters.* 1969. Autobiography of a noted writer and publicist.

2. Surveys

2493 Cox, Charles Brian and A. E. Dyson (eds.). *The twentieth-century mind: history, ideas and literature in Britain.* 1972, 3 vols. Useful essays.
2494 Hynes, Samuel Lynn. *The Edwardian turn of mind.* Princeton, N.J., 1968.
2495 Passmore, John Arthur. *A hundred years of philosophy.* 1968.
2496 Scott-James, Rolfe A. *Fifty years of English literature, 1900–1950, with a post-script, 1951 to 1955.* New ed., 1956. Excellent survey.
2497 Symons, Julian. *The thirties: a dream revolved.* 1960.
2498 Williams, Raymond. *Culture and society, 1780–1950.* 1958. Continued in *The long revolution.* 1961. 'Critical history of ideas and values'.

3. Monographs

2499 Allett, John. *New Liberalism: the political economy of J. A. Hobson.* Toronto, 1981. See also (2456).
2500 Ashley, Maurice. *Churchill as historian.* 1968.
2501 Ausubel, Herman, J. Bartlett Brebner, and Erling M. Hunt (eds.). *Some modern historians of Britain: essays in honor of R. L. Schuyler.* New York, 1951. Includes essays on a dozen twentieth-century historians.
2502 Ayerst, David. *The Manchester Guardian: biography of a newspaper.* Ithaca, N.Y., 1971.
2503 Balfour, Michael. *Propaganda in war, 1939–1945: organizations, policies and publics in Britain and Germany.* 1979. One of the better treatments.
2504 Barnes, James J. and Patience F. Barnes. *Hitler's Mein Kampf in Britain and America: a publishing history, 1930–39.* 1980.
2505 Berdahl, Robert O. *British universities and the state.* Berkeley, Calif., 1959.
2506 Beveridge, William H. *The London School of Economics and its problems, 1919–1937.* 1960.
2507 Bonham-Carter, Victor. *Authors by profession.* 2 vols. – 1979, 1981.
2508 Brendon, Piers. *The life and death of the press barons.* 1982.
2509 *The British Press.* 1971. Prepared by Reference Division, Central Office of Information, London. Brief analysis with historical reference.
2510 Cantor, Leonard M. and I. Francis Roberts. *Further education in England and Wales.* 1969. Other than universities and colleges.
2511 Cartsen, F. L. *War vs. war: British and German radical movements in the First World War.* 1982.
2512 Ceadel, Martin. *Pacifism in Britain in 1914–1945: the defining of a faith.* Oxford, 1980.
2513 Chapman, Arthur William. *The story of a modern university: a history of the University of Sheffield.* 1955.
2514 Charlton, Henry B. *Portrait of a university, 1851–1951.* Manchester, 1951. History of the University of Manchester.
2515 Clark, Ronald W. *A biography of the Nuffield Foundation.* 1972.
2516 Cole, George D. H. *A history of socialist thought.* 1953–60, 5 vols. Vols. 3–5 are on the twentieth century to 1939.
2517 Collini, Stefan. *Liberalism and sociology: L. T. Hobhouse and political argument in England, 1880–1914.* 1979.

2518 Craik, William W. *The Central Labour College, 1909–29: a chapter in the history of adult working class education.* 1964.
2519 Crossman, Richard H. S. (ed.). *New Fabian essays.* 1952.
2520 Deane, Herbert A. *The political ideas of Harold Laski.* New York, 1955.
2521 Dent, Harold Collett. *Universities in transition.* 1961. On 1930–60.
2522 *The Economist, 1843–1943: a centenary volume.* 1943. Essays.
2523 Elton, Godfrey, Baron (ed.). *The first fifty years of the Rhodes Trust and the Rhodes scholarships, 1903–53.* 1955.
2524 Gallie, Walter B. *A new university: A. D. Lindsay and the Keele experiment.* 1960.
2525 Gannon, Franklin Reid. *The British press and Germany, 1936–1939.* 1971.
2526 Ginsberg, Morris (ed.). *Law and opinion in England in the 20th century.* 1959. Text of 17 public lectures at London School of Economics.
2527 Gollin, Alfred M. *The Observer and J. L. Garvin, 1908–1914: a study in a great editorship.* 1960.
2528 Greenberger, Allen J. *The British image of India: a study in the literature of imperialism, 1880–1960.* 1969.
2529 Gross, John. *The rise and fall of the man of letters.* 1969.
2530 Halsey, Albert H. and M. A. Trow. *The British academics.* Cambridge, Mass., 1971. Evolution of the academic professional: statistical.
2531 Hardy, G. H. *Bertrand Russell and Trinity.* Cambridge, 1970.
2532 Harrison, John F. C. *Learning and living, 1790–1960: a study in the history of the English adult education movement.* 1961.
2533 Heindel, Richard H. *The American impact on Great Britain, 1898–1914.* Philadelphia, Pa., 1940.
2534 *The Historical Association, 1906–1956.* 1955. Brief, informative.
2535 Howard, Michael S. *Jonathan Cape, publisher.* 1971.
2536 Hutchison, Sidney C. *The history of the Royal Academy, 1768–1968.* 1968.
2537 Hyams, Edward. *The New Statesman: the history of the first fifty years, 1913–1963.* 1963.
2538 Hynes, Samuel Lynn. *The Auden generation: literature and politics in England in the 1930s.* 1976.
2539 Jackson, Ian. *The provincial press and the community.* Manchester, 1971.
2540 Johnstone, John K. *The Bloomsbury group: a study of E. M. Forster, Lytton Strachey, Virginia Woolf and their circle.* Reprinted, 1978. Originally published in 1954.
2541 Kelly, Thomas. *A history of adult education in Great Britain.* 2nd ed., Liverpool, 1970.
2542 —— *A history of public libraries in Great Britain, 1845–1965.* 1973.
2543 Kingsford, Reginald J. L. *The Publishers Association, 1896–1946.* Cambridge, 1970.
2544 Knickerbocher, Frances Wentworth. *Free minds: John Morley and his friends.* 1943.
2545 Koss, Stephen. *The rise and fall of the political press in Britain.* 1981–4, 2 vols.
2546 Lee, Alan J. *The origins of the popular press in England, 1855–1914.* 1976.
2547 Levy, Paul. *Moore: G. E. Moore and the Cambridge Apostles.* New York, 1979. See (2466).
2548 Mackenzie, Norman and Jeanne Mackenzie. *The Fabians.* 1977.
2549 McLaine, Ian. *Ministry of morale: home front morale and Ministry of Information in World War II.* 1979.
2550 Martin, Wallace. *The 'New Age' under Orage: chapters in English cultural history.* Manchester, 1967. See (2478).
2551 Maude, Angus. *The common problem.* 1969. Examination of modern economics and sociology.
2552 Miller, Edward. *That noble cabinet: a history of the British Museum.* 1973.
2553 Mitchell, G. Duncan. *A hundred years of sociology.* 1968.
2554 Moody, Theodore and James C. Beckett. *Queen's, Belfast, 1845–1949: the history of a university.* 1959, 2 vols.
2555 Mountford, James. *British universities.* 1966.
2556 Mumby, Frank and Ian Norris. *Bookselling and book publishing: a history from the earliest times to the present day.* 5th ed., 1974.

2557 Murray, George. *The press and the public: the story of the British Press Council.* Carbondale, Ill., 1972. Since its inception in 1953.
2558 O'Day, Alan (ed.). *The Edwardian Age: conflict and stability, 1900–1914.* Hamden, Conn., 1979. Eight essays by various authors.
2559 Panichas, George A. (ed.). *Promise of greatness, the war of 1914–1918.* 1968. Comment and reminiscence (literary, political, social) from a wide selection of writers including Blunden, Graves, and Liddell Hart.
2560 Partridge, Eric and John W. Clark. *British and American English since 1900.* New York, 1951. The only significant study of language change.
2561 Pease, Edward R. *The history of the Fabian Society.* 2nd ed., 1925.
2562 Pierson, Stanley. *British socialists: the journey from fantasy to politics.* Cambridge, Mass., 1979.
2563 [Pope, Wilson, et al.]. *The story of 'The Star', 1888–1938.* [1938].
2564 Porter, Bernard. *Critics of empire: British radical attitudes to colonialism in Africa, 1895–1914.* 1968.
2565 Pound, Reginald. *The Strand Magazine, 1891–1950.* 1966.
2566 Qualter, Terence H. *Graham Wallas and the great society.* New York, 1979.
2567 Radice, Lisanne. *Beatrice and Sidney Webb: Fabian socialists.* 1984.
2568 Robertson, William. *Welfare in trust: a history of the Carnegie United Kingdom Trust, 1913–1963.* Dunfermline, 1964.
2569 Robson, William A. (ed.). *The Political Quarterly in the thirties.* 1971.
2570 Sanders, Michael L. and Philip M. Taylor. *British propaganda during the First World War, 1914–1918.* 1982.
2571 Scott, George. *Reporter anonymous: the story of the Press Association.* 1968.
2572 Shackle, George L. S. *The years of high theory: invention and tradition in economic thought, 1926–1939.* Cambridge, 1967.
2573 Sharf, Andrew. *The British press and Jews under Nazi rule.* 1964.
2574 Soffer, Reba N. *Ethics and society in England: the revolution in the social sciences, 1870–1914.* Berkeley, Calif., 1978.
2575 Stansky, Peter and William Abrahams. *Journey to the frontier: Julian Bell & John Cornford: their lives and the 1930s.* 1966. See also their *The Unknown Orwell.* 1972.
2576 Stephen, Barbara. *Girton College, 1869–1932.* 1933.
2577 Storey, Graham. *Reuter's century, 1851–1951.* 1951. History of the leading news agency.
2578 Tawney, Richard H. *The radical tradition: twelve essays on politics, education and culture.* Ed. Rita Hinden. 1964.
2579 Taylor, Philip M. *The projection of Britain: British overseas policy and propaganda, 1919–1939.* 1981.
2580 *The Times. History of the Times.* III, *The twentieth century test, 1884–1912.* 1947. IV, *The 150th anniversary and beyond, 1912–1948.* 1952. V, *Struggles in War and Peace, 1939–66.* 1984.
2581 Toynbee, Arnold J. *A study of history.* 1934–54, 10 vols. See also D. C. Somervell. *Abridgement of Volumes VII–X.* 1957. See (2653).
2582 —— *Acquaintances.* 1967. Continued by *Experiences.* 1969.
2583 Truscot, Bruce [Edgar Allison Peers]. *Red brick university.* 1943. A book that aroused much interest.
2584 Tuke, Margaret J. *A history of Bedford College for Women, 1849–1937.* 1939.
2585 Tylecote, Mabel. *The education of women at Manchester University, 1883–1933.* Manchester, 1941.
2586 Watson, George. *Politics and literature in modern Britain.* 1977.
2587 Whates, Harry R. G. *The Birmingham Post, 1857–1957.* Birmingham, 1957.
2588 White, Cynthia L. *Women's magazine, 1693–1968.* 1970.
2589 Wiener, Martin J. *Between two worlds: the political thought of Graham Wallas.* Oxford, 1971.
2590 —— *English culture and the decline of the industrial spirit, 1850–1980.* 1981.
2591 Williams, Bernard and Alan Montefiore (eds.). *British analytical philosophy.* 1966.

2592 Wood, Neal. *Communism and British intellectuals.* 1959.
2593 Woodbridge, George. *The Reform Club, 1836–1978: a history from the club's records.* New York, 1978.
2594 Woods, Oliver and James Bishop. *The story of The Times.* 1984.
2595 Wright, A. W. G. *D. H. Cole and socialist democracy.* Oxford, 1979.

4. Biographies

2596 Barker, Nicolas. *Stanley Morison.* 1972. Morison was closely associated with a typographic revolution.
2597 Braddon, Russell. *Roy Thomson of Fleet Street.* 1965.
2598 Carpenter, Luther P. *G. D. H. Cole: an intellectual biography.* Cambridge, 1973. See also Margaret Cole. *The life of G. D. H. Cole.* 1971.
2599 Cecil, David. *Max, a biography.* 1964. Of Max Beerbohm.
2600 Clark, Ronald W. *The Huxleys.* 1968. On Julian and Aldous Huxley.
2601 —— *The life of Bertrand Russell.* New York, 1976.
2602 Cole, Margaret. *Beatrice Webb.* New York, 1946.
2603 Darlow, Thomas. *William Robertson Nicoll, life and letters.* 1925. Biography of the editor of *The British Weekly*, 1886–1923.
2604 Dillistone, Frederick William. *Charles Raven: naturalist, historian, theologian.* Grand Rapids, Mich., 1975.
2605 Eastwood, Granville. *Harold Laski.* 1977. See (2626).
2606 Eyck, Frank. *G. P. Gooch: a study in history and politics.* 1982.
2607 Ferris, Paul. *The house of Northcliffe: a biography of an empire.* New York, 1972. Private life of Lord Northcliffe.
2608 Forster, E. M. *Goldsworthy Lowes Dickinson.* 1934.
2609 Fyfe, Henry Hamilton. *T. P. O'Connor.* 1934. See (395).
2610 Gardiner, Alfred G. *Life of George Cadbury.* 1923. Cadbury was a cocoa merchant, newspaper proprietor, and social reformer.
2611 Grier, Lynda. *Achievement in education: the work of Michael Ernest Sadler, 1885–1935.* 1952.
2612 Hammond, John Lawrence Le Breton. *C. P. Scott of the 'Manchester Guardian'.* 1934.
2613 Harris, Henry Wilson. *J. A. Spender.* 1946. Spender was editor of the *Westminster Gazette*, 1896–1922.
2614 Havighurst, Alfred F. *Radical journalist: H. W. Massingham (1860–1924).* 1974.
2615 Henderson, Archibald. *George Bernard Shaw: man of the century.* 1956.
2616 Hendrick, George. *Henry Salt: humanitarian, reformer and man of letters.* 1977.
2617 Hobson, John A. and Morris Ginsberg. *L. T. Hobhouse: his life and work.* 1931.
2618 Hyman, Alan. *The rise and fall of Horatio Bottomley: the biography of a swindler.* 1972. See also (2637).
2619 Koss, Stephen F. *Fleet Street radical: A. G. Gardiner and the 'Daily News'.* 1973.
2620 Lees-Milne, James. *Harold Nicolson: a biography.* Vol. I (1886–1929). 1980.
2621 LeKachman, Robert. *The age of Keynes.* New York, 1966.
2622 Lysaght, Charles Edward. *Brendan Bracken.* 1974. Bracken was minister of information.
2623 McCarthy, John. *Hilaire Belloc, Edwardian radical.* Indianapolis, Ind., 1979.
2624 MacKenzie, Norman and Jeanne MacKenzie. *H. G. Wells: a biography.* 1973.
2625 McLachlan, Donald. *In the chair: Barrington-Ward of 'The Times', 1927–1948.* 1971.
2626 Martin, Kingsley. *Harold Laski (1893–1950): a biographical memoir.* 1953. Reestablished a leading figure in the intellectual world. See (2605).
2627 Minney, Rubeigh J. *Viscount Southwood.* 1954.
2628 Monroe, Elizabeth. *Philby of Arabia.* 1973. The life of an explorer, orientalist, and author.
2629 Muggeridge, Kitty and Ruth Adam. *Beatrice Webb: a life, 1858–1943.* New York, 1968. Lively, popular, informed.
2630 Namier, Julia. *Lewis Namier, a biography.* 1971. Of a distinguished historian.
2631 Ogg, David. *Herbert Fisher, 1865–1940: a short biography.* 1947.
2632 Pound, Reginald. *Arnold Bennett: a biography.* 1952.

2633 —— *A. P. Herbert: a biography.* 1976.
2634 —— and Geoffrey Harmsworth. *Northcliffe.* 1959.
2635 Scott, Drusilla. *A. D. Lindsay: a biography.* Oxford, 1971. Lindsay was master of Balliol and then vice-chancellor of Oxford, 1935–8.
2636 Strachey, Amy. *St. Loe Strachey: his life and his paper.* 1930. Concerning the editor of *Spectator*, 1898–1925.
2637 Symons, Julian. *Horatio Bottomley: a biography.* 1955. See also (2619).
2638 Taylor, Henry Archibald. *Robert Donald.* [1934]. Donald was editor of the *Daily Chronicle*, 1902–18.
2639 Terrill, Ross. *R. H. Tawney and his times: socialism as fellowship.* Cambridge, Mass., 1973.
2640 Unwin, Philip. *The publishing Unwins.* 1972.
2641 Ward, Maisie. *Gilbert Keith Chesterton.* 1943. Biography of a significant poet, novelist, and critic.
2642 Weintraub, Stanley. *Journey to Heartbreak: the crucible years of George Bernard Shaw, 1914–1918.* New York, 1971.
2643 West, Anthony. *H. G. Wells: aspects of a life.* 1984.
2644 West, Francis. *Gilbert Murray: a life.* 1984.
2645 West, Herbert Faulkner. *Modern conquistador: Robert Bontine Cunninghame Graham: his life and works.* 1932. Of a literary life closely associated with political and social questions.
2646 Wood, Alan. *Bertrand Russell, the passionate skeptic.* 1957.
2647 Wood, Herbert George. *Terrot Reaveley Glover: a biography.* 1953.
2648 Wrench, John Evelyn. *Geoffrey Dawson and our Times.* 1955. Dawson was editor of *The Times*, 1912–19 and 1923–41.

5. Articles

2649 Boyer, John W. 'A. J. P. Taylor and the art of modern history', *JMH*, XLIX (Mar. 1977), 40–72.
2650 Coppen, Helen (ed.). 'Symposium on mass media in the United Kingdom', *Year book of education, 1960* (1960), 294–312. Inquiry from 1939 of the use of media in education.
2651 Ferguson, John. 'The Open University in Britain', *World year book of education, 1972/3* (1972), 373–85.
2652 Freeden, Michael. 'J. A. Hobson as a New Liberal theorist: some aspects of his social thought until 1914', *JHI*, XXXIV (July–Sept. 1973), 421–43.
2653 Geyl, Pieter. 'Toynbee the prophet', *JHI*, XVI (no. 2, 1955), 260–74. Comment on Toynbee's *A study of history.* See (2581).
2654 Hernon, Joseph M., Jr. 'The last Whig historian and consensus history: George Macaulay Trevelyan, 1876–1962', *AHR*, LXXXI (Feb. 1976), 66–97.
2655 Hopkin, Deian. 'Domestic censorship in the First World War', *JHC*, V (no. 4, 1970), 151–69.
2656 Hyde, William J. 'The socialism of H. G. Wells in the early twentieth century', *JHI*, XVII (no. 2, 1956), 217–34.
2657 Irvine, William. 'Shaw, the Fabians, and the Utilitarians', *JHI*, VIII (no. 2, 1947), 218–31.
2658 Kitson Clark, George. 'A hundred years of the teaching of history at Cambridge, 1873–1973', *Hist. J.*, XVI (no. 3, 1973), 535–53.
2659 Lee, Alan J. 'Franklin Thomasson and the *Tribune:* a case study in the history of the Liberal press, 1906–1908', *Hist. J.*, XVI (no. 2, 1973), 341–60.
2660 Lockwood, John F. 'Haldane and education', *PA*, XXXV (autumn 1957), 232–44.
2661 McEwen, John M. 'National press during the First World War: ownership and circulation', *JCH*, XVII (July 1982), 459–86.
2662 Mitchell, Harvey. 'Hobson revisited', *JHI*, XXVI (no. 3, 1965), 397–416.
2663 Mowat, Charles Loch. 'Social legislation in Britain and the United States in the early twentieth century: a problem in the history of ideas', *Historical Studies*, VII (1969), 81–96.

2664 Parsons, Wayne. 'Keynes and the politics of ideas', *History of Political Thought*, IV (summer 1983), 367–92.
2665 Peters, A. J. 'The changing idea of a technical education', *BJES*, XI (May 1963), 142–66.
2666 Pierson, Stanley. 'Ernest Belfast Bax: 1854–1926 – the encounter of Marxism and the late Victorian culture', *JBS*, XII (Nov. 1972), 39–60.
2667 Samuels, Stuart. 'The Left Book Club', *JCH*, I (no. 2, 1966), 65–86.
2668 Seaman, John W. 'L. T. Hobhouse and the theory of Social Liberalism', *Canadian Journal of Political Science*, XI (Dec. 1978), 777–801.
2669 Szreter, R. 'History and the sociological perspective in educational studies', *University of Birmingham Historical Journal, XII* (1969–71), 1–19.
2670 Wiseman, Stephen. 'Higher degrees in education in British universities', *BJES*, II (Nov. 1953), 54–66.

INDEX OF AUTHORS, EDITORS, AND TRANSLATORS [by entry number]

INDEX